HIS HOLINESS THE DALAI LAMA

THE END OF SUFFERING AND THE DISCOVERY *of* HAPPINESS

The Path of Tibetan Buddhism

ALSO BY HIS HOLINESS THE DALAI LAMA

*All You Ever Wanted to Know from His Holiness the
Dalai Lama on Happiness, Life, Living, and Much More**

For the Benefit of All Beings:
A Commentary on The Way of the Bodhisattva

How to Practice: The Way to a Meaningful Life

*In My Own Words: An Introduction to
My Teachings and Philosophy**

Meditation on the Nature of Mind

A Profound Mind: Cultivating Wisdom in Everyday Life

Stages of Meditation

*Available from Hay House

Please visit:

Hay House UK: **www.hayhouse.co.uk**
Hay House USA: **www.hayhouse.com**®
Hay House Australia: **www.hayhouse.com.au**
Hay House South Africa: **www.hayhouse.co.za**
Hay House India: **www.hayhouse.co.in**

HIS HOLINESS THE DALAI LAMA

THE END OF SUFFERING AND THE DISCOVERY *of* HAPPINESS

The Path of Tibetan Buddhism

HAY HOUSE, INC.
Carlsbad, California • New York City
London • Sydney • Johannesburg
Vancouver • Hong Kong • New Delhi

First published and distributed in the United Kingdom by:
Hay House UK Ltd, 292B Kensal Rd, London W10 5BE. Tel.: (44) 20 8962 1230;
Fax: (44) 20 8962 1239. www.hayhouse.co.uk

Published and distributed in the United States of America by:
Hay House, Inc., PO Box 5100, Carlsbad, CA 92018-5100. Tel.: (1) 760 431 7695 or
(800) 654 5126; Fax: (1) 760 431 6948 or (800) 650 5115. www.hayhouse.com

Published and distributed in Australia by:
Hay House Australia Ltd, 18/36 Ralph St, Alexandria NSW 2015. Tel.: (61) 2 9669
4299; Fax: (61) 2 9669 4144. www.hayhouse.com.au

Published and distributed in the Republic of South Africa by:
Hay House SA (Pty), Ltd, PO Box 990, Witkoppen 2068.
Tel./Fax: (27) 11 467 8904. www.hayhouse.co.za

Published and distributed in India by:
Hay House Publishers India, Muskaan Complex, Plot No.3, B-2, Vasant Kunj,
New Delhi – 110 070. Tel.: (91) 11 4176 1620; Fax: (91) 11 4176 1630.
www.hayhouse.co.in

Distributed in Canada by:
Raincoast, 9050 Shaughnessy St, Vancouver, BC V6P 6E5. Tel.: (1) 604 323 7100;
Fax: (1) 604 323 2600

Originally published in India as *The Path of Tibetan Buddhism*

Cover design: Aeshna Roy • *Interior design:* Tricia Breidenthal

A catalogue record for this book is available from the British Library.

ISBN 978-1-84850-934-4

Printed and bound in Great Britain by CPI Group (UK) Ltd, Croydon, CR0 4YY.

CONTENTS

FOREWORD

His Holiness the 14th Dalai Lama is the preeminent voice not only of Tibetan Buddhism or Buddhism in general but for seekers of all traditions and faiths embodying, as he does, their highest aspirations. This is not because he is the Dalai Lama, but because of who the Dalai Lama is—a scholar and a practitioner of one of the richest and most sophisticated traditions of mind training in human history. He combines deep experiential insights and scriptural knowledge acquired from a long personal journey that began when he was not yet five years old, and continues to this day, more than 70 years later. He still engages in several hours of daily spiritual practice—in meditation, recitation, rituals, and the study of the scriptures. Asked about how much he has progressed as a spiritual aspirant in this lifetime—as one regarded by millions of his followers as a living Buddha, *Avalokiteshvara*—he describes himself as a "simple Buddhist monk" who has made "only little progress." Untouched by his global reputation, and the respect and adulation he evokes, he continues to receive teachings and initiations from other lamas and teachers with the humility and openness of the true aspirant.

His Holiness has authored more than 50 books. He teaches, lectures, gives talks, writes, and participates in numerous seminars, panel discussions, and other conferences with profound wisdom and seriousness, yet with a quality of lightness that touches and transforms hearts and minds. Though he often goes over familiar ideas, repeating and reaffirming them, they are, each time, freshly nuanced and are empowering to the reader or the listener, taking one to ever-deeper levels of insight and understanding, impacting us in new and exciting ways. This collection of his writings provides a rare overview of key aspects of Tibetan Buddhism, locating these first in the circumscribing ideas found in the simple and elegant insights in Chapter 1, "What Can Religion Contribute to Mankind?," responding to the simple human quest: "Everyone wants happiness and does not want suffering." This book is a road map to how we might end our experience of suffering, from a man who walks his talk.

The Foundation for Universal Responsibility of His Holiness the Dalai Lama feels very honored and privileged to present this important and illuminating compilation of the writings of His Holiness the Dalai Lama from the mid-1980s to the early 1990s. They are extracted from a remarkable publication—*Cho Yang: The Voice of Tibetan Religion and Culture*, edited by Jeremy Russell and Pedron Yeshi, an occasional publication of the Department of Religion and Culture of the Tibetan Administration in Exile and the Norbulingka Institute, under its umbrella. Our gratitude and appreciation go to the publishers for permission to publish these for the first time in book form so that they may reach a wide global audience.

I would like to acknowledge Kim Yeshe, the driving force and former director of the Norbulingka Institute from its inception, for her support; and Tempa Tsering, the Representative of His Holiness the Dalai Lama in Delhi, for mediating the permissions with the Tibetan Government in Dharamshala. His Holiness has been enabled to reach out to a global audience of readers and listeners thanks to the tireless work of a core group of translators and interpreters; many of them have become icons in their field. We owe them a deep debt. The real credit for bringing the contents of this book to the reader must go to them. I have been a mere compiler.

This book is based on the following essays:

- Chapter 1, "What Can Religion Contribute to Mankind?" (anonymous translator)

- Chapter 2, "A Survey of the Paths of Tibetan Buddhism" (translated by Geshe Thupten Jinpa, edited by Jeremy Russell)

- Chapter 3, "Teachings on Je Tsongkhapa's *Three Principal Aspects of the Path*" (translated by Lobsang Jordan, edited by Jeremy Russell)

- Chapter 4, "Je Tsongkhapa's *Abridged Stages of the Path to Enlightenment*" (translated by Geshe Lobsang Jordan, edited by Jeremy Russell)

- Chapter 5, "Generating the Mind of Enlightenment" (translated by Ven. Lhakdor, Dorje Tseten, and Jeremy Russell)

- Chapter 6, "Dependent Arising" (translated by Jeffrey Hopkins)

I am blessed and privileged to join the author, the translators, and the editors of the essays in this compilation in dedicating any merit gained from its publication to all sentient beings.

Rajiv Mehrotra
Secretary and Trustee
The Foundation for Universal Responsibility
of His Holiness the Dalai Lama

WORDS OF TRUTH

*This prayer was composed by
His Holiness Tenzin Gyatso, the 14th Dalai Lama of Tibet,
honoring and invoking the Great Compassion of the
Three Jewels: the Buddha, the Teachings, and the Sangha.*

O Buddhas of the past, present, and future, Bodhisattvas and
    disciples,
Having remarkable qualities immeasurably vast as the ocean,
And who regard all sentient beings as your only child,
Please consider the truth of my anguished pleas.

Buddha's teachings dispel the pain of worldly existence and self-
    centered peace;
May they flourish, spreading prosperity and happiness
    throughout this spacious world.
O holders of the Dharma: scholars and realized practitioners,
May your tenfold virtuous practice prevail.

Completely suppressed by seemingly endless and terribly
    negative karmic acts,
Humble sentient beings are immersed in misery, tormented by
    sufferings without cease;
May all their fears from unbearable war, famine, and disease be
    pacified,
To attain an ocean of happiness and well-being.

Barbarian hordes on the side of darkness by various means
Mercilessly destroy pious people, particularly in the Land of Snow;
Kindly let the power of compassion arise
To quickly stem the flow of blood and tears.

Through wild madness, brought on by the evils of delusion,
These objects of compassion do disservice to themselves and to
    others.
May the irresponsible attain the eye of wisdom to discern good
    from bad,
And be established in a state of love and friendship.

May this heart-felt wish of total freedom for all Tibet,
Which has been awaited for such a long time, be spontaneously
    fulfilled.
Please grant soon the great fortune to enjoy
The celebration of spiritual and temporal rule.

For the sake of the teachings and practitioners, the nation and its
    people,
Many have undergone myriad hardships,
Completely sacrificing their most cherished lives, bodies, and wealth.
O Protector Chenrezig, compassionately care for them.

Thus the great Patron of Boundless Love, before Buddhas and
    Bodhisattvas,
Embraced the people of the Land of Snow;
May good results now quickly dawn
Through the prayerful vows you have made.

By the power of the profound reality of emptiness and its relative
    forms,
Together with the force of great compassion in the Three Jewels
    and the Words of Truth,
And through the infallible law of actions and their effects,
May this truthful prayer be unhindered and quickly fulfilled.

Chapter 1

WHAT CAN RELIGION CONTRIBUTE TO MANKIND?

Before discussing what religion can contribute to mankind, it may be helpful to ask what is it that mankind needs. The simple answer is that all human beings, in fact all beings, constantly seek to find happiness and to overcome problems and avoid suffering. No matter what particular problems individual people or groups of people may face, whether they are rich or poor, educated or uneducated, what is equally common to all is the wish for lasting happiness. As human beings we all have a physical body which, at times, suffers from sickness and other problems, and we all have emotions, such as anger, jealousy, and greed, while on the positive side we have love, compassion, kindness, tolerance, and so forth. These are all part of human nature. Likewise, everyone wants happiness and does not want suffering.

Today, due to progress in science and technology, many people throughout the world experience some material improvement in their lives, and benefit from facilities and opportunities that previous generations never even dreamt of. However, if we ask whether this material development has really eliminated human suffering, the answer is no. Basic human distress remains. People continue not to get what they want and find themselves in unpleasant circumstances. Despite greater comfort, people experience loneliness, frustration, and mental restlessness.

Of the problems that face mankind as a whole, some, such as natural disasters, floods, and drought, we can do nothing about, but other problems are manmade. They include conflicts that arise between human beings over issues of race, ideology, religious faith, and so forth. This is very sad, for whatever race a person belongs to, he or she is primarily a member of the human family. With regard to ideology and religion, these things are intended to bring benefit to people and not to be a ground for antagonism and violence. It is important to remember that the purpose of different ideologies, religious systems, and so forth is to serve human beings and fulfill their needs. In this century alone there have already been two great world wars and many local conflicts, while killing continues to go on all around us all the time. In the meantime, we all live under the nuclear threat, largely because of ideological conflicts.

Another category of manmade problems concerns the relations between people and the earth or the environment, problems of ecology and pollution. Whatever difficulties deforestation and pollution of the earth, water, and air may present to our generation, they are clearly going to be much worse in the future unless something is done. And something can be done, because these are all problems made by man, and thus can be unmade or at least reduced if we choose.

There is no question that material development is good for mankind and provides many necessary benefits. But we have reached a point where it would be worthwhile examining whether there are areas of development other than the material one alone since, as I have already mentioned, there are certain side effects of material development: there is an increase of mental unease, worry, and fear, and this in turn sometimes expresses itself in violence. There is a decline in human feeling. For example, although it is true to say there has always been fighting throughout history, there is a difference between the hand-to-hand fighting between individuals in the past and the remotely controlled warfare of the present. If you were to try to kill someone with a knife, it would naturally be difficult because you would have to be able to cope with seeing his blood, witnessing his anguish, and hearing his screams of pain; natural restraint arises. But if you use a rifle with telescopic sights, it is so much easier, almost as if it did not concern you. The victim is unaware of you; you simply aim and pull the trigger, look away, and it is done. Of course, the situation is even worse with regard to nuclear and other remotely controlled weapons. What is lacking here is a sense of human feeling, a sense of responsibility.

If we look carefully at human beings, we will find that besides the physical aspect there is another very effective factor—consciousness or mind. Wherever there is a human being, there is always consciousness. So, in order to reduce manmade problems, the human mind is a key factor. Whether they are problems of economics, international relations, science, technology, medicine, ecology, or whatever, although these seem to be issues beyond anyone's control, the central point is still human motivation. If the motivation is careless or poorly considered, problems will arise; if the motivation is good, then the consequent action will develop in a positive way.

It seems that although the intellect—the "brain" aspect of human beings—has been much developed and put to use, we have somehow neglected the "heart" aspect, by which I mean the development of a good heart, love, compassion, kindness, and forgiveness. This lack of heart, although we may have much material progress, does not provide full satisfaction or mental peace. What is needed is mental development along with material development—if these are combined, we shall all feel happier and calmer. The key point is developing a basic human feeling, which means genuine sincerity, genuine openness, genuine love and kindness, and respect for others as brothers and sisters.

The question of genuine lasting world peace concerns human beings, so this human feeling is also the basis for that. Through inner peace, genuine world peace can be achieved. Here the importance of individual responsibility is quite clear, for an atmosphere of peace must be created within oneself; then it will be created in the family, and then in the community.

In order to create inner peace, what is most important is the practice of compassion and love, human understanding, and respect for human beings. The most powerful obstacles to these are anger, hatred, fear, and suspicion, so while people talk about disarmament in the world at large, some kind of internal disarmament is necessary. The question is whether or not we can minimize these negative thoughts and increase positive attitudes. We can examine our daily lives to see if there is any value in anger, and likewise we can think about the negative or positive effects of compassion and love. For example, since human beings are social animals, they have good friends and bad friends. People who are always angry have in most cases very little mental peace, but those who are calm by nature have more peace and more true friends— true friends who remain with them through success and failure. Such friends are not acquired through anger, jealousy, or greed; but through honest love, compassion, openness, and sincerity. So, it is quite clear that negative thoughts are destroyers of happiness, while positive thoughts are creators of it.

Although anger may sometimes seem like a defender, in fact it destroys our peace and happiness, and even destroys our ability to succeed. Success or failure depends on human wisdom and intelligence, which cannot function properly under the influence of anger. When we are under the sway of anger and hatred, our power of judgment is impaired. As a result, we pursue the wrong aims or apply the wrong method, and this leads to failure. Why, then, does anger arise? This is because deep down there is some kind of a fear; so fear is a cause of failure.

The best and the most powerful methods for eliminating anger are tolerance and patience. People sometimes have the impression that tolerance and patience are neutral and lack feelings, but they are not; they are much deeper and more effective than mere indifference. Some people also feel that tolerance and patience are signs of weakness. On the contrary, anger, hatred, and frustration are a sign of weakness. Anger comes from fear, and fear comes from weakness or a feeling of inferiority. If you have courage and determination, you will have less fear, and consequently you will be less frustrated and angry.

Now, the practice of methods to reduce anger and increase tolerance is adaptable to every religious system, even for those people who have no faith at all; for so long as you are a human being, you will always need tolerance and courage. From a Buddhist point of view, there are nine objects or situations which give rise to anger: situations in which I have been harmed, I am being harmed, or I will be harmed; similarly, situations in which my dear ones were harmed, are being harmed, or will be harmed; and situations in which my enemies were happy, are happy, or will be happy. Of these, perhaps the most important is the situation in which I am being harmed. At such times, a way to counter anger is to investigate the nature of the object which is actually harming us, examining whether it is harming us directly or indirectly. Suppose we are being hit with a stick; what is directly doing us harm is the stick. The root cause which harms us indirectly is not the person wielding the stick, but the anger which motivates him to hit us, so it is not the person himself with whom we should feel angry.

Another method which can be effective in certain circumstances when someone is harming us is to remember at the time that we could be experiencing far greater difficulties and worse sufferings. When we recognize that there are much worse things that could happen to us, the difficulties we face are reduced and become easier to cope with. This technique can be applied to all sorts of problems. If you look at a problem close up, it seems very big, but from a distance it appears much smaller, and this can help counter anger. Similarly, when a tragedy takes place, it can help if we analyze whether there is any way of overcoming it, and if not, then there is no use worrying about it.

Anger is our real enemy. Whether it is in our mind, our friend's mind, or our enemy's mind, anger is the real foe. It never changes; its nature is always harmful. However, a human being does not always have a harmful nature; he may be your worst enemy today, but tomorrow or the next year he may become your best friend. So, when a human being is behaving like an enemy and is doing

us harm, we should not blame the person—one day his motivation may change. The real blame should be put on his anger or
negative attitude. Whenever anger arises, whoever it arises in, it is
always a troublemaker.

In order to counter anger we need to increase patience and tolerance. In that sense, in order to practice patience and tolerance,
we need an enemy—a person who is an enemy. Otherwise we will
have no opportunity to practice them. Whether the enemy has a
good or a bad motivation, as far as we are concerned, the situation
will be beneficial, for his harming us provides an opportunity for
us to increase patience and test our inner strength. If we think in
this way, we can see our enemy as someone to whom we should be
grateful, rather than as an object of abuse.

Nevertheless, when it comes to taking action, if someone is behaving unreasonably and harmfully toward other beings and he
or she is doing so continually, then ultimately he or she will suffer. If you understand the situation clearly, then respectfully and
without scorn you can take necessary counteraction. In such situations, we should take action to stop other people from behaving
unreasonably, because unless we do so, things will just get worse.
We are not only allowed to take such counteraction, but indeed
we should; the difference being that we do so not out of anger but
with an altruistic intention.

A further way to counter anger is based on compassion and
deep respect for others; a genuine, altruistic attitude is very important here. Basically, human beings are social animals; without
others you simply cannot survive. Therefore, for your own survival, your own happiness, and your own success, you need others.
By helping other people, being concerned about their suffering,
and sharing in it, you will ultimately gain some benefit yourself.

This is also applicable on a larger scale, for example with regard to the world's economic problems. If you follow a one-sided
policy, although you may gain something temporarily, in the long
run you may lose more. If the policy is based on a wider perspective—a more altruistic attitude—it will produce better results. In
the field of economics today, we are all increasingly dependent on

each other, not only from country to country, but from continent to continent. The nations who consume the most ought to reflect on where they get the materials which allow such consumption to go on; otherwise, one day it will be a cause of big problems. These things are becoming steadily clearer as a result of the energy crisis and the widening gap between the North and the South, and the rich and poor countries. If the situation continues, it will definitely create problems, but if we think about how it can be changed, developing an altruistic attitude is the key point.

Now, developing such attitudes as love and compassion, patience and tolerance, and genuine understanding between human beings is not simply a religious matter, but a condition for survival. Sometimes I refer to it as a universal religion. To be a good human being in day-to-day life, neither philosophy nor rituals are necessary. To be a good human being means, if possible, to serve other people; if not, to refrain from harming them. Nevertheless, the various different religions do have responsibilities along these lines. It is not that everybody should become religious-minded, but rather that each of the various religions can contribute to mankind. All the great teachers of the past gave their various religious teachings for the benefit of humanity and, in some cases, even for the benefit of all sentient beings. Certainly, they did not teach us to disturb people.

The various different religious groups and systems have a special contribution to make, not toward material development, but toward mental development. The proper way to approach our future is a combination of these two; as human beings our physical and mental energy should be spent half on material development and half on inner or mental development. If we overemphasize the material side, it is insufficient because it is based on matter which has no feeling, no experience, and no consciousness. Until the world comes to be dominated by robots, we will need religion. Because we are human beings we have feelings and experiences, pains and pleasures, and as long as these circumstances persist, things like money alone cannot bring happiness. Whether or not we experience happiness is largely dependent on our mental attitude and way of thinking.

Each of the various religious systems, whether it be Buddhism, Christianity, Islam, Judaism, or one of the many kinds of Hinduism, has some special technique, some special method to achieve that goal. When we talk to religious scholars or practitioners, for example, when we meet sincere Christian practitioners, even without speaking to them we can feel that they have achieved something. This is a result of their own tradition and is an indication that all the world's religions are not only aiming at the same object, but have the ability and potential to produce good human beings. From this point of view we can easily develop respect for different religions.

It is a reality that there are many areas in which we human beings tend to fight, while religion is the only factor which acts as a remedy for human destruction. That religion itself can be used as an instrument for creating further divisions and provoking human beings to fight more is very unfortunate. It is another reality that it is impossible for all human beings to become religious-minded. There is no question of all human beings becoming Buddhists or Christians or anything else. Buddhists will remain Buddhists, Christians will remain Christians, and nonbelievers will remain nonbelievers. Whether we like it or not, this is a fact, so respect for other people's views is very important. If people have faith, accept some ideal, and feel they have found the most beneficial way of improving themselves, this is good. They are exercising their right to follow their own choice. Those who have no faith, who even feel religion is wrong, at least derive some benefit from their antireligious outlook, which is their right too.

As long as we remain human beings and citizens of this world, we have to live together, so we should not disturb each other, but realize that we are all brothers and sisters. There are very clear grounds for developing closer relations between the various different philosophies, religions, and traditions, and this is very important at present. I am glad to see positive signs of a movement in this direction, especially of a closer understanding between the

Tibetan Buddhist community and Christian monks and nuns. We Tibetans have many things to learn from other traditions.

However, it is important to understand that the future of religion and what it can contribute to mankind is not merely a matter of preserving institutions, but depends very much on individuals' own practice. If you accept religion, you should practice it sincerely, not artificially. Therefore, it is important to grasp the essence, to understand what the aim of your religion is, and what its results will be. If you then practice properly, you yourself will present an example of the benefits of religion.

In the field of philosophy there are significant differences between religions. For instance, according to the Jain and Buddhist teachings there is no "creator," there is no God. Ultimately, one is like a creator oneself, for according to the Buddhist explanation there is within one's own consciousness an innermost subtle consciousness, sometimes called clear light, which resembles a creator but is deep within oneself. Consequently, there is no other force involved such as God. Now, as far as most other religions are concerned, the central belief is in God, so we can see here wide differences in philosophy.

However, instead of dwelling on differences, a more important question is, what is the purpose of these different systems and philosophies? The answer is that the purpose is the same, to bring the maximum benefit to humankind. There are so many different mental dispositions among human beings that for certain people certain traditions are more effective, while for other people other traditions and practices are more effective. Flowers are very pleasing, one flower is beautiful, but a combination is even more beautiful. If there is more variety, you have the opportunity to choose according to your taste and liking. Similarly, it is good to have many different religious teachings and many different philosophies. Just as we eat food to support our physical bodies, religions and ideologies are food for the mind.

There are differences between us even in the limited physical sphere, for our small human faces contain many distinguishing features. Our minds are not of solid substance, but are vast as space, so naturally there are many different mental dispositions. For these reasons, one religion and one philosophy are not sufficient to satisfy all human beings. What we should aim at, with the welfare of mankind in mind, is not to hope to convert everyone to one religion, or not to try to evolve a single eclectic religion from all the others. We can appreciate and admire the features we find in common and respect the areas in which we differ. Certainly, there are aspects in which different religions can learn from each other, but they do not have to surrender their identity to do so. Christians, for example, might find Buddhist techniques for developing concentration or focusing the mind on one point, to be useful. There are many ways to do this, such as through meditation, as there are also many techniques which aim to develop tolerance, compassion, love, kindness, and so forth. Similarly, Buddhists may find Christian practices of social action helpful and conducive to their mind training. The essential point to remember here, bearing in mind that the aim of the religion is the welfare of human beings, is that whatever we may learn or borrow from each other, the benefits that religion can bring and the contribution they can make to mankind depend upon ourselves and whether we really put them into practice.

Chapter 2

A Survey of the Paths of Tibetan Buddhism

In giving an overview of the Buddha-dharma as practiced by the Tibetans, I generally point out that the Buddhism we practice is an integrated form comprising teachings of the Lower, Bodhisattva, and Tantric vehicles, including such paths as the Great Seal [Mahamudra]. Because quite a number of people have already received initiations, teachings, and so on, they might find it helpful to have an explanation of the complete framework.

We pass our lives very busily. Whether we behave well or not, time never waits for us, but goes on forever changing. In addition, our own lives continually move on, so if something goes wrong, we cannot repeat it. Life is always running out. Therefore, it is very important to examine our mental attitudes. We also constantly need to examine ourselves in day-to-day life, which is very helpful to give ourselves guidelines. If we live each day with mindfulness and alertness, we can keep a check on our motivation and behavior. We can improve and transform ourselves. Although I haven't changed or improved myself much, I have a continuing wish to do so. And in my own daily life, I find it very helpful to keep a check on my own motivation from morning until night.

During these teachings, what I will be describing is essentially a kind of instrument with which to improve yourself—just as you might take your brain to a laboratory to examine your mental functions more deeply so that you can reshape them in a more positive way. Trying to change yourself for the better is the point of view a Buddhist practitioner should adopt.

People of other religious traditions, who have an interest in Buddhism and who find such features of Buddhist practice as the meditative techniques for developing love and compassion attractive, could also benefit by incorporating them into their own tradition and practice.

In Buddhist writings, many different systems of belief and tradition are explained. These are referred to as vehicles—the vehicles of divine beings and human beings, and the Lower Vehicle (Hinayana), the Great Vehicle (Mahayana), and the vehicle of Tantra.

The vehicles of human and divine beings here refer to the system which outlines the methods and techniques for bringing about a betterment within this life or attaining a favorable rebirth in the future as a human or a god. Such a system highlights the importance of maintaining good behavior. By performing good deeds and refraining from negative actions, we can lead righteous lives and be able to attain a favorable rebirth in the future.

The Buddha also spoke of another category of vehicle, the Brahma Vehicle, which comprises techniques of meditation by which a person withdraws his or her attention from external objects and draws the mind within, trying to cultivate single-pointed concentration. Through such techniques, one is able to attain the highest form of life possible within cyclic existence.

From a Buddhist point of view, because these various systems bring great benefit to many living beings, they are all worthy of respect. Yet these systems do not provide any method for achieving liberation, that is, freedom from suffering and the cycle of existence. Methods for achieving such a state of liberation enable us to overcome ignorance, which is the root cause of our spinning in the cycle of existence. And the system containing methods for obtaining freedom from this cycle of existence is referred to as the Hearer's Vehicle or the Solitary Realizer's Vehicle.

In this system, the view of selflessness is explained only in terms of the person, not of phenomena, whereas in the Great

Vehicle system, the view of selflessness is not confined to the person alone, but encompasses all phenomena. When this view of selflessness gives rise to a profound understanding, we will be able to eliminate not only ignorance and the disturbing emotions derived from it, but also the imprints left by them. This system is called the Great Vehicle.

The highest vehicle is known as the Tantric Vehicle, which comprises not only techniques for heightening your own realization of emptiness or mind of enlightenment, but also certain techniques for penetrating the vital points of the body. By using the body's physical elements, we can expedite the process of realization, eliminating ignorance and its imprints. This is the main feature of the Tantric Vehicle.

According to the viewpoint of Shakyashri, a great pandit [scholar] of Kashmir who came to Tibet, Lord Buddha lived in India 2,500 years ago. This accords with the popular Theravadan view, but according to some Tibetan scholars, Buddha appeared in the world more than 3,000 years ago. Another group says it was more than 2,800 years. These different proponents try to support their theories with different reasons, but in the end they are quite vague.

I personally feel it is quite disgraceful that nobody, not even Buddhists, knows when our teacher, Shakyamuni Buddha, actually lived. I have been seriously considering whether some scientific research could be done. Relics are available in India and Tibet which people believe derive from the Buddha himself. If these were examined with modern techniques, we might be able to establish some accurate dates, which would be very helpful.

We know that, historically, the Buddha was born as an ordinary person like ourselves. He was brought up as a prince, married, and had a son. Then, after observing the suffering of human beings, aging, sickness, and death, he totally renounced the worldly way of life. He underwent severe physical penances and with great effort undertook long meditation, eventually becoming completely enlightened.

I feel the way he demonstrated how to become totally enlightened set a very good example for his followers, for this is the way in which we should pursue our own spiritual path. Purifying your own mind is not at all easy; it takes a lot of time and hard work. Therefore, if you choose to follow this teaching, you need tremendous willpower and determination right from the start, accepting that there will be many, many obstacles, and resolving that despite all of them you will continue the practice. This kind of determination is very important. Sometimes, it may seem to us that although Shakyamuni Buddha attained enlightenment through great sacrifice and hard work, we his followers can easily attain Buddhahood without the hard work and difficulties that he underwent. So, I think that the Buddha's own story has something to tell us.

According to popular legend, after his complete enlightenment, the Buddha gave no public teaching for 49 days. He gave his first discourse to the five who had formerly been his colleagues when he lived as a mendicant. Because he had broken his physical penances, they had abandoned him, and even after he had become totally enlightened they had no thoughts of reconciliation toward him. However, meeting the Buddha on his way, they naturally and involuntarily paid him respect, as a result of which he gave them his first teaching.

The First Turning of the Wheel of Dharma

He gave the first teaching, known as the first turning of the wheel of Dharma, on the basis of the four noble truths. These four noble truths are the truth of suffering, the truth of its origin, the truth of cessation, and the path leading to cessation.

He taught the four noble truths, according to the sutra we find in the Tibetan edition, in the context of three factors: the nature of the truths themselves, their functions, and their effects.

The four truths are really very profound, for the entire Buddhist doctrine can be presented within them. What we seek is happiness, and happiness is the effect of a cause, and what we don't want is suffering, and suffering has its own causes too.

In view of the importance of the four noble truths, I often remark that both the Buddhist view of dependent arising and the Buddhist conduct of not harming emphasize the conduct of non-violence. The simple reason for this is that suffering comes about unwanted due to its cause, which is basically our own ignorance and undisciplined mind. If we want to avoid suffering, we have to restrain ourselves from negative actions which give rise to suffering. And because suffering is related to its causes, the view of dependent arising comes in. Effects depend upon their causes, and if you don't want the effects, you have to put an end to their causes.

So, in the four noble truths we find two sets of causes and effects: suffering is the effect and its origin is the cause. In the same manner, cessation is peace and the path leading to it is the cause of that peace.

The happiness we seek can be achieved by bringing about discipline and transformation within our minds; that is, by purifying our minds. Purification of our minds is possible when we eliminate ignorance, which is at the root of all disturbing emotions, and through that we can achieve that state of cessation which is true peace and happiness. That cessation can be achieved only when we are able to realize the nature of phenomena and penetrate the nature of reality, and to do this the training in wisdom is important. When it is combined with the faculty of single-pointedness, we will be able to channel all our energy and attention toward a single object or virtue. Therefore, the training in concentration comes in here, and for the training of concentration and wisdom to be successful, a very stable foundation of morality is required; the practice of morality or ethics comes in here.

Ethics

Just as there are three types of training—in wisdom, concentration, and morality—the Buddhist scriptures contain three divisions—discipline, sets of discourses, and knowledge.

Both male and female practitioners have an equal need to practice these three trainings, although there are differences in the vows they take. The basic foundation of the practice of morality is restraint from the ten unwholesome actions: three pertaining to the body, four pertaining to speech, and three pertaining to thought.

The three physical nonvirtues are:

1. Taking the life of a living being, from an insect up to a human being.

2. Stealing, taking away another's property without his consent, regardless of its value, and whether or not you do it yourself.

3. Sexual misconduct, committing adultery.

The four verbal nonvirtues are:

1. Lying, deceiving others through spoken word or gesture.

2. Divisiveness, creating dissension by causing those in agreement to disagree or those in disagreement to disagree further.

3. Harshness, abusing others.

4. Senselessness, talking about foolish things motivated by desire and so forth.

The three mental nonvirtues are:

1. Covetousness, desiring to possess something that belongs to another.

2. Harmful intent, wishing to injure others, be it in a great or small way.

3. Wrong view, viewing some existent thing, such as rebirth, cause and effect, or the Three Jewels, as nonexistent.

The morality practiced by those who observe the monastic way of life is referred to as the discipline of individual liberation (Pratimoksha). In India there were four major schools of tenets, later producing 18 branches, which each preserved their own version of the Pratimoksha, the original discourse spoken by the Buddha, which laid down the guidelines for monastic life. The practice observed in the Tibetan monasteries follows the Mulasarvastavadin tradition in which 253 precepts are prescribed for fully ordained monks, or *bhikshus*. In the Theravadan tradition, the individual liberation vow of monks comprises 227 precepts.

In providing you with an instrument of mindfulness and alertness, the practice of morality protects you from indulging in negative actions. Therefore, it is the foundation of the Buddhist path. The second phase is meditation; it leads the practitioner to the second training, which is concerned with concentration.

Concentration

Meditation in the general Buddhist sense is of two types—absorptive and analytical meditation. The first refers to the practice of the calmly abiding or single-pointed mind, and the second to the practice of analysis. In both cases, it is very important to have a firm foundation of mindfulness and alertness, which is provided by the practice of morality. These two factors—mindfulness and alertness—are important not only in meditation, but also in our day-to-day lives.

We speak of many different states of meditation, such as the form or formless states. The form states are differentiated on the basis of their branches, whereas the formless states are differentiated on the basis of the nature of the object of absorption.

We take the practice of morality as the foundation and the practice of concentration as a complementary factor, an instrument, to make the mind serviceable. So, later, when you undertake the practice of wisdom, you are equipped with such a single-pointed mind that you can direct all your attention and energy to the chosen object. In the practice of wisdom, you meditate on the selflessness or emptiness of phenomena, which serves as the actual antidote to the disturbing emotions.

The 37 Aspects of Enlightenment

The general structure of the Buddhist path, as outlined in the first turning of the wheel of Dharma, consists of the 37 aspects of enlightenment. These begin with the four mindfulnesses, which refer to mindfulness of the body, feelings, mind, and phenomena. Here, however, *mindfulness* refers to meditation on the suffering nature of cyclic existence, by means of which practitioners develop a true determination to be free from this cycle of existence.

Next are the four complete abandonments, because when practitioners develop a true determination to be free through the practice of the four mindfulnesses, they engage in a way of life in which they abandon the causes of future suffering and cultivate the causes of future happiness.

Since overcoming all negative actions and disturbing emotions, and increasing positive factors within your mind, which are technically called the class of pure phenomena, can be achieved only when you have a very concentrated mind, there follow what are called the four factors of miraculous powers.

Next come what are known as the five faculties, five powers, eightfold noble path, and seven branches of the path to enlightenment.

This is the general structure of the Buddhist path as laid down in the first turning of the wheel of Dharma. Buddhism as practiced in the Tibetan tradition completely incorporates all these features of the Buddhist doctrine.

THE SECOND TURNING OF THE WHEEL OF DHARMA

In the second turning of the wheel of Dharma, the Buddha taught the *Perfection of Wisdom* or *Prajnaparamita* sutras on the Vulture's Peak, outside Rajgir.

The second turning of the wheel of Dharma should be seen as expanding upon the topics which the Buddha had expounded during the first turning of the wheel. In the second turning, he not only taught the truth of suffering, that suffering should be recognized as suffering, but emphasized the importance of identifying both your own suffering as well as that of all sentient beings, so it is much more extensive. When he taught the origin of suffering in the second turning of the wheel of Dharma, he referred not to the disturbing emotions alone, but also to the subtle imprints they leave behind, so this explanation is more profound.

The truth of cessation is also explained much more profoundly. In the first turning of the wheel of Dharma, cessation is merely identified, whereas in the *Perfection of Wisdom* sutras the Buddha explains the nature of this cessation and its characteristics in great detail. He describes the path by which sufferings can be ceased and what the actual state called cessation is.

The truth of the path is similarly dealt with more profoundly in the *Perfection of Wisdom* sutras. The Buddha taught a unique path comprising the realization of emptiness, the true nature of all phenomena, combined with compassion and the mind of enlightenment, the altruistic wish to achieve enlightenment for the sake of all sentient beings. Because he spoke of this union of method and wisdom in the second turning of the wheel of Dharma, we find that the second turning develops and expands on the first turning of the wheel of Dharma.

Although the four noble truths were explained more profoundly during the second turning of the wheel of Dharma, this is not because certain features were explained in the second that were not explained in the first. That cannot be the reason, because many topics are explained in non-Buddhist systems which are not explained in Buddhism, but that does not mean that other systems are more profound than Buddhism. The second turning of the wheel of Dharma explains and develops certain aspects of the four noble truths, which were not explained in the first turning of the wheel, but which do not contradict the general structure of the Buddhist path described in that first discourse. Therefore, the explanation found in the second is said to be more profound.

Yet, in the discourses of the second turning of the wheel we also find certain presentations that do contradict the general structure of the path as described in the first; thus, the Great Vehicle speaks of two categories of sutras, some which are taken at face value and are thought of as literally true, whereas others require further interpretation. So, based on the Great Vehicle approach of the four reliances, we divide the sutras into two categories—the definitive and the interpretable.

These four reliances consist of advice to rely on the teaching, not on the person; within the teachings rely on the meaning, not on mere words; rely on definitive sutras, not those requiring interpretation; and rely on the deeper understanding of wisdom, not on the knowledge of ordinary awareness.

This approach can be found in the Buddha's own words, as when he said, "O *bhikshus* and wise men, do not accept what I say just out of respect for me, but first subject it to analysis and rigorous examination."

In the second turning of the wheel of Dharma, the *Perfection of Wisdom* sutras, the Buddha further explained the subject of cessation, particularly with regard to emptiness, in a more elaborate and extensive way. Therefore, the Great Vehicle approach is to interpret those sutras on two levels: the literal meaning, which concerns the presentation of emptiness, and the hidden meaning, which concerns the latent explanation of the stages of the path.

THE THIRD TURNING OF THE WHEEL OF DHARMA

The third turning of the wheel contains many different sutras, the most important of which is the *Tathagata Essence* sutra, which is actually the source for Nagarjuna's *Collection of Praises* and also Maitreya's treatise the *Sublime Continuum*. In this sutra, the Buddha further explores topics he had touched on in the second turning of the wheel, but not from the objective viewpoint of emptiness, because emptiness was explained to its fullest, highest, and most profound degree in the second turning. What is unique about the third turning is that Buddha taught certain ways of heightening the wisdom which realizes emptiness from the point of view of subjective mind.

The Buddha's explanation of the view of emptiness in the second turning of the wheel, in which he taught about the lack of inherent existence, was too profound for many practitioners to comprehend. For some, to say phenomena lack inherent existence seems to imply that they do not exist at all. So, for the benefit of these practitioners, in the third turning of the wheel the Buddha qualified the object of emptiness with different interpretations.

For example, in the *Sutra Unraveling the Thought of the Buddha,* he differentiated various types of emptiness by categorizing all phenomena into three classes: imputed phenomena, dependent phenomena, and thoroughly established phenomena, which refers to their empty nature. He spoke of the various emptinesses of these different phenomena, the various ways of lacking inherent existence, and the various meanings of the lack of inherent existence of these different phenomena. So, the two major schools of thought of the Great Vehicle, the Middle Way (Madhyamika) and the Mind Only (Chittamatra), arose in India on the basis of these differences of presentation.

Next is the Tantric Vehicle, which I think has some connection with the third turning of the wheel. The word *tantra* means "continuity." The Yoga Tantra text called the *Ornament of the Vajra Essence Tantra* explains that tantra is a continuity referring to the continuity of consciousness or mind. It is on the basis of this mind that on the ordinary level we commit negative actions, as a result of which we go through the vicious cycle of life and death. On the spiritual path, it is also on the basis of this continuity of consciousness that we are able to make mental improvements, experience high realizations of the path, and so forth. And it is also on the basis of this continuity of consciousness that we are able to achieve the ultimate state of omniscience. So, this continuity of consciousness is always present, which is the meaning of *tantra*, or continuity.

I feel there is a bridge between the sutras and tantras in the second and third turnings of the wheel, because in the second, the Buddha taught certain sutras which have different levels of meaning. The explicit meaning of the *Perfection of Wisdom* sutra is emptiness, whereas the implicit meaning is the stages of the path which are to be achieved as a result of realizing emptiness. The third turning was concerned with different ways of heightening the wisdom which realizes emptiness. So I think there is a link here between sutra and tantra.

Different Explanations of Selflessness

From a philosophical point of view, the criterion for distinguishing a school as Buddhist is whether or not it accepts the four seals: that all composite phenomena are impermanent by nature, contaminated phenomena are of the nature of suffering, all phenomena are empty and selfless, and nirvana alone is peace. Any system accepting these seals is philosophically a Buddhist school of thought. In the Great Vehicle schools of thought, selflessness is explained more profoundly, at a deeper level.

Now, let me explain the difference between selflessness as explained in the second turning of the wheel and that explained in the first.

Let us examine our own experience, how we relate to things. For example, when I use this rosary here, I feel it is mine and I have attachment to it. If you examine the attachment you feel for your own possessions, you find there are different levels of attachment. One is the feeling that there is a self-sufficient person existing as a separate entity independent of your own body and mind, which feels that this rosary is "mine."

When you are able, through meditation, to perceive the absence of such a self-sufficient person, existing in isolation from your own body and mind, you are able to reduce the strong attachment you feel toward your possessions. But you may also feel that there are still some subtle levels of attachment. Although you may not feel a subjective attachment from your own side in relation to the person, because of the rosary's beautiful appearance, its beautiful color, and so forth, you feel a certain level of attachment to it in that a certain objective entity exists out there. So, in the second turning of the wheel, the Buddha taught that selflessness is not confined to the person alone, but that it applies to all phenomena. When you realize this, you will be able to overcome all forms of attachment and delusion.

Just as Chandrakirti said in his *Supplement to Nagarjuna's "Treatise on the Middle Way,"* the selflessness explained in the lower schools of tenets, which confine their explanation of selflessness only to the person, is not a complete form of selflessness. Even if you realize that selflessness, you will still have subtle levels of clinging and attachment to external objects, like your possessions and so forth.

Although the view of selflessness is common to all Buddhist schools of thought, there are differences of presentation. That of the higher schools is more profound in comparison with that of the lower schools of thought. One reason is that even though you may have realized the selflessness of persons, as described by the lower schools, in terms of a person not being a self-sufficient or substantially existent entity, you may still cling to a certain misconception of self, apprehending the person as inherently, independently, or truly existent.

As realization of the selflessness of persons becomes increasingly subtle, you realize that the person lacks any form of independent nature or inherent existence. Then there is no way you can apprehend a self-sufficient person. Therefore, the presentation of selflessness in the higher schools is much deeper and more profound than that of the lower schools.

The way the higher schools explain selflessness is not only more powerful in counteracting the misconception of the true existence of persons and phenomena, but also does not contradict phenomena's conventional reality. Phenomena do exist on a conventional basis, and the realization of emptiness does not affect this.

The Buddha's different presentations of selflessness should be viewed in order, as providing background for the Buddhist view of dependent arising. When Buddhists speak of dependent arising, they do so in terms of afflictive phenomena which are causes of suffering, whose consequences are suffering. This is explained in terms of the "12 links of dependent arising," which comprise those factors completed within one cycle of rebirth within the cycle of existence. Therefore, dependent arising is at the root of the Buddhist view.

If you do not understand selflessness in terms of dependent arising, you will not understand selflessness completely. People's mental faculties are different. For some, when it is explained that all phenomena are empty of inherent existence, it may seem that nothing exists at all. Such an understanding is very dangerous and harmful, because it can cause you to fall into the extreme of nihilism. Therefore, Buddha taught selflessness roughly for persons with such mental faculties. For practitioners of higher faculties, he taught selflessness on a subtler level. Still, no matter how subtle the realization of emptiness may be, it does not harm their conviction in phenomena's conventional existence.

So, your understanding of emptiness should complement your understanding of dependent arising, and that understanding of emptiness should further reaffirm your conviction in the law of cause and effect.

If you were to analyze the higher schools' presentation from the viewpoint of the lower schools, you should find no contradiction or logical inconsistencies in them. Whereas, if you were to consider the lower schools' presentation from the viewpoint of the higher schools, you would find many logical inconsistencies.

The Four Seals

The four seals have profound implications for a Buddhist practitioner. The first seal states that all compounded phenomena are impermanent. The question of impermanence has been expounded most fully by the Sutra Follower (Sautrantika) school, which explains that all compounded phenomena are by nature impermanent, in the sense that due to its being produced from a cause, a phenomenon is by nature impermanent or disintegrating. If something is produced from a cause, no secondary cause is required for it to disintegrate. The moment that it was produced from the cause, the process of disintegration has already begun. Therefore, its disintegration requires no further cause. This is the subtle meaning of impermanence, that anything produced by causes is "other-powered" in the sense that it depends upon causes and conditions and therefore is subject to change and disintegration.

This is very close to the physicists' explanation of nature, the momentariness of phenomena.

The second seal states that all contaminated phenomena are of the nature of suffering. Here, contaminated phenomena refer to the type of phenomena which are produced by contaminated actions and disturbing emotions. As explained above, something that is produced is "other-powered" in the sense that it is dependent on causes. In this case, causes refer to our ignorance and disturbing emotions. Contaminated actions and ignorance constitute a negative phenomenon, a misconception of reality, and as long as something is under such a negative influence, it will be of the nature of suffering. Here, suffering does not only imply overt physical suffering, but can also be understood as of the nature of dissatisfaction.

By contemplating these two seals concerning the impermanent and suffering nature of contaminated phenomena, we will be able to develop a genuine sense of renunciation, the determination to be free from suffering. The question then arises, is it possible for us ever to obtain such a state of freedom? This is where the third seal, that all phenomena are empty and selfless, comes in.

Our experience of suffering comes about due to causes and conditions, which are contaminated actions and the ignorance which induced them. This ignorance is a misconception. It has no valid support and, because it apprehends phenomena in a manner contrary to the way they really are, it is distorted, is erroneous, and contradicts reality. Now, if we can clear away this misconception, the cessation of suffering becomes possible. If we penetrate the nature of reality, it is also possible to achieve that cessation within our minds, and as the fourth seal states, such a cessation or liberation is true peace.

When we take into account the different explanations of various philosophical schools within Buddhism, including the Great Vehicle schools, it is necessary to discriminate those sutras that are definitive and those requiring further interpretation. If we were to make these distinctions on the basis of scriptural texts alone, we would have to verify the scripture we used for determining whether something was interpretable or definitive against another sutra, and because this would continue in an infinite regression, it would not be a very reliable method. Therefore, we have to determine whether a sutra is definitive or interpretable on the basis of logic. So, when we speak of the Great Vehicle philosophical schools, reason is more important than the scripture.

How do we determine whether something is interpretable? There are different types of scriptures belonging to the interpretable category; for instance, certain sutras mention that one's parents are to be killed. Now, since these sutras cannot be taken literally, at face value, they require further interpretation. The reference here to parents is to the contaminated actions and attachment which brings about rebirth in the future.

Similarly, in tantras such as *Guhyasamaja*, the Buddha says that the Tathagata or Buddha is to be killed and that if you kill the Buddha, you will achieve supreme enlightenment.

It is obvious that these scriptures require further interpretation. However, other sutras are less obviously interpretable. The sutra which explains the 12 links of dependent arising states that because of the cause, the fruits ensue. An example is that because of ignorance within, contaminated actions come about. Although the content of this type of sutra is true on one level, it is categorized as interpretable, because when ignorance is said to induce contaminated action, it does not refer to the ultimate point of view. It is only on the conventional level that something can produce something else. From the ultimate point of view, its nature is emptiness. So, because there is a further, deeper level not referred to in these sutras, they are said to be interpretable.

Definitive sutras are those sutras, like the *Heart of Wisdom*, in which the Buddha spoke of the ultimate nature of phenomena, that form is emptiness and emptiness is form; apart from form, there is no emptiness. Because such sutras speak of the ultimate nature of phenomena, their ultimate mode of existence, emptiness, they are said to be definitive. However, we should also note that there are different ways of discriminating between definitive and interpretable sutras among different Buddhist schools of thought.

In short, the texts of the Middle Way Consequentialist (Madhyamika Prasangika) school, particularly those by Nagarjuna and his disciple Chandrakirti, are definitive and expound the view of emptiness the Buddha taught to its fullest extent. The view of emptiness expounded in these texts is not contradicted by logical reasoning, but rather is supported by it.

Nagarjuna

Among the definitive sutras are also included sutras belonging to the third turning of the wheel of Dharma, particularly the *Tathagata Essence* sutra, which is actually the fundamental source of such Middle Way treatises as the *Sublime Continuum* [by Maitreya] and the *Collection of Praises* written by Nagarjuna. Also included in the third turning were other sutras, such as the *Sutra Unraveling the Thought of the Buddha*, which according to some Tibetan masters are also categorized as definitive.

Emptiness

These scholars (such as the Jonangpas) maintain a unique view of emptiness, which is technically called "emptiness of other," and they speak of different kinds of emptiness qualifying different phenomena. They maintain that conventional phenomena are empty of themselves and ultimate phenomena are empty of conventional phenomena.

You could interpret this explanation of emptiness, that conventional phenomena are empty of themselves, to mean that because conventional phenomena are not their own ultimate nature, they are empty of themselves. But these Tibetan scholars do not interpret it in such a way; they maintain that because phenomena are empty of themselves, they do not exist.

As we know from history that many masters belonging to this group of scholars actually achieved high realizations of the generation and completion stages of tantra, they must have had a profound understanding of their particular interpretation of emptiness. But if we were to interpret emptiness as things being empty of themselves in such a manner that they do not exist at all, it would be like saying that nothing exists at all.

Because they maintain that conventional phenomena do not exist, being empty of themselves, they maintain that their ultimate nature is a truly existent phenomenon that exists in its own right, and is inherently existent. And when they speak of the emptiness of this ultimate truth, they refer to its being empty of being a conventional phenomenon.

Dharmashri, the son of Yumo Mingyur Dorje, one of the proponents of this view, stated in a text I once read that Nagarjuna's view of emptiness was a nihilistic view.

So, these systems of thought maintain that since conventional phenomena are empty of themselves, the only thing that exists is ultimate truth, and that ultimate truth exists truly and inherently.

It is obvious that adherence to such a philosophical point of view directly contradicts the view of emptiness explained in the *Perfection of Wisdom* sutras, in which the Buddha has stated explicitly and clearly that as far as empty nature is concerned, there is no discrimination between conventional and ultimate phenomena. He has explained the emptiness of ultimate phenomena by using many different synonyms for ultimate truth, indicating that from form up to omniscience, all phenomena are equally empty.

Although Middle Way Consequentialists, proponents of the highest Buddhist philosophical tenets, speak of phenomena being empty and having an empty nature, this is not to say that phenomena do not exist at all. Rather, phenomena do not exist in or of themselves, in their own right, or inherently. The fact is that phenomena have the characteristics of existence, such as arising in dependence on other factors or causal conditions. Therefore, lacking any independent nature, phenomena are dependent. The very fact that they are by nature dependent on other factors is an indication of their lacking an independent nature. So, when Middle Way Consequentialists speak of emptiness, they speak of the dependent nature of phenomena in terms of dependent arising. Therefore, an understanding of emptiness does not contradict the conventional reality of phenomena.

Because phenomena arise in dependence on other factors, causal conditions and so forth, the Middle Way Consequentialists use their dependent nature as the final ground for establishing their empty nature. Lacking an independent nature, they lack inherent existence. The reasoning of dependent arising is very powerful, not only because it dispels the misconception that things exist inherently, but because at the same time it protects a person from falling into the extreme of nihilism.

In Nagarjuna's own writings, we find that emptiness has to be understood in the context of dependent arising. In *Fundamental Wisdom,* Nagarjuna says, "Since there is no phenomenon which is not a dependent arising, there is no phenomenon which is not empty."

It is clear that Nagarjuna's view of emptiness has to be understood in the context of dependent arising, not only from his own writings, but also those of later commentators such as Buddhapalita, who is very concise but clear, and Chandrakirti in his *Commentary on Nagarjuna's "Treatise on the Middle Way"; Clear Words,* his Supplement to Nagarjuna's *Treatise on the Middle Way;* his autocommentary to it; and also his *Commentary on Aryadeva's "Four Hundred."* If you were to compare all these texts, it would become very clear that the view of emptiness as expounded by Nagarjuna has to be understood in terms of dependent arising. And when you read these commentaries, you begin to feel great appreciation for Nagarjuna.

INTRODUCTION TO THE TANTRAS

There is an explanation of the evolution of the tantras from a historical point of view, according to which the Buddha taught the different tantras at certain times and so forth. However, I think that the tantric teaching could also have come about as a result of individuals having achieved high realizations and having been able to explore the physical elements and the potential within the body to its fullest extent. As a result of this, they might have had high realizations and visions, and so may have received tantric teachings. Therefore, when we think about tantric teachings, we should not have this rigid view of a particular historical time.

In the fundamental tantra of Kalachakra, the Buddha himself says that when he gave the second turning of the wheel of Dharma at Vulture's Peak, he also gave a different system of tantric teachings at the place called Dhanyakataka. There is a difference of opinion among Tibetan scholars concerning the evolution of the tantric teachings, including the *Kalachakra Tantra*. One system maintains that the Buddha gave the tantric teachings on the full-moon day one year after his complete enlightenment; whereas a second system maintains that he gave the tantric teachings one month prior to his *parinirvana.*

The second view seems to be more consistent because the *Kalachakra Tantra* itself says that just as the Buddha gave the second turning of the wheel of Dharma at Vulture's Peak, he gave tantric teachings at Dhanyakataka. It seems that among the lower sets of tantra there are a few which the Buddha taught in his normal form as a fully ordained monk, or *bhikshu*, but in general, when he taught most of the tantras, he assumed the form of the principal deity of the particular tantra.

The practice of tantra can be undertaken when a person has gained a firm foundation in the path presented in the sutra system. This consists of a correct view of emptiness, as it was explained in the second turning of the wheel, and a realization of the altruistic aspiration to achieve enlightenment for the benefit of all living beings, based on love and compassion, together with the practices of the six perfections. So only after you have laid a proper foundation in the common paths can you undertake the practice of tantra as an additional factor.

The greatest profundities can be found in the Highest Yoga Tantra. This is where you can come to understand the term "Buddha-nature" or "essence of Buddhahood," in other words, the uncontaminated awareness explained in the *Sublime Continuum*. The deepest meaning of this can only be understood in the Highest Yoga Tantra.

Irrespective of whether we maintain that the *Sublime Continuum* itself deals with Buddha-nature in its fullest form, it is very clear that the ultimate intent of Buddhahood is the fundamental innate mind of clear light as explained in the Highest Yoga Tantra.

What is so unique and profound about the Highest Yoga Tantra is that it not only explains and outlines methods for realizing spiritual progress on the path on the level of the gross mind, but also explains techniques and methods for utilizing the subtlest level of the mind, the fundamental innate mind of clear light. When you are able to transform the fundamental innate mind of clear light into the entity of the path, you are equipped with a very powerful practice.

Usually, in practicing single-pointed meditation, we are functioning on a gross mental level and so require a strong degree of mindfulness and alertness to prevent our concentration from being distracted. If there were a technique or method by which we could do away with the distractions associated with these gross levels of mind, there would be no need for such rigorous vigilance and mindfulness. Highest Yoga Tantra explains methods by which you can dissolve and withdraw all the gross levels of mind and bring your mind to a level at which there is no possibility of distractions arising.

In addition, the method for bringing that fundamental innate mind of clear light, the subtlest level of mind, into the entity of the path according to Highest Yoga Tantra, is to dissolve or withdraw the gross levels of mind and the energies that propel them. There are three major ways of doing this. One is by means of wind yoga, another is through experiencing the four types of bliss, and the third is through meditation on nonconceptuality.

Here, it should be remembered that although these are different methods, we can achieve these feats by means of any of these three techniques. We should be aware that these feats can be achieved not only by one method, but through a collection of many different methods. For example, if we generate a virtuous thought today, although this virtuous thought can serve as a cause for attaining omniscience in the future, this does not mean that this virtuous thought alone is the cause of omniscience.

A text called the *Sacred Words of Manjushri*, composed by the Indian master Buddhajnana, mentions that because of the physical structure of our bodies and the elements that we possess as human beings inhabiting this planet, even on an ordinary level there are certain occasions when we experience the subtle level of clear light, naturally. These occur during sleep, yawning, fainting, and sexual climax.

This shows that we have within ourselves a certain potential which we can explore further. And among these four states, the best opportunity for further development is during sexual intercourse.

Although I am using this ordinary term, "sexual climax," it does not imply the ordinary sexual act. The reference here is to the experience of entering into union with a consort of the opposite sex, by means of which the elements at the crown are melted, and through the power of meditation the process is also reversed.

A prerequisite of such a practice is that you should be able to protect yourself from the fault of seminal emission. According to the explanation of the *Kalachakra Tantra* in particular, such emission is said to be very damaging to your practice. Therefore, because you should not experience emission even in dreams, the tantras describe different techniques for overcoming this fault.

This contrasts with the Vinaya explanation, which sets out the code of discipline for Buddhist monks, in which exception is made for emission in dreams, because it is beyond your control, whereas in tantra it is considered an offense. The experience of melting the mind of enlightenment is brought about by ordinary afflicted desire, so the practitioner must be able to generate it.

The point is that due to the force of desire, you are able to melt the elements within your body. Consequently, when you experience the nonconceptual state, you should be able to direct your attention to meditation on emptiness. So, when you experience a nonconceptual state as a result of the elements melting within your body, if you are able to generate that understanding into a realization of emptiness, you will have achieved the feat of transforming a disturbing emotion, desire, into the wisdom realizing emptiness.

When you are able to employ this nonconceptual blissful mind in realizing emptiness, the result is a powerful wisdom that serves as an antidote to counteract and eliminate disturbing emotions. Therefore, it is a case of wisdom derived from disturbing emotions counteracting and eliminating them, just as insects born from wood consume it.

This is the significance of the Buddha's assuming the form of a meditational deity, the principal deity of the mandala, and entering into union with the consort when he taught the tantric path. Therefore, in the course of their practice, practitioners generate themselves on an imaginary level into such deities in union with a consort.

Another unique and profound feature of tantra concerns the process for attaining the twofold body of the Buddha, the form body and the truth body. According to the sutra system, the practitioner works to attain the form and the truth bodies of a Buddha as a result of cultivating the altruistic aspiration for enlightenment. However, the body of the Buddha does not come about without causes and conditions, and these causes and conditions must be commensurate with their effects. That is to say, cause and effect should have similar aspects.

The sutra systems speak of the causes of the Buddha's form body in terms of a unique mental body attained by highly evolved Bodhisattvas, which, serving as the substantial cause of the Buddha's body, eventually becomes the form body of the Buddha. This is also mentioned in the writings of the Lower Vehicle. Although they do not describe a complete method for actualizing the omniscient state, they do speak of certain types of practices which are geared toward achieving the major and minor marks of the Buddha.

Highest Yoga Tantra, on the other hand, outlines the unique causes and methods for actualizing both the truth body and the form body of a Buddha.

In order to undertake the practice of a method which serves as the principal or substantial cause for attaining the form body of the Buddha, the practitioner of tantra should first ripen his mental faculties. In other words, he should rehearse this unique cause. The importance of deity yoga, which employs imagination in meditation, is that the practitioner generates himself or herself into the aspect of a deity.

Texts such as the explanatory tantra called the *Vajrapanjara Tantra* and related Indian commentaries point out that attainment of the Buddha's truth body requires meditation and practice of a path that has features similar to the resultant truth body. This refers to meditation on emptiness through direct perception in which all dualistic appearances and conceptual elaborations have been withdrawn. Similarly, in order to attain the form body of the Buddha, one should also cultivate a path that has similar features to the resultant form body. Engaging in a path that has similar features to the resultant state of Buddhahood, particularly the form body, is of indispensable significance and power. The tantras present a path that has features, technically called the four complete purities, similar to the resultant state in four ways: the complete purity of enlightenment, the complete purity of the body, the complete purity of the resources, and the complete purity of activities.

All Great Vehicle systems assert that in order to achieve the resultant state, which is the union of the two bodies, it is essential to engage in a path in which there is a union of method and wisdom. However, the union of wisdom and method according to the sutra system is not a complete union. Although it refers to wisdom in terms of the wisdom realizing emptiness and method in terms of the practice of the six perfections such as giving, ethics, and so forth, the union of method and wisdom here refers only to the practice of wisdom realizing emptiness being complemented by a factor of method such as the mind of enlightenment, and the practice of the mind of enlightenment and aspects of method being complemented and supported by a factor of wisdom such as the realization of emptiness. In other words, they maintain that it is not possible for both factors of the path, the wisdom factor and the method factor, to be present within one entity of consciousness. Such a form of practice is a relative union of method and wisdom. The practice of wisdom is not isolated from factors of method, nor is the practice of method isolated from factors of wisdom, yet it is not a complete form of union of method and wisdom. Tantra alone can serve as the ultimate cause or path for realizing the resultant state of Buddhahood, in which there is a complete unity between the form body and the truth body.

The question is what form of practice or path is possible where method and wisdom are inseparably united. In the practice of tantra, it is deity yoga, in which the divine form of a deity is visualized in a single moment of consciousness, while at the same time there is mindfulness of its empty nature, its emptiness. There, within one entity of consciousness, is meditation on both the deity as well as apprehension of emptiness. Therefore, such a moment of consciousness is a factor of both method and wisdom.

Also, when we try to cultivate divine pride or the sense of identity as a divine being in the practice of deity yoga, we try to overcome the feeling and perception of ordinariness. I think this helps us to make the potential of Buddhahood within ourselves manifest more.

To attain a firm pride of being a deity requires a stable visualization of the form and appearance of the deity. Normally, because of our natural tendency and consequent notion of self, we have an innate feeling of "I" and self based upon our body and mind. If we similarly cultivate a strong perception of our own appearance as a deity, we will also be able to cultivate divine pride, the sense of identity as a deity, by focusing on the divine body.

In order to actualize the omniscient mind within ourselves, we need to develop the substantial cause for such a mind, which is not just any form of consciousness, but a consciousness with an enduring continuity. That is to say, the mind whose emptiness we realize in order to actualize omniscience should be a special type of mind which, in terms of its continuity, is permanent. Contaminated states of mind, such as disturbing emotions and so forth, are adventitious. Therefore, they are occasional. They arise at a certain moment, but they disappear. So, although they are disadvantageous, they do not endure, whereas the mind whose nature we realize when we become omniscient should be permanent in terms of its continuity, not adventitious.

This means that we should be able to realize the empty nature of the purified mind, the mind that has never been polluted by the influence of disturbing emotions.

Now, from the point of view of emptiness itself, although there is no difference between the emptiness of external phenomena, such as a sprout, and the emptiness of a deity, such as oneself generated into a deity like Vairochana, from the point of view of the subjects qualified by emptiness, there is a difference.

The importance of deity yoga is that it is the special type of wisdom that realizes the emptiness of this deity that eventually serves as the substantial cause for the omniscient mind of Buddhahood. Deity yoga, therefore, is a union of clarity, which is the visualization of the deity, and the profound, which is the realization of emptiness.

Now, according to the sutra system, the Buddha never approved the generation of disturbing emotions for one's own welfare, or from the point of view of one's own realization of the path. But there are occasions mentioned in the sutras where a Bodhisattva, who finds that the application of certain disturbing emotions is useful and beneficial for the purpose of others, is given such approval.

The Buddha said that although excrement is dirty in the town, it is helpful when used as fertilizer in a field. The Bodhisattva's special use of delusions can similarly be of benefit to others.

While, according to the sutra system, the Buddha never approved a Bodhisattva's generating anger or hatred, we often find that for us ordinary people, hatred or anger, being very strong emotional forces, actually help us to get things done.

In the tantras we find that the Buddha has made an exception for the generation of hatred, because we find here techniques and methods for using hatred and anger for positive purposes. However, we must be aware that even when utilizing hatred and anger for positive purposes, the fundamental motive should be the altruistic thought of achieving enlightenment for the benefit of others. When it is induced by such a motive, circumstantial anger or hatred is condoned. The significance of the wrathful aspect of some deities can be understood in this context.

So, these are just some of the differences between the sutra system and the tantric system or, as we might say, the superior features of the tantric path.

THE FOUR CLASSES OF TANTRA

The tantric system is divided into four classes, as stated in the explanatory tantra *Vajrapanjara*. As we discussed above, it is only in the Highest Yoga Tantra that the most profound and unique features of tantra come to their fulfillment; therefore, we should view the lower tantras as steps leading up to the Highest Yoga Tantra. Although the explanation of ways of taking desire into the path is a common feature of all four tantras, the levels of desire differ. In the first class of tantras, Action Tantra, the method for taking desire into the path is to glance at the consort. In the subsequent classes of tantra, the methods include laughter, holding hands, or embracing and union.

The four classes of tantras are termed according to their functions and different modes of purification. In the lowest class of tantra, mudras, or hand gestures, are regarded as more important than the inner yoga, so it is called Action Tantra.

The second class, in which there is equal emphasis on both aspects, is called Performance Tantra. The third, Yoga Tantra, is where inner yoga is emphasized more than external activities. The fourth class is called Highest Yoga Tantra, not only because it emphasizes the importance of inner yoga, but because there is no tantra superior to it.

The explanation of the Nyingma Great Perfection [Dzogchen] School speaks of nine vehicles. The first three refer to the Hearer (Shravaka), Solitary Realizer (Pratyekabuddha), and Bodhisattva vehicles, which constitute the sutra system. The second three are called the external vehicles, comprising Action Tantra, Performance Tantra, and Yoga Tantra, since they emphasize the practice of external activities, although they also deal with the practitioner's outer and inner conduct. Finally, there are the three inner tantras, which are referred to in the Great Perfection terminology as Mahayoga, Anuyoga, and Atiyoga. These three inner vehicles are termed the methods or vehicles for gaining control, because they contain methods for making manifest the subtlest levels of mind and energy. By these means a practitioner can place his or her mind in a deep state beyond the discriminations of good or bad, clear or dirty, which enables him or her to transcend such worldly conventions.

Empowerments

The form of the empowerment or initiation ceremony is quite uniform among the three lower tantras. In Highest Yoga Tantra, however, because of the wide diversity among the tantras belonging to this category, there are also different initiations which serve as ripening factors for the particular tantra to which they belong.

Different types of empowerment are necessary for specific classes of tantras. For example, in the case of Action Tantra, two types of initiations are indispensable: the water empowerment and the crown empowerment. In Performance Tantra, the five wisdom empowerments are indispensable, and in the Highest Yoga Tantra, all four empowerments—vase, secret, wisdom-knowledge, and word initiations—are essential.

Nevertheless, many different terms are used in different traditions. In the tradition of the Old Transmission, or Nyingma School, for example, the Vajra master initiation is called the "initiation of illusion," and the disciple initiation is called the "beneficial empowerment," and so forth. There is also an "all-encompassing Vajra initiation." In the Great Perfection, the fourth initiation itself is further divided into four, the initiation with elaboration, and so on.

The term "initiation," *abhisheka* in Sanskrit, has many different connotations in different contexts. In a broad sense, initiation may be explained as a ripening factor, or as a causal initiation; and then in terms of the path, which is the actual path of release; and finally, initiation of the resultant state, which is the purified result. The Great Perfection also mentions one more type of initiation, the initiation of the basis. This refers to the clear light, which serves as a basis and enables other initiations to take place. If a person were to lack the basic faculty of the fundamental innate mind of clear light, it would be impossible for the subsequent empowerments to occur.

In the case of an external phenomenon like a vase or a sprout, we cannot talk of a ripening factor, path, and resultant state and so on. It is only on the basis of an individual who possesses this kind of faculty within that one can speak of a ripening factor and a path that leads to an eventual resultant state. Thus, broadly speaking, there are four initiations.

Preparations for Empowerment

To conduct a ceremony of empowerment one requires a mandala, which is the inestimable mansion or divine residence of the deity. There are different types of mandalas: mandalas created by concentration, painted mandalas, sand mandalas, and also, in Highest Yoga Tantra, body mandalas based on the body of the guru, and mandalas of the conventional mind of enlightenment.

Among all of these, the sand mandala is principal because it is the only one in preparation of which all the rituals concerning consecration of the site, the strings, etc., can be conducted. It also incorporates the performance of ritual dance, which includes various hand gestures and steps.

There are different types of ritual dance. One is conducted when consecrating the site where the mandala is to be built. Another is performed after the completion of the mandala as an offering to the mandala deities. In addition, there is another type of ceremonial dance called Cham, which is associated with activities for overcoming obstacles.

Many small monasteries are expert in performing these ritual dances, but we might question their understanding of the symbolism and significance behind them. Most people consider their performance as a spectacle, a kind of theatrical show. This is a reflection of the sad fact that the tantras are degenerating. I have read in Indian history that one of the factors for the degeneration of tantra and the Buddhist doctrine in India was the excessive proliferation of tantric practices. If a practitioner lacks the basic foundations which are prerequisites for tantric practice, then tantric techniques and meditation may prove to be more harmful than beneficial. That is why tantric practices are called "secret."

We should bear in mind that even in tantric writings, the monastic vows of individual liberation are highly praised. The fundamental tantra of Kalachakra, which is king of all Highest Yoga Tantras, mentions that of the varieties of Vajra masters conducting teachings and ceremonies, fully ordained monks are the highest, novices are middling, and the laymen are the lowest. Moreover, in the course of receiving an initiation there are different types of vows to be taken. Bodhisattva vows can be taken in the presence of an image of the Buddha, without a guru in human form. Individual liberation vows and tantric vows, on the other hand, must be taken from a living person in the form of a guru.

If you are to make successful progress in the tantric path, it is essential that you receive the inspiration and blessings of the uninterrupted lineage originating with Buddha Vajradhara from your own guru, in order to arouse the latent potential within your mind to actualize the resultant state of Buddhahood. This is achieved by the empowerment ceremony. Therefore, in the practice of tantra, the guru is very important.

Since the guru plays such an important role in the practice of tantra, many tantric texts have outlined the qualifications of a tantric master.

The person giving an initiation should be properly qualified. So before we take initiation, it is important to examine whether the guru has these qualifications. It is said that even if it takes 12 years to determine whether the master possesses the right qualifications, you should take the time to do it.

A qualified Vajra master is a person who guards his or her three doors of body, speech, and mind from negative actions; a person who is gentle and well versed in the three trainings of ethics, concentration, and wisdom. In addition, he or she should possess the two sets, inner and outer, of ten principles. The *Fifty Verses on the Guru* describes a person who lacks compassion and is full of spite, is governed by strong forces of attachment and hatred, and, having no knowledge of the three trainings, boasts of the little knowledge he has, as unqualified to be a tantric master. But, just as the tantric master should possess certain qualifications, so should the disciples. The current tendency to attend any initiation given by any lama, without prior investigation, and having taken initiation, then to speak against the lama, is not good.

On the part of the gurus, it is also important to give teachings in accordance with the general structure of the Buddhist path, taking the general framework of the Buddhist path as the rule by which you determine the integrity of your teachings.

The point is that the teacher should not arrogantly feel that within the close circle of his disciples, he is almighty and can do whatever he wants. There is a saying in Tibetan, "Even though you may rival the deities in terms of realization, your lifestyle should conform to the ways of others."

Maintaining the Vows

Once you have taken the initiation, you have a great responsibility to observe the pledges and vows. In the Action and Performance Tantras, although Bodhisattva vows are required, there is no need to take the tantric vows. Any tantra that includes a Vajra master initiation requires the disciples to observe the tantric vows as well.

If you are paying particular attention to observing practices of the three lower tantras, it is important to maintain a vegetarian diet. Although it was reasonable for Tibetans to eat meat in Tibet, because of the climatic conditions and the scarcity of vegetables, in countries where there are vegetables in abundance, it is far better to avoid or reduce your consumption of meat. Particularly when you invite many people to a party, it is good if you can provide vegetarian food.

There is a story of a nomad who visited Lhasa and was surprised to see people eating vegetables. He said, "People in Lhasa will never starve; they can eat anything green."

The Buddhist position with regard to diet, even as it is presented in monastic discipline, with the exception of the flesh of certain specific animals, is that there is no general prohibition of meat. Monks in Sri Lanka, Burma, and Thailand eat meat.

In the scriptural collections of the Bodhisattvas, eating meat is generally prohibited. However, the prohibition is not very strict. In his text called *Heart of the Middle Way*, Bhavaviveka deals with the question of vegetarianism in the Buddhist way of life, and concludes that since the animal is already dead when its meat is eaten, it is not directly affected. What is prohibited is eating meat which you know or suspect has been killed for you.

In the three lower classes of tantra, eating meat is strictly prohibited. But in the Highest Yoga Tantra, practitioners are recommended to partake of the five meats and five nectars. The perfect practitioner of Highest Yoga Tantra is someone who is able to transform the five meats and five nectars into purified substances through the power of meditation, and is then able to utilize them to enhance the body's energy. But if someone tried to justify eating meat by claiming to be a Highest Yoga Tantra practitioner, when they came to eat the five meats and nectars they could not be choosy, relishing some and rejecting the others in disgust.

Women and Buddhism

I think it is also appropriate for me to say something about feminism and women's rights within Buddhism.

In the case of the monastic way of life, although male and female practitioners are afforded equal opportunities in the Discipline [Vinaya] texts to take the monastic vows, we find that fully ordained monks are treated as superior in terms of being objects of respect and veneration. From this point of view, we might say that there is some discrimination.

Also in the writings of the Lower Vehicle, we find that a Bodhisattva on the highest level of path who is sure to gain enlightenment in that lifetime is said to be a male. We find a similar explanation in the Great Vehicle sutras, that a Bodhisattva on the highest level of path who will definitely achieve enlightenment in the same lifetime is a male abiding in the Blissful Pure Land (Sukhavati). This is also true of the three lower classes of tantra, but the explanation in Highest Yoga Tantra is different.

In Highest Yoga Tantra, even the first step of receiving empowerment is possible only on the basis of the presence of a complete assembly of male and female deities. The Buddhas of the five families must be accompanied by their consorts.

The female role is strongly emphasized in Highest Yoga Tantra. To despise a woman is a transgression of one of the root tantric vows, although no corresponding transgression is mentioned in relation to male practitioners. Also, in the actual practice of meditating on mandala deities, the deity concerned is often female, such as Vajra Yogini or Nairatmaya.

In addition, tantra speaks of the point in the completion stage when the practitioner is advised to seek a consort as an impetus for further realization of the path. In such cases of union, if the realization of one of the partners is more advanced, he or she is able to bring about the release, or actualization of the resultant state, of both practitioners.

Therefore, it is explained in Highest Yoga Tantra that a practitioner can become totally enlightened in this lifetime as a female. This is explicitly and clearly stated in tantras such as *Guhyasamaja*.

The basic point is that in tantra, and particularly in Highest Yoga Tantra, what practitioners are engaged in is a method of exploring and developing the latent potency within themselves. That is the fundamental innate mind of clear light, and from that point of view, since males and females possess that faculty equally, there is no difference whatsoever in their abilities to attain the resultant state.

So, the Buddhist position on the question of discrimination between the sexes is that from the ultimate point of view, that of Highest Yoga Tantra, there is no distinction at all.

THE ACTUAL PATHS OF TANTRIC PRACTICE: ACTION TANTRA

In the lower classes of tantra, two levels of the path are referred to, technically called yoga with signs and yoga without signs.

From another point of view, Action Tantra presents its paths in terms of methods to actualize the body of the Buddha, the speech of the Buddha, and the mind of resultant Buddhahood. The path for actualizing the body of the Buddha is explained in terms of visualization of the deity. The path for actualizing the speech is explained in terms of two types of mantra repetition—one actually whispered and the other repeated mentally. The path for actualizing the mind of the Buddha is explained in terms of what is technically called "the concentration which bestows liberation at the end of sound." This type of concentration requires as a prerequisite the concentration abiding in fire and the concentration abiding in sound.

Actualizing the Body of the Buddha

Whether or not Action Tantra incorporates a practice of generating oneself into the deity is a point on which masters have differing opinions. However, we can say that ordinary trainees of Action Tantra have no need to generate themselves into the deity. Their meditation is confined simply to visualizing the deity in their presence. But the principal trainees of Action Tantra are those who can actually generate themselves into deities and who visualize deities on such a basis.

Deity Yoga

Visualization of a deity such as Avalokiteshvara, or deity yoga, as it is explained in an Action Tantra and intended for the principal trainees of that tantra, can be described in six stages: the emptiness deity, mantra deity, letter deity, form deity, mudra deity, and sign deity.

Meditation on the emptiness deity refers to meditation on the emptiness of your own self and the self of the deity—reflecting on their common basis in terms of their empty nature.

Generally speaking, as Aryadeva's *Four Hundred Verses* explains, from the point of view of their ultimate nature, there is no difference whatsoever between phenomena—they are all similar in that they lack inherent existence. From the ultimate point of view, they are of one taste; therefore it speaks of a multiplicity becoming of one taste. And though they all have identical empty natures, on the conventional level, phenomena have many different appearances; therefore it speaks of multiplicity from unity.

With meditation on the mantra deity, you visualize a resonant mantra arising from this state of emptiness, the ultimate nature of your own self and that of the deity. This is not in the form of letters, just the sound of the deity's mantra resounding. Maintaining that, contemplation is the second step, meditation on the mantra or sound deity.

During meditation on the letter deity, the practitioner imagines the syllables of the self-resounding mantra emerging in the shape of letters standing on a white moon disk, within him- or herself.

Next, the practitioner visualizes the letters of the mantra being generated into the actual form of the deity, which is meditation on the form deity.

Meditation on the mudra deity occurs when the practitioner, having arisen in the form of the deity, performs the specific hand gesture, which in the case of the Lotus family is performed at the heart.

Finally, meditation on the sign or symbol deity refers to visualizing the crown of your head, throat, and heart being marked respectively by the three syllables OM AH HUM and inviting the wisdom beings to enter into your body.

The Importance of Realizing Emptiness

One basic feature of all Buddhist tantric practices is that you should always meditate on emptiness before generating yourself into a deity, whether the manual you are using includes such Sanskrit words as *am svabhavashuddha sarva-dharma* or not. The significance of this meditation is to emphasize the importance of generating your own wisdom realizing emptiness into the appearance of the deity. Although at the initial stage this is only done on an imaginary level, it serves as a rehearsal for the occasion when the practitioner's awareness of the wisdom realizing emptiness actually arises in the form of a divine body. For this reason, if the practitioner lacks an understanding of emptiness as explained by either the Yogic Practitioner [Yogachara] or the Middle Way [Madhyamika] School, it is difficult to practice tantric yoga.

The appearance or form of the deity, generated from your own wisdom realizing emptiness, is said here to represent the practice of method. Then the practitioner has occasionally to reaffirm his mindfulness of the empty nature of the deity. This is the meditation on what is called the "Great Seal ripening the faculties to actualize the form body," in the context of Action Tantra.

It is good if practitioners already possess the faculty of one-pointedness or a calmly abiding mind. Otherwise, if you are cultivating single-pointedness in conjunction with tantric practice, you should do the practice after having generated yourself into the deity, but before doing the mantra repetition.

Many tantric manuals say that if you feel tired of the meditation, then perform the mantra repetition. So, when those who do not perform intensive meditations at this point feel tired of repeating mantras, they will only be able to end their session. The actual structure of the ritual texts emphasizes meditation first of all and treats mantra repetition as secondary.

Meditation here refers to training in the profound and vast paths. Training in the profound path refers to meditation on emptiness: not meditation on any emptiness, but rather an emptiness which is the unique nature of the deity you have visualized. Focusing upon the empty nature of such a deity constitutes this practice.

Meditation on the vast path consists of two aspects: firstly, trying to develop a very clear visualization of the deity, for once this appearance of yourself as the deity is firm and clear, you will be able to develop the second aspect, which is divine pride. Once you have a clear vision of yourself as a deity, you will be able to develop a very strong sense of divine pride, of actually being the deity.

In one of the Indian master Buddhajnana's meditation manuals, the question is raised that although ignorance is the root cause of cyclic existence, in the deity yoga of the generation stage there is no specific meditation on emptiness. How, then, can one maintain that deity yoga serves as an opponent force to this ignorance? In reply, Buddhajnana says that what is meant by deity yoga in the generation stage of tantra is a practice in which you meditate on the empty nature of the form of the deity, not meditation on the deity alone. You meditate upon the emptiness of the deity while retaining its visualized appearance. So, the practice of deity yoga consists of two aspects: that focused on conventional truth and that focused on ultimate truth.

The tantras also refer to three attitudes: regarding all appearances as the form of deities, everything you hear as the form of mantra, and any conscious experience you have as the wisdom of the deity.

The first attitude should be understood, not in the sense of developing such a perception through conviction, but to achieve a very particular purpose: that is, to overcome our sense of ordinariness. On an imaginary level you try to perceive everything that appears to you as the form of the deity. Therefore, the apprehension of that attitude is always founded on emptiness.

Another explanation of this attitude, particularly as presented in the Sakyapa tradition, discusses the meaning of the threefold tantra. Their teaching, known as Path and Fruit, describes "causal tantra" as the fundamental ground, and the practitioner is trained to understand the significance and meaning of this fundamental ground in order to attain a perception of everything as pure and divine.

Another explanation, found in the works of one of the masters of the Great Perfection School, Dodrup Jigme Tenpai Nyima, called *General Topics of the Essence of Secrets*, explains the cultivation of this perception from the point of view that everything that occurs within this cycle of existence and peace is in fact a different manifestation or play of the fundamental ground known as primordial awareness in the terminology of the Great Perfection.

This primordial awareness is the source of everything that occurs and appears in the expanse of reality; cyclic existence and peace are just manifestations of primordial awareness, which is in fact the subtlest level of clear light.

This resembles the Middle Way explanation that emptiness is the source or the origin of all conventional phenomena, because all phenomena are manifestations of the same ultimate nature, emptiness. Similarly, the Sakya and Nyingma explanations that all phenomena appearing within the cycle of existence and peace are manifestations or the play of primordial awareness, have the same kind of intention.

This primordial awareness, the subtle clear light, is permanent in terms of its continuity and its essential nature; unpolluted by disturbing emotions, it is basically pure and clear. From that point of view it is possible to extend your vision of purity to include all phenomena, which are actually manifestations of this fundamental ground.

We should remember that these different explanations are given from the point of view of Highest Yoga Tantra.

So, that is the point at which you have to undertake the meditation. If, after having done so, you feel tired, you can do the mantra repetition actualizing the speech of the Buddha; Action Tantra speaks of two types of mantra repetition: one is whispered, which means you recite quietly so you can hear yourself, and the other is mental repetition, which means you do not voice but imagine the sound of the mantra.

Actualizing the Mind of the Resultant Buddha

The "concentration abiding in fire" is a term given to the meditation in which the practitioner visualizes different mantras, seed syllables, and so on, at the heart of the meditational deity and imagines flames arising from them.

The "concentration abiding in the sound" refers to a meditation in which the practitioner imagines and concentrates on the tone of the mantra, not as if he or she were reciting it themselves, but rather listening to the tone of mantra as though it were recited by someone else.

So, the practitioner cultivates single-pointedness or a calmly abiding mind in these ways, which is why we find passages in the Action Tantras which say that through the practice of concentration abiding in fire, the practitioner will gain physical and mental suppleness. Then, through the concentration abiding in the sound, the practitioner will actually attain a calmly abiding mind.

The third type of yoga, called "bestowing liberation at the end of the sound," is a technique which provides the practitioner with eventual realization of liberation.

Generally speaking, if we were to classify the tantric teachings among the three scriptural collections of Discipline [Vinaya], Discourses [Sutra], and Knowledge [Abhidharma], the tantric teachings would be included among the second, the sets of discourses. Therefore, in the tantras, Buddha himself has said that he would teach tantra in the style of the sutras.

The significance of this is that the unique or profound features of tantra come about through techniques for cultivating meditative stabilization. The unique feature, common to all four tantras, that distinguishes tantric practice from practices of the sutras, is the tantras' special technique for cultivating meditative stabilization.

One thing I would like to clarify here is that, generally speaking, calm abiding is an absorptive state of mind in which a person is able to maintain his or her attention to a chosen object undistractedly. Therefore, techniques for cultivating such a state are also absorptive rather than contemplative.

Special insight is an analytical type of meditation, so the methods for cultivating special insight are also analytical in nature.

Calm abiding is a heightened state of mind in which not only is your concentration single-pointed, but it is also accompanied by faculties of mental and physical suppleness. Similarly, special insight is a heightened state of mind in which your analytical power is so developed that it is also equipped with mental and physical suppleness.

So, because meditation on calm abiding is absorptive in nature and meditation on special insight is analytical, when we speak about meditation in general, we must be aware that there are many different types. Certain types of meditation are states of mind which focus on an object, such as meditation on emptiness, in which emptiness is the object, whereas in meditation on love, you generate your mind into a state of love. In addition, there are different types of meditation in which the focus is on imagining or visualizing something.

According to explanations in the sutras and the three lower tantras, when you cultivate calm abiding in a meditative session, you are thoroughly absorbed, maintaining single-pointedness and not employing any analysis. The two different types of meditation are usually distinct from one another, but Highest Yoga Tantra contains a unique method of penetrating the vital points of the body. It is by pinpointing these sensitive points of the body that even special insight can be cultivated through concentrated or absorptive meditation.

In the practice of the sutra path and three lower tantras, attainment of calm abiding and special insight is always sequential. Calm abiding is attained first, leading on to special insight, whereas in Highest Yoga Tantra, some of the most able practitioners can attain the two simultaneously.

The third type of yoga referred to earlier, the "concentration bestowing liberation at the end of the sound," is a technical term given to the meditation on emptiness according to the tantric system. It is also known as the yoga without signs, while the two earlier concentrations are referred to as the yoga with signs.

PERFORMANCE TANTRA

Mandalas belonging to Performance Tantra are quite rare in the Tibetan tradition, but when they do occur, the most common deity is Vairochana Abhisambodhi.

Performance Tantra also presents the path in terms of the yoga with signs and yoga without signs. Here, yoga without signs refers to meditation, the emphasis of which is on emptiness, while the emphasis of the yoga with signs is not.

Both Action and Performance Tantra speak of the requirement to practice deity yoga and undertake the appropriate meditation retreat, which is followed by engaging in the activities of the practice. In the Action and Performance Tantras this refers mainly to certain types of activities, such as the prolongation of life on the basis of a long-life deity. Other types of activity, such as achieving the highest liberation and so on, are not described in detail.

Yoga Tantra

The most important tantra of this class translated into Tibetan is the *Compendium of the Principles of All the Tathagatas* (*Sarvatathagata-tattva-samgraha*), which concerns the vajra realm and includes the Sarvavid tantras.

The general procedure of the path of Yoga Tantra is explained on the basis of three factors: the basis of purification, the purifying path, and the purified result. The basis of purification here refers to the practitioner's body, speech, mind, and activity, while the purifying paths refer to the practice of the great seal, the phenomenal seal, the pledge seal, and the wisdom or action seal. Just as there are four bases of purification—the body, speech, mind, and activity of the practitioner, and four corresponding paths of purification—there are four purified results: the body, speech, mind, and activities of Buddhahood. This is why the principal text of this class of tantra, the *Compendium of Principles*, has four sections.

Highest Yoga Tantra

Highest Yoga Tantra for us Tibetans is like our daily diet. I have found that the practice of the *Compendium of Principles* and the *Vairochana Abhisambodhi Tantra* is widespread in Japan, where there are quite a lot of practitioners of the lower tantras. But it seems that Highest Yoga Tantra is found only in the Tibetan tradition, although I cannot state this definitively.

The trainees for whom Highest Yoga Tantra was intended are human beings belonging to the desire realm, whose physical structure is comprised of six constituents. These refer to the three constituents we obtain from our father and the three we obtain from our mother.

One unique feature of the profound paths of Highest Yoga Tantra is that they employ techniques which correspond not only to phenomena related to the basis of purification as they occur on the ordinary level, such as death, intermediate state, and rebirth, but also to features of the resultant state of Buddhahood, the three bodies of the Buddha.

Highest Yoga Tantra explains the term *tantra* on three levels: causal tantra, which is the basis; method tantra, which is the path; and resultant tantra. All three levels of tantra arise from the fundamental innate mind of clear light.

If you understand the significance of this, you will understand the explanation of the Sakya tradition, which speaks of a causal tantra called the basis of all, or the fundamental basis, referring to the mandala and the deities within it, all of which actually arise from this fundamental basis.

This tradition explains that the fundamental basis is present in our basic faculties and all phenomena on an ordinary level in the form of characteristics. All the phenomena on the path are present within this fundamental basis in the form of qualities, and all the phenomena of the resultant state of Buddhahood are present within this fundamental basis in the form of potential. Similarly, we find statements such as "the equality of the basis and the result" in the writings of the Nyingmapa.

Since all the phenomena of the resultant state are complete or present in this fundamental basis in the form of potential, we can also understand such statements as the body of the Buddha and his wisdom being inseparable. But it is also important to understand these statements and concepts correctly, otherwise there is a danger of mistakenly asserting something like the Enumerator's (Samkhya) view that the sprout is present at the time of its seed.

Keeping the ultimate intent of such points in mind, we can understand that what Maitreya wrote in his *Sublime Continuum*—"All the stains of the mind are temporary and adventitious, all the qualities of the mind are present within it naturally"—doesn't mean that all the qualities and realizations of the mind are actually present within the mind, but [means that they] exist in the form of potential, because all of them are present as potential in the fundamental innate mind of clear light. From this point of view we can also understand such statements as "Recognizing one's true nature is equivalent to becoming totally enlightened."

There are similar passages in other tantras, such as *Hevajra Tantra*, where we read, "Sentient beings are completely enlightened, but they are obscured by mental stains." The *Kalachakra Tantra* also speaks very emphatically on this point, the fundamental innate mind of clear light, but it employs different terminology, giving it the name—"all-pervasive vajra space."

In his commentary on the fivefold completion stage of *Guhyasamaja Tantra*, titled *Lamp Illuminating the Five Stages*, Nagarjuna mentions that the practitioner abiding in an illusory meditation perceives all phenomena in the same aspect. The implication here is that at the completion stage, when the practitioner is able to arise in a very subtle body, technically known as an illusory body, which is of the nature of the very subtlest energy and mind, he extends his perception to all phenomena, perceiving them as manifestations of this fundamental mind of clear light.

Now, although we may be able to understand perceiving all living beings as manifestations of the fundamental innate mind of clear light, because ultimately this is the fundamental source from which they all arose, the question is, how logically do we justify the whole environment being a manifestation of this fundamental innate mind of clear light? I don't think the reference here is to the environment or phenomena being of the nature of the mind, although the Mind Only School of Buddhist thought maintains that that is the nature of all external reality. Here the meaning is slightly different. We should understand the whole environment, all external phenomena, as creations, manifestations, or appearances of this fundamental innate mind of clear light, rather than being of the nature of it.

So, when a person goes through the manifest experience of this fundamental innate mind of clear light, which is the subtlest level of the mind, at that point all the gross levels of energy and mental processes are withdrawn or dissolved. What then appears to the mind at such a level is only pure emptiness.

In tantra, techniques and methods are explained by which a person is able to utilize the fundamental innate mind of clear light that naturally manifests at the time of death or other occasions. Generally, in the sutra system, the last moment of a dying consciousness is said to be neutral though very subtle, but methods are explained in tantra to put that state of mind to positive use, by generating it into something virtuous.

I have read in the works of the Indian master Vasubhandu that compared to negative states of mind, virtuous states are more powerful. The reason being, from one point of view, that virtuous states of mind have a valid basis because they are rational and unmistaken. Another reason is that it is only virtuous states of mind that can be generated at moments of generating the fundamental innate mind of clear light, such as the time of death, and even extended beyond it. Negative states of mind could never be generated once the fundamental innate mind of clear light has become manifest.

The view of the Great Seal, the Mahamudra of the Kagyu tradition, and the view of the Great Perfection, Dzogchen, all come down to the same point—understanding the fundamental innate mind of clear light.

You might want to question that, because normally the Great Perfection is presented as the peak of the nine vehicles, for the reason that in practicing it we utilize our basic awareness, while in the preceding vehicles we used our minds. If that is the case, how can we say that the view of the Great Perfection comes to the same thing, that is, an understanding of the fundamental innate mind of clear light, which is also referred to in Highest Yoga Tantra?

The answer to this question has been given by the Dzogchen master Tenpai Nyima. He says that, while it is true that in Highest Yoga Tantra much emphasis is given to exploring and developing the fundamental innate mind of clear light, this is also a feature of Great Perfection practice. The difference lies in their methods.

In Highest Yoga Tantra practices, techniques for exploring and developing the fundamental innate mind of clear light are explained as a very gradual process leading from the generation stage on to the subsequent stages of completion, and eventually to actualization of the clear light. In the practice of Great Perfection, the development and enhancement of the fundamental innate mind of clear light has been explained, not as a gradual process, but as directly grasping the mind of clear light itself, right from the beginning, by using our basic awareness.

When studying Highest Yoga Tantra, we must keep in mind that in tantric treatises a single word can have many different levels of interpretation, just as in the case of the *Perfection of Wisdom* sutras that we discussed earlier, which had two levels of interpretation, a literal meaning and a hidden meaning. In the tantric case, the interpretation is much deeper; one word can have many different levels of meaning and interpretation.

It is said that one word of the tantra can have four interpretations, four modes of explanation: the literal meaning; the explanation common to the sutra system and the lower tantras; the hidden or concealed meaning, which is of three types (that which conceals the method for taking desire into the path, that which conceals appearance, and that which conceals conventional truth the—illusory body); and finally, the ultimate meaning, which refers here to the ultimate clear light and union.

There is also a mode of interpretation called the six boundaries: the interpretive and definitive, the intentional and nonintentional, and the literal and nonliteral meaning.

In this complex approach to tantra, there are two ways of actually explaining it to the disciples. One refers to the presentation given at a public teaching or gathering, and the other refers to the manner of the teacher-disciple relationship.

In order to validate the practice of tantra as a Buddhist practice that will eventually lead to the achievement of Buddhahood, reference is always made in tantric treatises to the mode of procedure on the sutra path. The complexity and subtle differences in the various tantras are due to the differences in the practitioners' mental disposition, physical structure, and so on. Therefore, tantras begin with a preface in which the qualifications of the appropriate trainees are identified. There are four types of practitioners of tantra, the chief being called the jewel-like practitioners.

The purpose of explaining the tantras to an appropriate trainee in such a complex way is to enable the trainee to realize the two truths. The two truths here do not refer to the two truths explained in the sutra system, which are ultimate and conventional truths. These are the two truths in the context of Highest Yoga Tantra.

According to the sutra explanation, both ultimate and conventional truths in the context of the Highest Yoga Tantra would both be conventional truths. This mode of interpreting a tantric treatise is explained in a tantra called *Compendium of Wisdom Vajras*, which is an explanatory tantra.

One feature of tantra is that almost all the tantras begin with two words: *E vam*. These two words encompass the entire meaning of tantra, not only the literal but also the definitive meaning of tantras. All tantras, because they are treatises, are composed of many different letters, which ultimately are all derived from vowels and consonants, therefore all of them are contained in these two words *E vam*, and since the entire meaning of tantra is encompassed in the three factors—base, path, and result—all of them are also included in the meaning of *E vam*.

E vam actually encompasses the entire subject matter of tantra, as Chandrakirti explained when he summarized the whole content of tantra in one verse in his renowned commentary, the *Brilliant Lamp*. It was so famous that at one time it was said that just as the sun and the moon are the two sources of light in the sky, on earth there are two sources of clarity, referring to *Clear Words*, which is Chandrakirti's commentary on Nagarjuna's *Treatise on the Middle Way*, and the *Brilliant Lamp*, which is his extensive commentary on the *Guhyasamaja Tantra*.

The verse says:

> The generation stage actualizing the deity's body is first,
> Meditation on the nature of the mind is second,
> Attaining a stable conventional truth is third,
> Purification of conventional truth is fourth,
> Conjoining the two truths in union is fifth.

In essence, this is the entire subject matter of Highest Yoga Tantra. Chandrakirti's treatise divides the entire tantric path into five stages: the generation stage and the four stages of completion.

Just as there are different stages on the path, so there are different initiations which are ripening factors for these paths. The initiation that empowers the practitioner to undertake the generation stage is called the vase initiation. The factor that empowers the practitioner to undertake the practice of the illusory body, which includes the three isolations—isolated body, isolated speech, and isolated mind—that are actually preliminaries to the illusory body and make up the three first stages of the completion stage, which is the second or secret initiation. With the wisdom-knowledge initiation, the practitioner is empowered to undertake meditation on clear light. And with the fourth initiation, the practitioner is empowered to undertake meditation on union.

Bliss and Emptiness

There are two different connotations of the term *union*. One is the union of emptiness and bliss, and the other is the union of conventional and ultimate truths. When we speak of union in the sense of conventional and ultimate truth, the union of emptiness and bliss is one part of the pair, and the illusory body is the other.

When these two are united or inseparably conjoined, they form the union of the two truths.

One meaning of the union of emptiness and bliss is that the wisdom realizing emptiness is conjoined with bliss—the wisdom realizing emptiness is generated in the aspect of bliss, such that they are one entity. Another interpretation of joining bliss and emptiness is that you utilize a blissful state of mind to realize emptiness, and such a realization of emptiness through that blissful state of mind is called the union of bliss and emptiness.

As to the sequence for attaining bliss and the realization of emptiness, there are two modes. In some cases, experience of a blissful state of mind comes first, followed by the realization of emptiness. However, for most practitioners of Highest Yoga Tantra, realization of emptiness precedes the actual experience of bliss.

Certain practitioners' realization of emptiness may not be as complete as that of the Middle Way Consequentialist School. They may adhere to a view of emptiness as propounded by the Yogic Practitioner or Middle Way Autonomist School, but by applying certain tantric meditative techniques, such as ignition of the inner heat or penetrating the vital points of the body through wind yoga, you may be able to generate an experience of bliss. This may eventually lead to a state where you are able to withdraw or dissolve the gross level of mind or energies.

Such a deep level of experience, when conjoined with a little understanding of emptiness, may lead to a subtler understanding of emptiness, an understanding that all phenomena are mere mental imputations, mere designations, imputed to the basis, lacking inherent existence, and so on. For that type of person, bliss is attained earlier and the realization of emptiness later.

The practitioner with sharp faculties, who is the main trainee of Highest Yoga Tantra, should be equipped with a realization of emptiness before taking a Highest Yoga Tantra initiation. For such a practitioner, therefore, the wisdom realizing emptiness is attained earlier than experience of bliss.

During an actual tantric meditation session, a practitioner with sharp high faculties uses methods such as ignition of the inner heat or deity yoga or penetrating vital points of the body through wind yoga, and so on. Through the force of desire which he has generated, he is able to melt the mind of enlightenment or elements within his body and experiences a state of great bliss. At this point the experience is the same, whether the practitioner is male or female. He or she recollects the realization of emptiness and conjoins it with the experience of great bliss.

The way great bliss is experienced is that when the mind of enlightenment or elements within the body are melted, you experience a physical sensation within the central channel which gives rise to a very powerful experience of bliss. This in turn induces a subtle mental bliss. When the meditator then recollects his or her understanding of emptiness, the experience of mental bliss is conjoined with it. That is the conjunction of bliss and emptiness.

According to the tantric explanation, when we speak of a blissful experience here, we are referring to the bliss that is derived from the emission of the element of regenerative fluid, another type of bliss which is derived from the movement of that element within the channels, and a third type of bliss which is derived through the state of immutable bliss. In tantric practice it is the two latter types of bliss that are utilized for realizing emptiness.

Because of the great significance of utilizing bliss in the realization of emptiness, we find that many of the meditational deities in Highest Yoga Tantra are in union with a consort. As I explained before, this experience of bliss is very different from the ordinary bliss of sexual experience.

Death, Intermediate State, and Rebirth

Since the practice of Highest Yoga Tantra is intended to benefit the trainee or practitioner whose physical structure possesses the six constituents, the processes of the path resemble ordinary experiences and have similar features to the experiences of death, intermediate state [bardo], and rebirth.

Because of human beings' unique physical structure, they naturally pass through three stages: death, intermediate state, and rebirth. Death is a state when all the gross levels of mind and energy are withdrawn or dissolved into their subtlest levels. It is at that point that we experience the clear light of death. After that, we assume a subtle body known as the intermediate state, and when the intermediate-state being assumes a coarser body, visible to other persons, it has taken rebirth into a new life.

Although we naturally pass through these different states, in their tantric treatises, Nagarjuna and Aryadeva have described unique techniques and methods whereby practitioners can put these experiences to positive use. Rather than going through them helplessly, they can gain control of these three states and use them to achieve the resultant state of Buddhahood.

The procedures for achieving the three bodies of Buddha, the truth body, the enjoyment body, and the emanation body, have features similar to the states of death, intermediate state, and rebirth. Thus, there is a possibility of achieving the three bodies by utilizing these three states.

As the path of Highest Yoga Tantra is explained in terms of meditation on the three bodies of the Buddha, any generation-stage practice in Highest Yoga Tantra should incorporate these three aspects.

The Nyingma texts describe this process in different terms, referring to the three meditative stabilizations instead of the meditation on the three bodies, the meditative stabilization of suchness, the meditative stabilization of arising appearances, and the causal meditative stabilization. These meditative stabilizations are equivalent to those generation-stage practices explained in both Yoga Tantra and Highest Yoga Tantra, comprising the meditative stabilization of the initial stage, the victorious mandala meditative stabilization, and the victorious activities meditative stabilization.

"Meditation on the three bodies" refers to the meditation in which you take death, intermediate state, and rebirth into the process of the path. For instance, taking death into the process of the path as the truth body is where you transform the condition of dying by imagining or visualizing going through the process of death. On the imaginary level you withdraw and dissolve all the processes of your mind and energies. The death process begins with dissolution of elements within your own body; consequently it has eight stages, starting with the dissolution of the earth, water, fire, and wind elements.

This is followed by four stages, technically referred to as the experiences of white appearance, red increase, black near-attainment, and the clear light of the death. This dissolution is experienced during the generation stage only on an imaginary level, while deeper experiences of the dissolution process arise as the practitioner progresses and advances in his realization during the completion stage. This will eventually lead to a point where he will be able to go through the experience of the actual death process.

Nowadays, scientists have been conducting experiments to examine the death process to find out how it works. The process of dissolution will be much clearer in a person going through the death process gradually, such as someone who has been sick for a long time, and more conclusive results may be achieved in this way.

A tantric practitioner who has attained an advanced state of realization will be able to recognize the experience of death for what it is, and will be able to put it to positive use, maintaining his awareness and not simply being overwhelmed by it. Generally speaking, ordinary people may remain in the clear light of death for up to three days at most, but some meditators may abide in it for a week or more. What indicates that a person, although externally he or she may appear to be dead, has remained in the clear light of death, is that the body does not decompose.

The point at which the meditator goes through the experience of clear light on an imaginary level during the generation stage is the point at which he or she should enter into meditative equipoise on emptiness.

Just as an ordinary person enters into the intermediate state and assumes a very subtle body following the experience of the clear light of death, in the generation-stage practice, after arising from this meditative equipoise on emptiness, the practitioner assumes a subtle body on an imaginary level, which is the factor that ripens the intermediate state. This is meditation on the enjoyment body.

Then, just as on an ordinary level a person in the intermediate state assumes a gross physical body, marking their rebirth into a new life, so a practitioner of the generation stage, following the adoption of an enjoyment body, assumes an emanation body.

There are many manuals describing meditations on the generation stage for generating yourself as a deity. In some practices you find yourself arising first as a causal vajra-holder and then as the resultant vajra-holder; in other cases, you find that you generate yourself into a deity through a process known as the "five clarifications," and so forth.

Although there are a lot of ways to visualize yourself as a deity in the practices of the generation stage which are very important, the most significant part of the meditation is the point at which you give special emphasis to meditation on the vast and the profound by cultivating the clarity of the visualization and divine pride. I have already mentioned this when I explained that the practitioner should cultivate clarity in the visualization of the deity and divine pride based on that.

As a serious practitioner you should try to undertake all these meditations, always relating them to your own mental state and level of realization, and always watching that your own meditation is free from the influences of mental laxity and excitement. Such forms of meditation should be undertaken in a sustained and concerted manner.

The greatest obstacle to obtaining and maintaining single-pointedness of mind is mental distraction. This includes many different types of mental states, such as mental scattering, but among them all, the greatest obstacle is mental excitement. This arises when your mind is distracted by a desirable object. In order to overcome and counteract such influences, the meditator is recommended to try to relax the intensity of the meditation, to withdraw the attention from external objects and so on, so that the mind can be calmed down.

Because mental excitement comes about when your mind is too alert or your meditation is too intense, it helps to reflect on the nature of suffering of cyclic existence and so on. This will enable you to reduce the intensity of your alertness.

In order to develop firm single-pointedness of mind, it is necessary to have both clarity of mind and clarity of its object, for without clarity, even though you may be able to withdraw your mind from external objects, you will not be able to achieve single-pointedness. Clarity here is of two types, clarity of vision and clarity of the subjective experience itself. The factor that disrupts clarity of mind is mental sinking. This can be overcome by raising your level of awareness.

When you engage in meditation to develop single-pointedness, you should judge for yourself whether your mind is too intensely alert or whether it is too relaxed, and so on. Assessing the level of your own mind, you should cultivate single-pointedness correctly.

Because the object of meditation in the practice of Highest Yoga Tantra is yourself in the form of a deity, and also because of the practice of single-pointedly focusing your attention on certain points within your body, you are able to bring about movement of the elements in the body. Some meditators have related their experiences of this to me. When you are able to hold a clear image of the deity single-pointedly for a long period of time, this obstructs your normal sense of ordinariness and so leads to a feeling of divide pride. However, during all these stages of meditation, it is very important constantly to reaffirm your awareness of emptiness.

When you undertake practice properly in this way, you will reach a point where you will have a clear visualization of the entire mandala and the deities within it of such vividness that it is as if you could see them and touch them. This indicates realization of the first stage of generation.

If, as a result of your further meditation, you are able to reach the stage where you have a clear vision of the subtle deities that are generated from different parts of your body in a single instant, you will have achieved the second level of the generation stage.

Once you have attained firm meditative stabilization, different meditations, such as emanating deities, dissolving them back into your heart, and so on, are explained in order to train yourself to gain further control over this single-pointedness. These meditations include visualization of subtle hand symbols at the opening of the upper end of the central channel and visualization of subtle drops and syllables at its lower end. Then, if you feel exhausted as a result of all this meditation, the next step is to do the mantra repetitions.

Mantra repetition in Highest Yoga Tantra is of many varieties: mantra repetition that is a commitment, mantra repetition that is gathered up like a heap, wrathful mantra repetition, and so on.

The Postmeditation Period

Following this there are practices for the postmeditation period. Since a tantric practitioner has to lead a life in which he is never separated from his practice of union of method and wisdom, the postmeditation periods are very important. There are different yogas to be practiced in these periods, such as the yoga of sleeping, the yoga of eating (which includes the proper way of maintaining your diet), the yoga of washing, and so on. There are even certain practices to be observed while relieving yourself.

Just as the great masters say, "The progress made during the meditation session should complete and reinforce the practices during the postmeditation period, and the progress made in the period after your meditation session should reinforce and complement your practices during the session."

It is during the postmeditation period that you can really judge whether your practice during the meditation sessions has been successful or not. If you find that despite having undertaken meditation for years, your way of thinking, your lifestyle, and your behavior during the postmeditation period remain unchanged and unaffected, it is not a good sign.

We don't take medicine in order to try it or test it for taste, color, or size, but in order to improve our health. If after taking it for a long time it has done us no good, there is no point in continuing to take it. Whether your practices are short or elaborate, they should bring about some transformation or change for the better.

THE COMPLETION STAGE

There are different kinds of activities that can be done on the basis of the deity yoga practiced in the generation stage. Consistently engaging in such forms of practice, the meditator will reach a point where he or she will begin to feel the physical effect of these practices. Experiencing this special physical effect within your body marks the attainment of the first level of the completion stage.

There are many different types of completion-stage practices, such as the yoga of inner heat, wind yoga—that is, yoga that makes use of the currents of energy—and the yoga of the four joys and so forth. Wind yoga includes such techniques as holding the vase breath, or what is technically referred to as vajra repetition.

At that point a lay practitioner can seek the assistance of a consort. But if the practitioner is an ordained person holding monastic vows, the point has not yet been reached. In order to engage in such profound practices of the completion stage, the practitioner should first be aware of the structure of his or her own body. This means understanding the stationary channels, the flowing energies, and the drops that reside in certain parts of the body.

When we speak of channels, we generally refer to three main ones—the central, right, and left channels—and also the five channel wheels or energy centers. These three main channels branch and rebranch so that there are, according to the tantric texts, 72,000 channels in the body. Some sutras also mention 80,000 channels within the body.

Then, there are the flowing energies. These are of ten types, five major energies and five minor ones. The drops refer to the white element and the red element. The *Kalachakra Tantra* refers to four types of drops: the drop between the brows, which becomes manifest during the waking period; the drop at the throat, which becomes manifest during the dream state; the drop at the heart, which becomes manifest at the time of deep sleep; and the drop at the navel, which becomes manifest at the fourth stage (death).

In the Kalachakra we find very detailed explanations of these things. The entire structure of the practitioner's body, with its channels, energies, and drops, is called the internal Kalachakra, which is the basis of purification. The *Kalachakra Tantra* speaks of three types of Kalachakras or wheels of time: the outer, inner, and the alternative Kalachakras.

Based on a proper knowledge of the physical structure of his or her body, when the meditator focuses on certain vital points and penetrates them, he or she is able to withdraw and dissolve the flow of the gross level of wind and mind. Eventually, the practitioner will be able to generate the subtlest level of clear light, the clear light of death, into an entity of the path which is the wisdom realizing emptiness. Gaining such a realization is like having found the key which provides access to many treasures.

Once you achieve that stage and you have the key, you can attain the complete enlightenment of Buddhahood through the path of *Guhyasamaja*, that is, by actualizing the illusory body as explained in the *Guhyasamaja*, or through the path of Kalachakra, which speaks of the achievement of empty form, or through the rainbow body as explained in the *Mayajala Tantra*, which is also explained in the Great Perfection practices.

When a meditator has gained a certain control over his mind during the waking state, he or she begins to utilize even the dream state in the practice of the path, and certain techniques are described for doing this. These kinds of meditation are called "mixings," mixing during the waking state, during the dream state, and during death.

Highest Yoga Tantra explains that the best practitioner is someone who is able to attain complete enlightenment within his or her lifetime. Those with middling faculties are able to attain complete enlightenment during the intermediate state, and those of inferior ability will be able to attain it during their future lives. For those practitioners who will become enlightened during the intermediate state or during their future lives, practices such as the transference of consciousness are explained. There is also another practice quite similar to the transference of consciousness, but with the difference that the consciousness is transferred into another being's body or corpse.

These techniques belong to what are called the Six Yogas of Naropa, which are techniques Naropa extracted from many different tantras. These are among the basic practices of the Kagyu tradition. There is also a Gelug practice of the Six Yogas of Naropa derived from Marpa's tradition. These meditations can also be found in the Sakya practices of Path and Fruit and in the Nyingma practice of the Heart's Drop.

We have been discussing the Highest Yoga Tantra procedures according to the New Tradition. But the Old Tradition or Old Transmission School, the Nyingma, refers to the Great Perfection Vehicle, whose practices consist of the Mind Collection, the Centeredness Collection, and the Collection of Quintessential Instructions.

Although there are many works on these topics, it is very difficult to perceive the subtleties of these different practices. Among these three collections, the Collection of Quintessential Instructions is said to be the most profound. We can say that the practices of the first two Collections lay the foundations for the practice of "breakthrough."

The view of emptiness explained in the Mind and Centeredness Collections must have some features that distinguish it from the view of emptiness expounded in the Lower Vehicle, but it is difficult to explain this clearly in words. The practices of the Collection of Quintessential Instructions have two aims: actualization of the truth body and actualization of the enjoyment body.

The paths by which you actualize these two bodies of the Buddha are the practice of "breakthrough" and "leap-over."

Through understanding these elements of the Great Perfection School, you can understand what is meant by the Great Perfection of the base, the Great Perfection of the path, and the Great Perfection of the result. As I have remarked before, these are factors that can be understood only through experience and cannot be explained merely through words. However, you can appreciate the extent of their profundity and difficulty by reading Longchenpa's text on the Great Perfection practices, called *Treasury of the Supreme Vehicle*, although the fundamental text as well as the commentary to it is very large and difficult to understand. He has also composed a text called the *Treasury of Reality*, which also outlines the practices of the Great Perfection.

You can only hope to gain a good understanding of the Great Perfection if you are able to explain the practices of the Great Perfection according to these two texts of Longchenpa. It is also important to study Kunkhyen Jigme Lingpa's text on the Great Perfection called the *Treasury of Virtue*, in the second volume of which you will find explanations of Great Perfection practices.

There are also very short and succinct texts composed by masters who have themselves had experience of the Great Perfection. I myself believe that these texts were composed by highly realized masters who have been able to extract the essence of all the elements of the Great Perfection and its practices and as a result have been able to recount their experiences in very few words. However, I think it would be very difficult to try to understand the practice of the Great Perfection on the basis of these short texts.

For example, when Lord Buddha taught the *Perfection of Wisdom* sutras, the shortest one consisted of the single syllable *AH*. This sutra is said to encompass the entire meaning of the *Perfection of Wisdom* sutras, but it would be either too simple or too difficult if we were to try to study the Perfection of Wisdom on the basis of that sutra. To say "AH" is very simple, but it doesn't mean we have understood the meaning of the sutra.

When we study the Middle Way philosophy in all its complexity, studying the different reasons through which we can arrive at the conclusion that all phenomena lack inherent existence, if we are to understand all the subtleties and implications of such a philosophical view, it is also necessary to understand the viewpoint of the lower schools of thought. The conclusion you then arrive at is very simple. Because things are interdependent, and rely on other causal factors, they lack an independent nature or inherent existence.

But if you were to approach the Middle Way Consequentialist view of emptiness right from the beginning with that simple statement, "Because things are interdependent or dependently arising, they are empty of inherent existence," you would not fully understand what it meant or implied. If, in a similar way, you were to read a short text composed by an experienced lama on the Great Perfection and were to conclude that the view of the Great Perfection was very simple, that would be a sign that you had not understood it properly. It would also be very ironic if the highest of the nine vehicles could also be said to be the simplest.

Chapter 3

TEACHINGS ON JE TSONGKHAPA'S THREE PRINCIPAL ASPECTS OF THE PATH

INTRODUCTION

Whatever teachings are being given, both the listener and the teacher should have a pure motivation. Especially when you listen to a Mahayana teaching, you should first take refuge in the Buddha, Dharma, and Sangha to protect yourself from following the wrong path, and second you should generate an altruistic awakening mind [Bodhichitta] to differentiate yourself from followers of lower paths. Therefore, we should visualize two points: first, taking refuge in the Buddha, Dharma, and Sangha for the benefit of all sentient beings, and then generating the altruistic aspiration to enlightenment for the sake of all sentient beings. So with this motivation, we should recite the verse for taking refuge in the Buddha, Dharma, and Sangha three times, clearly visualizing that we are doing so for the benefit of all sentient beings.

After the Incomparable Buddha had attained enlightenment at Bodhgaya, he taught the four noble truths: true sufferings, the true causes of suffering, true cessations, and true paths. This became the basis or foundation for all the later teachings he gave. Although the Buddha taught the four noble truths during his first turning of the wheel of the Dharma, the meaning of true cessation was most explicitly taught during the second turning of the wheel of doctrine. At that time he taught the meaning of emptiness directly, and implicitly taught the stages of the path. In other words, while teaching emptiness directly, he taught the meaning of the two truths, conventional and ultimate truth, and the complete meaning of nirvana and cessation.

A scene from the life of Je Tsongkhapa

During the third turning of the wheel of the Dharma, the Buddha taught the meaning of Buddha-nature in the Tathagata

Essence Sutra that forms the basis for Maitreya's *Sublime Science* (*Uttaratantra*) [also translated as *Sublime Continuum*]. He explained that sentient beings have a Buddha-nature, or an ability to become enlightened, mainly in terms of the nature of the mind, which is empty of inherent existence and thus suitable to be transformed into enlightenment. It is very clearly explained in the *Sublime Science* that the mind is by nature very pure and free of defilement, which makes it suitable for attaining enlightenment. This is because anything which lacks inherent existence is changeable, and subject to causes and conditions. As Nagarjuna says in his text called *Fundamental Wisdom*:

> For whichever [system] emptiness is possible,
> For that all is possible.
> For whichever [system] emptiness is not possible,
> For that nothing is possible.

The meaning of emptiness is being empty of inherent existence, and that means being dependent on something else, being dependent on causes and conditions. When we say something is dependent on other phenomena, it means that when those phenomena change, that particular thing will also change. If it were not dependent on something else and had inherent existence, then it would not be subject to change due to other conditions.

So, during the second turning of the wheel of doctrine, teaching that phenomena lack inherent existence, the Buddha taught clearly that phenomena can be made to change because they are dependent on causes and conditions. Now, although phenomena lack inherent existence, when they appear to us, we think that they exist inherently. Not only do phenomena appear as if they are inherently existent, but we also become attached to them and determine that they exist inherently. In this way we generate craving, desire, anger, and so forth. When we encounter some pleasant or interesting object, we generate a lot of attachment, and if we see something distasteful or unappealing, we get angry. Therefore, problems like anger and attachment arise because of conceiving phenomena as inherently existent.

The conception of phenomena as inherently existent is a wrong consciousness mistaken toward its referent object, which provides the foundation for all delusions. However, if we generate an understanding that phenomena are not inherently existent, it will act as a counterforce to that wrong consciousness. This shows that the defilements of the mind can be removed. If the delusions which defile the mind are removable, then the seeds or potencies left behind by these delusions can also be eliminated. The total purity of the nature of the mind, which is its lack of inherent existence, is taught very explicitly in the second turning of the wheel of the doctrine. During the third turning of the wheel, it is explained again, not only from the ultimate but also from the conventional point of view, that the ultimate nature of the mind is pure, and in its pure state it is only neutral and clear light.

For example, whoever we are, delusions do not manifest within us all the time. What is more, the same object toward which we sometimes generate anger, we sometimes generate love toward, which ought not to be possible. This clearly shows that the real nature of the principal mind, the mind itself, is pure, but due to mental factors or the minds that accompany the principal mind, it sometimes appears to have a virtuous quality like love, and at others it appears in a deluded form like anger. The nature of the principal mind is therefore neutral, but being dependent on its accompanying mind, it may change from a virtuous to a nonvirtuous mind.

So, the mind by nature is clear light, and the defilements or delusions are temporary and adventitious. This indicates that if we practice and cultivate virtuous qualities, the mind can be transformed positively. On the other hand, if it encounters delusions, then it will take on the form of delusions. Therefore, all such qualities as the ten powers of the Buddha can also be attained because of this quality of the mind.

For example, all the different kinds of consciousness have the same quality of understanding and knowing their object clearly, but when a particular consciousness encounters some obstacle, it is not able to understand its object. Although my eye-consciousness has the potential to see an object, if I cover it up it will be obstructed from seeing the object. Similarly, the consciousness may not be able to see the object because it is too far away. So the mind already has the potential to understand all phenomena, a quality that need not be strengthened, but it may be obstructed by other factors.

With the attainment of the higher qualities of a Buddha, like the ten powers, we attain a full state of consciousness, able to see the object very clearly and completely. This, too, can be attained merely by recognizing the real nature of the mind and removing the delusions and obstructions from it.

During the third turning of the wheel of the doctrine, of the four noble truths initially taught during the first turning of the wheel, the meaning of the true path is explained very clearly by defining the meaning of Tathagatagarbha, or Buddha-nature. This makes possible the attainment of omniscience, the ultimate state of consciousness able to see phenomena and their ultimate mode of being.

Therefore, a complete explanation of the meaning of true cessation is given during the second turning of the wheel of the doctrine, and a very detailed explanation of the true path is given during the third turning of the wheel. It explains the mind's potential to know phenomena's ultimate mode of existence and how omniscience can be achieved if you promote and develop that.

Now, when it comes to explaining the ultimate nature of the mind and its suitability for attaining enlightenment, we have the accounts of both sutra and tantra. These are differentiated by the detail of their explanation of the nature of the mind. The tantric teachings give a very clear explanation of the subtlest state of enlightenment within the highest class of tantra that is Highest Yoga Tantra. The first three classes of the tantra form a foundation for that.

In essence, this is a brief explanation of the Buddha's teaching from the four noble truths up to the highest class of tantric teaching. However, even if we have a clear understanding of the ultimate nature of the mind and the possibility of attaining enlightenment with it, if we do not practice and make effort to achieve that goal, then enlightenment will not be attainable. So while on the one hand it is important to know the ultimate nature of the mind, on the other, we should generate an intention to practice and realize this potential.

In teaching the first two noble truths, the Buddha described the faults, the defects that must be given up and eliminated, that is, true suffering and the true origin of suffering. In teaching the second pair of the four noble truths, that is, the true path and true cessation, the Buddha explained that there is a method, a path to get rid of these sufferings and delusions through which the complete cessation of those delusions can be attained. If there were no cure or method to eliminate suffering and attain a state of complete cessation and peace, it would not be necessary to discuss, think about, or meditate on suffering, because it would merely engender pessimism and create more suffering for yourself. It would be better to remain bewildered and carefree. However, in fact we do have a chance, there is a path and method to get rid of suffering, so it is worthwhile to talk and think about suffering. This is the importance and encompassing quality of the Buddha's teaching of the four noble truths, for they provide the basis and foundation of all practices.

When we think about true suffering and the true origin of suffering, and we come to an understanding of these two truths, we will generate a wish to rid ourselves of suffering and its causes. In other words, because we dislike true suffering and the true origin of suffering, we will generate a wish to reject them. This is called the determination to be free.

When you carefully consider suffering, it is not only you who are under its power, for other sentient beings also suffer in the same way. Then you should think that as other sentient beings are suffering just like me, how marvelous it would be if they could also eliminate suffering and its causes. Such a wish for other sentient beings to eliminate suffering and its causes is called compassion. When, induced by compassion, you decide that you will help them yourself to eliminate suffering and its causes, that is the special resolve or the mind that wishes actively to benefit other sentient beings.

Then, if you look carefully at how sentient beings can be benefited not just temporarily but ultimately, you will come to the conclusion that you will only be able to benefit them completely if you help them attain enlightenment, and to do that, you must attain enlightenment yourself. This compassionate mind, wishing to attain Buddhahood in order to help all sentient beings attain enlightenment, is called the mind of enlightenment.

It is feasible to get rid of suffering and attain the ultimate status of enlightenment because phenomena do not have independent or inherent existence. Therefore, it is important to understand the nature of phenomena, their lack of inherent existence. This understanding of phenomena's lack of inherent existence is called "right view."

It is these three qualities—the determination to be free, the mind of enlightenment, and the right or correct view—which are treated here as the three principal paths. They are so called because they provide the real motivation for attaining liberation from cyclic existence and form the framework for attaining enlightenment.

The principal means of attaining liberation from cyclic existence is the determination to be free, and the principal means of attaining enlightenment is the mind of enlightenment. Both of these are augmented by the right view, or wisdom realizing emptiness.

Now I will begin to explain the text.

THE TEXT

The Homage

I pay homage to the foremost venerable lamas.

This line is the author's expression of respect before composing the text. I will explain the meaning of some of the words here. The term *lama* denotes not only a position of status and power in the mundane sense, but rather indicates someone who is truly kind and possesses immense qualities. The Tibetan word *je* or "foremost" here [in the phrase "vernerable lamas"] signifies someone who cares less about the immediate or sensual pleasures of this world, this life in cyclic existence, than for the next life. It refers to someone who is more concerned about other sentient beings' long-term benefit over many lives to come. The Tibetan word *tsun*, meaning venerable or disciplined, refers to the lama because he has understood that, however pleasing or attractive they might be, the pleasures and attractions of cyclic existence are worthless. He has seen the lack of any lasting value among worldly phenomena, and has turned his mind toward the longer-lasting happiness of future lives. In other words, the lama is one who has disciplined his mind and is not hankering after the delights of this world but aspires for the attainment of liberation. The word *lama* actually means "supreme," indicating one who has greater care for other sentient beings than for himself and neglects his own interests for their sake.

"I pay homage" implies bowing down. You bow down to the lama on seeing his quality of concern for other sentient beings and their happiness at the cost of his own. In paying respect to this quality in the lama, by bowing down to him, you make an aspiration to attain such qualities yourself.

The Promise to Compose the Text

> *I will explain, as well as I can,*
> *The essence of all the teachings of the Conqueror,*
> *The path praised by the Conqueror's Children,*
> *The entrance for the fortunate desiring liberation.*

The first line expresses the author's promise to compose the text. The second implies the determination to be free, because all the Buddha's teachings are aimed toward liberation. It is from this point of view, the aim of attaining liberation, that we should be able to see faults in the attractions of cyclic existence and generate a wish to renounce them. This is actually imperative if we wish to achieve liberation. So this line implies renunciation of cyclic existence.

The words "Conqueror's Children" in the third line have three connotations. They can refer to those born from the Buddha's body, speech, or mind. Rahula was his physical son. The offspring of his speech refers to the Hearers and Solitary Buddhas [or Solitary Realizers]. But in this context the "Conqueror's Children" refers to those born from the mind of the Buddha, those who have generated the mind of enlightenment. You become a Bodhisattva or child of the Buddha only if you have this altruistic aspiration for enlightenment. Bodhisattvas are called offspring of the Buddha's mind because they are born from qualities found in the mindstream of the Buddha.

The last line of the verse implies right view, as the attainment of liberation is dependent on whether you have realized emptiness. So, these three lines summarize the meaning of the determination to be free, the mind of enlightenment, and the view of emptiness that are explained in this text.

Exhortation to Disciples

Those who are not attached to the joys of cyclic existence
Strive to make meaning of this leisure and opportunity,
Rely on the path pleasing to the Conqueror;
Those fortunate ones, listen with a clear mind.

Most of us here have sufficient resources so we do not have to work very much to obtain food, clothing, and so forth. But it is clear that in this life, merely having something to wear and something to eat is not enough. We want something else. We still yearn for something more. This clearly illustrates that unless pleasure and happiness are brought about through transforming the mind, it is not possible to achieve lasting happiness through external means, however favorable the external conditions may be. Happiness and discomfort are very much dependent on our mental attitude. So it is important that we should bring about some internal transformation of the mind. Since lasting happiness can only be attained in this way, it is important to rely on the power of the mind and to discover the mind's ultimate nature.

There are many diverse teachings in different religious traditions on how to bring about such a transformation. The Buddha's teaching, which we are discussing here, contains a very clear, detailed, and systematic explanation.

We do more or less qualify as "fortunate ones," as referred to in this verse, because we are trying to reduce our attachment, we are trying to make meaningful use of this precious life as a free and fortunate human being, and we are relying on the teachings of the Buddha. So, this line tells us to pay attention to the teaching that the author is going to impart.

The Need to Generate the Determination to Be Free

Without a pure determination to be free, there is no means to achieve peace
Due to fixation upon the pleasurable effects of the ocean of existence.
Embodied beings are thoroughly bound by craving for existence;
Therefore, in the beginning seek a determination to be free.

Here we begin the actual body of the text, the actual teaching it contains. This verse explains the necessity of generating a determination to be free or a mind seeking release from cyclic existence. Seeing the faults and shortcomings of cyclic existence and generating a very strong wish to abandon it and attain liberation is called a determination to be free. As long as you are unable to see the worthlessness of the pleasures of cyclic existence, but continue to see some meaning or attraction in them and cling to them, you will neither be able to turn your mind toward liberation nor will you realize how you are bound.

So the first line of this verse says that unless you have a pure determination to free yourself from the ocean of cyclic existence, your attempts to achieve peace will be in vain. It is our fascination with cyclic existence due to craving and attachment that binds us within it. Therefore, if we really seek the peace of liberation, the right course to adopt is to generate the determination to be free, to recognize the faults of cyclic existence and reject them. The biography of Buddha himself can provide us with a clear understanding of the meaning of the determination to be free for our own practice.

He was born a prince in a wealthy family, was well educated, had a wife and son, and enjoyed all imaginable worldly pleasures. Yet, despite all the alluring pleasures available to him, when he came across examples of the sufferings of birth, sickness, old age, and death, he was provoked by the sight of others' suffering. He discovered for himself that, no matter how attractive external comforts may be, so long as you have a physical body like ours, which is the short-lived product of contaminated action and delusion, then such attractive external pleasures are illusory. Understanding this, he tried to find a path to liberation from suffering and renounced all worldly pleasures, including his wife and son. Through gradually increasing his determination to be free in this way, he was able to attain not only liberation, but also enlightenment.

Therefore, it is taught that we need to develop a determination to be free. Merely renouncing the comforts of cyclic existence and checking attachment and craving toward it is not enough. We must cut the stream of births. Rebirth comes about due to craving and desire, and we must cut its continuity through the practice of meditation. Hence, the Buddha entered into deep meditative stabilization for six years. Finally, by means of a union of calm abiding and special insight, he attained the power to overcome the hindrances presented by the aggregates and external evil forces. He eliminated the very source of disturbing emotions, and because they were extinguished he also overcame death. In this way he conquered all four evil forces or hindrances.

As followers of the Buddha, we too should try to see faults in the alluring attractions of cyclic existence, then without attachment toward them, generate concentration and focus on the view of selflessness—understanding the real nature of phenomena.

Now, should you wonder how to practice this determination to be free, how to generate a mind that wishes to renounce cyclic existence, the next verse says:

> *Contemplating how freedom and fortune are difficult to find,*
> *And that in life there is no time to waste, blocks the attraction to*
>   *captivating appearances of this life.*
> *Repeatedly contemplating action's infallible effects*
> *And the sufferings of cyclic existence blocks the captivating appear-*
>   *ance of future lives.*

This verse explains how to check attachment first to this life and then toward future lives. In order to cut attachment toward the pleasures of this life, it is important to think about the preciousness of this human life, how it is difficult to find, and the many qualities it provides. If we think clearly about those points, we will be able to extract meaning from having attained a human birth. Life as a human being is precious because with it we attain a status, quality, and intelligence which is absent in all other animals, even in all other sentient beings. We have the power to achieve great benefit and destruction. If we were to just while away our time and waste this precious potential in silly and meaningless activities, it would be a great loss.

Therefore, it is important that we recognize our capacity, our qualities, and supreme intelligence, which other sentient beings do not possess. If we can identify these things, we will be able to appreciate and use them. The power of the human brain and human intelligence is marvelous. It is capable of planning ahead and can engage in deep and extensive thought, as other sentient beings cannot. Since we have such a powerful brain or intelligence, it is very important that we first recognize the strength and character of this awareness. We should then steer it in the right direction, so that it can contribute significantly to peace and harmony in the world and within all sentient beings.

Let us take the example of nuclear energy. There is great power within a nuclear particle, but if we use that power wrongly or mishandle it, it can be very destructive. Nowadays we have nuclear missiles and other weapons, the very names of which make us afraid because they are so destructive. They can cause mass destruction in a fraction of time. On the other hand, if we put nuclear power to use in a constructive way, it can be of great service to humanity and sentient beings at large. Similarly, since human beings have such capacity and power, it is very important that they use it for the benefit of all sentient beings. Properly employed, human ingenuity can be a great source of benefit and happiness, but if misused it can bring great misery and destruction.

It is from the point of view of this keen intelligence that we should think about the significance of our precious human life. However, it is also important to understand that the life of a free and fortunate human being is not only meaningful and difficult to find, but it is also short-lived.

The next two lines say that if we think repeatedly about the infallible connection between causes, our actions, and the sufferings of cyclic existence, we will be able to cut our attachment to the next life. At present we engage in many levels of activity to obtain clothing, food, and a good name. In addition, our experiences in the latter part of our lives are dependent on the actions that we have performed in the earlier part. This actually is the meaning of actions and results. Although it is not the subtlest interpretation, when we talk about actions and results, actions include any of the things we do in order to obtain any kind of happiness or pleasure. The results are the effects that we achieve thereby. Therefore, in the first part of our lives we engage in certain kinds of activity that we think will lead to some kind of happiness or success in the future. Similarly, we engage in certain kinds of action in this life so that we may be able to achieve a good result in our next life. In other words, our experiences in the latter part of our lives are dependent on the actions we have performed in the earlier part of our lives, and our experiences in future lives, whether pleasant or unpleasant, are dependent on the actions that we have committed in former lives.

These actions are done by either body, speech, or mind and so are termed physical, verbal, and mental actions. From the point view of the result that they produce, they can be termed wholesome, unwholesome, or neutral actions. Wholesome actions give rise to pleasant results, unwholesome actions give rise to unpleasant results, and neutral actions lead to a feeling of equanimity. Then there are actions that will definitely give rise to a result and those that will not. For example, when an action comes into being, it is first motivated, there is an intention, then it is actually implemented, and finally it is brought to a conclusion.

Now, when the intention, action, and conclusion are all very strong, it is definite that the action will give rise to a result, whether good or bad. On the other hand, if the intention is very strong but you do not put it into effect, or if at the end, instead of thinking that you have completed the deed, you regret what you have done, then that particular action may not produce an effect at that time. If these three aspects—intention, application, and conclusion—are not present, the action is classified as indefinite. From the point of view of the basis experiencing the result, there are actions that give fruit in this very life, actions that give fruit in the immediate next life, and actions whose fruits will be experienced in many lives after the next.

Then there are two levels of action which can be classified as projecting and completing actions. Projecting actions are those actions which are responsible for projecting us into a particular life through birth as a human being, animal, or other state of being. Completing actions are those that determine the quality of whatever life you are born into. For example, despite being a human being you may be perpetually poor. Right from birth, your sense faculties may be damaged or your limbs crippled. On the other hand, your complexion may be radiant and you may have a natural strength. Even born as an animal, you might, like a pet dog, have a comfortable home. These kinds of qualities or defects that you inherit right from birth, that are additional to the actualization of a particular birth, are the result of completing actions. So actions can be termed projecting or completing according to their function. It is possible that although the projecting action is wholesome, the completing action is nonvirtuous, and that although the completing action is unwholesome, the projecting action is virtuous.

Whether a particular action is positive, like faith in the Buddha, or negative, like attachment, if in its own terms it is pure, it can be seen as completely white and virtuous or completely black and unwholesome. If the preparation, application, and conclusion of a particular action are totally virtuous, then that action can be seen as a virtuous action. But if it results from impure preparation, application, and conclusion, then it can be seen as an unwholesome action. If it is a result of a mixed intention, pure application, and impure conclusion—in other words, if it is a mixture of both positive and negative qualities—then it can be called a mixed action.

It is the "I," or the person, who accumulates an action and experiences its results. Although these different levels of actions are the product of the thinking of particular sentient beings, they are not produced by a creator of the world. There is someone who creates the action, because when we talk about action, the word itself clearly implies that there is an actor or agent who performs that action, but it is not an external agent.

How does an action give rise to a result? For example, when I snap my fingers, I stop immediately and the action is complete, leaving behind a result. If you ask what that result is, it is the mere disintegration of the action, and the disintegration of an action goes on continuously. So, when we talk about the result of a particular action, it is the mere disintegration or part of the disintegration or the cessation of that particular action. To clarify the point, it is a kind of potency left behind by the disintegration of that action, which is responsible for bringing forth many other conditioned phenomena.

If you wonder where the imprint of that potency of the disintegration or cessation of that particular action is left, the answer is on the continuum of the consciousness existing during the immediate moment of the cessation of the action. There are occasions when the consciousness is alert and awake, and there are occasions when the consciousness is latent, for example when we are in deep sleep or when we faint. Therefore, the consciousness is not a wholly reliable place to deposit such potency. Sometimes it is very subtle and sometimes it is very coarse, so the consciousness provides only a temporary basis for such imprints.

Hence, if we seek an ultimate explanation, it is the mere I, or the person, which carries the potency of a particular action. This explanation is based on the ultimate explanation of the highest school, that is, the Middle Way Consequentialist School. I used the words *mere I* to clarify that the "I" or the person has only nominal, not inherent, existence. It is only designated and does not exist by itself. It is not something that you can point at with your finger. The word *mere* indicates an "I" which is merely designated by name and thought, and negates a self-supporting or independent "I." The negation of an inherently existent or self-supporting "I" does not mean that the "I" does not exist at all; it has a nominal existence. This mere "I" or person becomes the basis on which the imprint or potency of an action is left. In general, the "I" is designated to the collection of the physical and mental aggregates.

When we talk about the physical body and the consciousness, which is the basis of designation of the "I," with reference to a human being, it is principally the consciousness which becomes the basis of designation of the term *I*. The consciousness has many levels, some of them coarse and some of them subtle. The physical body of a human being can also be divided into many parts, such as the eye, the ear, and so forth. These physical parts again become a basis for the designation of consciousness. For example, the eye-consciousness is designated to the eye, the ear-consciousness to the ear, and so forth. But if you try to find the subtlest basis of designation of consciousness, it seems that the nerves and pathways of the brain are actually the basis of designation of mental consciousness. Then there is also talk of the bases of the sense powers, and these are supposed to be very subtle. It is not clear whether such bases of the sense faculties can be found in the brain or somewhere else. It will be an interesting object of research.

Let us take an example: in order to generate an eye-consciousness, many conditions or causes are necessary. The dominant cause is an indefectible eye sense-power. Having a particular form within its focus becomes the objective condition. However, despite the presence of such conditions, it is not definite that an eye-consciousness will arise. This indicates that a third condition, the immediately preceding condition, which is a consciousness, is required, in addition to the external objective condition and internal dominant condition of a sense power. Therefore, in order for the eye sense-consciousness to arise, all three conditions are necessary.

As an example to elucidate this point, there are occasionally cases of people who after a long illness become so physically weak that their heartbeat and all physical functions stop. When they enter into such a deep coma that no physical activity or function can be perceived, the doctor declares them clinically dead. However, sometimes after a few minutes or even hours, despite the apparent lack of physical activity, the person starts breathing again, the heart starts beating, and physical functions are regained. This revival, despite the previous cessation of all physical functions, shows the unavoidable presence of a mental condition that immediately preceded it. When that immediately preceding condition—a consciousness—is present, the person can come back to life again. Similarly, in the case of a sense consciousness, the mere presence of the dominant condition and the objective condition is not sufficient to generate a particular consciousness.

According to the Buddhist view, when we talk about the various levels of consciousness of a particular human being which are designated to the various parts of his body, then we are referring to the coarser levels of consciousness of a person. These consciousnesses are called consciousnesses of a human being because they are dependent on particular parts of a human body. Therefore, when a human being dies, all the coarser levels of consciousness that are dependent on the physical body also seem to disappear, but it is interesting to note that their arising as entities of consciousness does not come about merely due to the presence of the physical body. They are produced as entities of clarity and awareness, such as eye-consciousness, ear-consciousness, and so forth, in dependence on conditions other than the body. There is a fundamental cause that generates these consciousnesses as entities of clarity and awareness, and according to the various conditions it encounters, consciousnesses cognizing form, sound, and so forth arise. This shows that there is a consciousness independent of the coarser physical body, but when it encounters coarser conditions, it appears in the form of coarser consciousness.

Consciousness has a much subtler nature, and if you examine that subtler nature, then the real, substantial cause of that consciousness can only be another continuum of consciousness which preceded it, irrespective of whether there is a physical body or not. Therefore, there is plainly a kind of innate natural mind, which is totally pure and clear. When this pure state of the mind comes into contact with different levels of the physical body, consciousness also manifests itself more or less coarsely, depending upon what particular physical body it is being designated to. But if you examine the real nature of the mind, it has an existence independent of the coarser levels of the physical body.

Such a pure, natural state of mind, which exists independently of the physical body, is called the primordial clear light or the primordial consciousness—a consciousness which has always been present. Compared to this, coarser consciousnesses are adventitious because they are sometimes present and at other times absent. This primordial innate clear light consciousness is the real basis of designation of a sentient being or person. So, whoever has this kind of consciousness, this pure state of the mind, is termed a sentient being, and this is the main criterion that differentiates sentient beings from other living things and other phenomena. No doubt a person, or "I," is attributed to the total aggregate of the physical body and the consciousness, but it is the primordial innate clear light that is the exclusive basis of designation of a person, and not the physical body. Even plants and flowers have a kind of physical body, but since they lack this kind of innate subtle consciousness they are not referred to as persons. Whatever your shape, form, or outer aspect, anyone who possesses a continuity of consciousness and has feelings, perception, and so on is referred to as a person. Therefore, different texts explain that the "I" or the person has been attributed to the continuity or stream of consciousness.

Although specific consciousnesses vary according to different occasions, and coarser levels of consciousness are dependent upon various physical bodies, the subtlest level of consciousness, the mere entity of clarity and awareness, the primordial innate clear light consciousness, is independent of the physical body. The nature of consciousness has no beginning. If you try to trace the origin of consciousness, you can go further and further back, but you will not reach a point at which you can say, this is where this consciousness came into being. Therefore, it is a kind of natural law that consciousness came into existence from beginningless time.

This is also a more realistic explanation, because if you accept a beginning of consciousness, you either have to assert a creator of consciousness, or you have to say that consciousness arises without any cause. This is preposterous, out of concern for which consciousness has been explained as beginningless. If you ask why it is beginningless, we can only say that it is a natural law. If we observe carefully, there are so many things in this world whose continuity can be traced from beginningless time. But if you ask, what their real and ultimate origin is, you can find no answer. This is simply their nature. If you ask why physical forms appear in the entity of form, it is simply due to their nature. If we say that this comes about without cause or from unrelated causes, why can it not occur causelessly now when it could previously occur without cause?

Therefore, according to the Buddhist view, if you ask whether there is a beginning to consciousness, the answer is that the continuum of consciousness is beginningless, the origin of the "I" or the person is beginningless, and birth is beginningless. And if you ask whether these things have an end, again the answer is negative if you are thinking about the mere continuum of consciousness or the mere continuum of a person. But there is an end to the impure state of mind, the impure state of a person, and there is also a limit to birth, because normally when we talk about birth, we are referring to something which has been produced through contaminated action and delusion.

So because of the beginninglessness of birth, later experiences of suffering and pleasure are connected to actions performed earlier. The different kinds of deluded actions or virtuous actions that a person accumulates in different lives are connected to results in different lives. For example, if you commit some virtuous or negative actions in this life, then you will have to experience their results later on. Similarly, you may have committed some virtuous or unwholesome actions in a past life, whose result you will have to experience in that very life or in this life. If you have not accumulated such actions, then you will never experience their effects. On the other hand, if you have accumulated a particular action, then generally speaking you will never escape the result: sooner or later it will bear fruit. Similarly, if one has accumulated a positive action, the result will be definitely positive. Those kinds of actions are called definite actions, but there are also actions whose results are not very definite because the proper conditions or situations were not present. Furthermore, there are actions which seem of minor importance, but whose results multiply rapidly, depending upon the circumstances, situation, and conditions. So, there are many kinds of action: definite action, indefinite action, actions that multiply greatly, as well as the fact that the results of actions not done will not be encountered and that actions once done will not dissipate.

Usually, all our daily actions arise from some wish or desire. For example, if you wish to go somewhere, then you actually set out and go; if you wish to eat something, then you look for something to eat and eat it. Desire can be classified into two types, one which is negative and another which is logical and creative. For example, the wish to attain liberation from cyclic existence results in a reasonable undertaking, therefore it is a sound and logical desire. On the other hand, to generate attachment toward a particular object, such that you wish to obtain or achieve something, is an impure desire and usually arises from a misconception of phenomena as existing independently or inherently. Most of the work that we do in cyclic existence, and the desires that we generate, are the result of this kind of illogical reasoning.

Familiarizing our minds with positive qualities and trying to achieve goals like liberation are logical desires. Still, it is possible that in particular cases an individual's wish to attain liberation is assisted by the conception of true existence. However, every wish for worldly perfection is based on the ignorance that conceives of true existence. On these grounds, it is better to classify desire in two ways: one, the result of correct reasoning, and the other, the result of incorrect reasoning.

The result of desire based on the conception of true existence is cyclic existence. Still, there is another kind of desire based on sound reasoning that does not project cyclic existence, but aspires to attain the supreme attainments and qualities of the Buddha, the Dharma, the Sangha, and Nirvana, the state beyond suffering. There is a wish and desire to attain them.

If we did not classify desire into two types as mentioned above, we might think that desiring liberation was improper, that desiring religious practice was improper, and that even wishing for happiness was also improper. No doubt there are different modes of desiring your own happiness, but what is clear is that so long as we have attachment and a conception of a truly existent self, those actions characteristic of cyclic existence will continue to be created.

Generally speaking, once an action has been accumulated, the result has to be experienced. Therefore, although we may be enjoying the delights of cyclic existence just now and intense sufferings are not manifest, since we are not free from the actions' shackles and snares, we have no security and no guarantee of lasting happiness. This is the perspective from which this particular text says:

If you think repeatedly about the infallible law of actions
    and results
And the sufferings of cyclic existence,
You will be able to stop attachment to the next life.

By understanding the infallible law of actions and results, you will be able to see that unless you completely purify your actions, whatever kind of apparent enjoyment and pleasure you find in cyclic existence will be unreliable. Having understood this, you will not be confused by the pleasures of cyclic existence and will be able to curb your attachment to the next life.

As a human being in cyclic existence we normally encounter four kinds of suffering: the sufferings of birth, old age, sickness, and death. Right from birth, we are faced with sufferings; our life begins with suffering. At the same time, the process of aging begins and we start to encounter different degrees of sickness. Even when we are healthy, we encounter a lot of disturbances and confusion. Finally, the chapter of our life is closed with the sufferings of death.

When we talk about someone who is in cyclic existence, we are referring to a sentient being who is uncontrollably under the sway of contaminated actions and delusions. Because we are overpowered by contaminated actions and delusions, we repeatedly have to take birth in a cycle; therefore it is called cyclic existence. Of the two, contaminated actions and delusions, it is delusions which are mainly responsible for casting us into cyclic existence. When we are free of delusions, we attain liberation. Delusions are states of mind which, when they arise within our mental continuums, leave us disturbed, confused, and unhappy. Therefore, those states of mind which delude or afflict us are called delusions or afflictive emotions. They are the negative qualities which make us unhappy when they arise within us. It is these internal disturbances, and not external conditions, that really make us suffer.

As long as we have these evildoers residing within us, happiness is impossible. So, if we really want to transform ourselves and achieve maximum happiness, we must identify these deluded states of mind and eliminate them. Enlightenment, the state of greatest happiness, cannot be actualized by any other means than by transforming our minds. Usually, on an ordinary level, we think of delusions like attachment and anger as qualities that make life meaningful and colorful. We think that without attachment and anger our whole society or community would become colorless and without life. But if you think carefully about it and weigh up the qualities and disadvantages of delusions like attachment and anger, you may find that in the short term they give you some relief and make your life colorful. But on closer scrutiny, you will find that the fewer of these delusions we have, even though life may be less colorful, the more we will develop inner calm, inner strength, and lasting happiness. Consequently, our minds will be happy, our physical health will improve, and we will be able to engage successfully in virtuous activities.

Of course, you might feel that your life now is colorless, unattractive, and without meaning. But if you think carefully and look for your own and other sentient beings' long-term benefit, you will notice that the more you control your delusions, the greater your peace of mind and physical well-being will be. In pursuit of physical health many people do various kinds of yoga exercises. No doubt this is very good for them, but if they were also to do some mental yoga that would be even better. In short, as long as your mind is disturbed and unsound, you will continue to encounter problems and sufferings. And as long as your mind is under control, disciplined, and free from these faults, the more you will gain inner strength, calm, peace, and stability, due to which you will be able to be more creative. From our own experience that we have more suffering when our minds are more disturbed by faults, we can deduce that when our minds are completely clear, our experience of happiness will be stable.

Up to this point we have been discussing the faults, sufferings, and delusions of cyclic existence. On the one hand, we have to think about the faults and sufferings of cyclic existence and generate aversion to them, and on the other we need to ascertain the possibility of attaining nirvana, the cessation of suffering—the complete elimination of delusions. If you were to ask, "Is there really a method by which we can attain liberation, or a method by which we will be able to eliminate sufferings and delusions completely?" it would be worthwhile asking whether nirvana or liberation actually exists.

Liberation or cessation is the nature of the mind on the occasion of the complete annihilation of defilements by their antidotes. When you think about the sufferings of cyclic existence and you weary of them, you look forward to nirvana, liberation, as an alternative. Let us say that we have a defiled and deluded mind. When the defilements of the previous moment of the continuum of this particular consciousness are completely eliminated, the very nature of that purified consciousness is liberation, nirvana or true cessation. In other words, the teachings say that the cyclic existence that we are presently experiencing is not eternal, because it has arisen from causes and conditions, and they can be counteracted.

If you ask what the cause of cyclic existence is: it is ignorance, the conception of true existence. And what is the remedy for such ignorance? It is the wisdom realizing emptiness or wisdom realizing the real nature of phenomena. Now, these two qualities, ignorance, which is the cause of cyclic existence, and the wisdom realizing emptiness, which is the antidote to ignorance, cannot abide simultaneously in the continuum of one human being, because they are mutually exclusive. Although both observe the same object, their modes of apprehension are completely opposed to each other. Therefore, they cannot both abide in one person's continuum with equal strength. As one is strengthened, the other is weakened.

If you examine these two qualities carefully, you will find that whereas ignorance has no valid support or foundation, the wisdom realizing emptiness does. Any quality that has a valid foundation can be strengthened and developed limitlessly. On the other hand, because the conception of true existence lacks a valid foundation, when it encounters the wisdom realizing emptiness, a valid mind based on correct reasoning, it is weakened such that it can finally be eliminated altogether. So, ultimately, the wisdom realizing the nature of phenomena will be able to uproot ignorance, the source of cyclic existence.

If we examine how attachment and anger arise within us when our minds are calm and clear, in what way we crave the object, how it appears to us, and how we generate a conception of true existence toward it, we will be able to see how these delusions arise within us. Although we may not gain a direct understanding, we can make some correct assumptions.

How are attachment and anger supported by the conception of true existence? When, for example, you are very angry with somebody, notice how at that time you see that person as completely obnoxious, completely unpleasant. Then, later, a friend tells you: no, that person is not completely unpleasant, because he has this or that quality. Just hearing these words, you change your mind and no longer see the person you were angry with as completely obnoxious or unpleasant. This clearly shows that right from the beginning, when you generate attachment, anger, and so forth, the mental tendency is to see that particular person or object not as merely pleasant or unpleasant, but as completely unpleasant or completely pleasant. If the person is pleasant, you see him or her as completely attractive, 100 percent attractive, and if you are angry with them, you see that person as completely unattractive. In other words, you see whatever quality they have as existing inherently or independently. Therefore, this mode of apprehending phenomena as existing inherently or truly provides a strong basis for the arising of delusions like attachment and anger.

From such explanations you can make an assumption that in general this quality, liberation or nirvana, does exist. It is a phenomenon. Not only does it exist, but it is something that you can achieve within your mental continuum. If you train yourself in the twin practices of [1] thinking about the disadvantages and sufferings of cyclic existence, and the advantages of being able to get rid of these sufferings; and [2] the possibility of attaining liberation, then you will be able to generate a determination to become completely free from cyclic existence.

The Measure of Having Generated a Determination to Be Free

The next verse explains how to gauge whether you have generated a determination to be free of cyclic existence:

Having familiarized yourself in this way, if you do not generate admiration
For the prosperity of cyclic existence even for an instant,
And if you wish for liberation day and night,
At that time you have generated the determination to be free.

The next verses explain the generation of the mind of enlightenment. First the need and purpose of generating altruism is explained.

The Purpose of Generating the Mind of Enlightenment

If this determination to be free is not influenced by a pure mind of enlightenment,
It will not become a cause for unsurpassable enlightenment, the perfect bliss.
Therefore, the intelligent should generate a mind of enlightenment.

However strong your familiarity with the determination to be free of cyclic existence may be, unless you generate an altruistic attitude, a strong wish to benefit sentient beings, it will be impossible for you to attain enlightenment. In this regard, Nagarjuna's *Precious Garland* says:

If you and this world wish
To actualize supreme enlightenment,
Its root is the mind of enlightenment.

The basis for generating an altruistic aspiration for enlightenment is compassion, of which there are many types. One kind of compassion is to think how nice it would be if sentient beings were free from suffering. There are other degrees of compassion which not only include this thought, but also have greater courage. This induces a special resolve to take responsibility personally for getting rid of sentient beings' sufferings. Even the Hearers and Solitary Buddhas [or Solitary Realizers] strongly wish that sentient beings be separated from suffering. Similarly, we ourselves sometimes generate the kind of compassion which thinks how nice it would be if sentient beings were free from sufferings. For example, seeing the misery or neglected condition of a particular person or animal, we might generate a strong sense of compassion, wishing that the sufferings of that particular sentient being be eliminated.

It is also important to note that when the object of our compassion is someone we like, our sympathy is based on attachment rather than compassion. On the other hand, if, seeing the sufferings of a neglected animal, such as a stray dog to whom you have no attachment at all, you generate compassion, that is pure compassion.

Now, the compassion generated by Hearers and Solitary Buddhas is of a much higher quality than the compassion we normally generate, because, seeing the suffering that pervades the whole of cyclic existence, they generate compassion for all sentient beings. Unable to see the sufferings of all cyclic existence, we see only the sufferings of particular beings, which we see only as some kind of fault or demerit in them. However, Hearers and Solitary Buddhas do not have a compassion that induces them to take responsibility for liberating sentient beings themselves.

The compassion generated by Bodhisattvas is of the highest kind. They not only wish that sentient beings be separated from suffering, but voluntarily take responsibility for ridding them of their sufferings. This is called great compassion. It is this compassion which underlies the altruistic aspiration for enlightenment and which induces the special attitude. For this reason, we often come across statements in the scriptures that it is compassion which acts as the root of the mind of enlightenment. In order to generate such compassion, on the one hand you must identify the suffering by which the particular sentient being is afflicted. On the other hand you should regard that being as pleasant and dear to your heart.

The Means of Generating the Mind of Enlightenment

Carried away by the four torrential rivers,
Bound by tight bonds of actions, difficult to undo,
Caught in the iron net of the conception of self,
Thoroughly enveloped by the thick darkness of ignorance,
Born into boundless cyclic existence,
And in their rebirths unceasingly tormented by the three sufferings:
Contemplating the state of mother sentient beings in such
*   conditions, generate the supreme mind.*

The words "mother sentient beings" here clearly show that suffering sentient beings are not totally unrelated to you. They have acted as your mother in many previous lives and have been extremely kind to you. Therefore, you should see them as very pleasing. Understanding how your mothers suffer will provoke in you a feeling of being unable to bear it. Through the mental process of recognizing how you are intimately connected to sentient beings, you will be able to generate the great compassion that gives rise to the mind of enlightenment. This verse says that sentient beings are being carried away by four torrential rivers. These four could refer to the four causes that project sentient beings into birth in cyclic existence, and they could also refer to their four results. But here, the four rivers refer to the four unwanted sufferings that we encounter in cyclic existence: that is, birth, aging, sickness, and death. In other words, we are completely under the control of very strong, irreversible contaminated action because of which we experience these four sufferings.

Such strongly contaminated actions also arise from potent delusions like anger and attachment. These in turn arise from a powerful conception of (a truly existent) self. This is compared to a strong iron net, due to which we are ensnared in cyclic existence.

A strong conception of self means that it is stable and unchallenged. The stronger the conception of self is, the stronger delusions like anger and attachment will be. And the stronger the delusions are, the stronger the actions that project us into cyclic existence will be. And the stronger the actions that project us into cyclic existence are, the more powerful our sufferings will be.

The misconception of self arises because we are obscured on all sides by the darkness of ignorance. In this context the misconception of self that entraps us in cyclic existence actually refers to the misconception of self of persons, because the next line says that sentient beings are completely confused and enshrouded by the great darkness of ignorance. Usually the misconception of self itself is referred to as ignorance, but when we find two things explained, like the misconception of self and ignorance, the first, the misconception of self, refers to the misconception of self of persons, and ignorance in the next line refers to the misconception of self of phenomena, the misconception of phenomena as truly existent.

Our misconception of the true existence of phenomena—in other words, our strong grasping for the attractions of our physical body—acts as the foundation for generating too much attachment toward our own person. Therefore, the misconception of phenomena acts as a foundation for the misconception of the person. When you observe the "I" in your continuum and generate a feeling of "I," a conception of a truly existent self, that is called the view of the transitory collection. So, the misconception of self of phenomena gives rise to this view of the transitory collection, and this in turn stimulates the accumulation of action. And because of the misconception of self of phenomena and the misconception of self of persons, we involuntarily take birth in cyclic existence and for an immeasurable time experience an unceasing chain of suffering like birth, aging, sickness, and so forth.

Now, the cessation of subsequent results depends on the cessation of the preceding causes. If strong causes have been created, then you have to experience their result, no matter how reluctant you are. If you think in this way, then the more you resent your sufferings, the more you will loathe their causes. These verses explain two ways of generating renunciation and a determination to be free through thinking about true suffering. These are to think about the faults and sufferings of cyclic existence and to reflect on the true origins of suffering. When the verse explains the four levels of sufferings and so forth, it is explaining true suffering, and when it explains factors like the conception of true existence, ignorance, and contaminated action, it is explaining the true origins of suffering. In this way it explains the first two noble truths.

If you think about this cycle of suffering and its origins with reference to other sentient beings, it will lead to training in compassion. But if you think about these sufferings and their origins with reference to yourself, it leads to generation of a determination to be free.

We were discussing the different levels of suffering and how to generate an altruistic attitude wishing to benefit all sentient beings; in this context the text says seeing the sufferings of the mother sentient beings that are in such a situation, we should generate the supreme mind.

In other words, we must first observe the sufferings of sentient beings, and then generate a strong feeling of closeness and affection for them. The closer you feel to other sentient beings the easier it will be to generate a feeling of being unable to bear their suffering. Therefore, we should view all sentient beings as our relatives, such as our mother.

In order to generate this mental attitude of concern for other sentient beings, we must first understand the beginningless nature of cyclic existence. The sentient beings who have taken birth in cyclic existence are also beginningless; therefore, there is no sentient being who you can say has not been connected to you as a relative such as your mother.

In order to generate a strong sense of affection and closeness to all other sentient beings, you must first generate a strong sense of equanimity toward all sentient beings. Based on this feeling, you can generate a sense of kinship with the rest of sentient beings and view them as your mother. Then you will be able to reflect on the kindness of these sentient beings, which is the same as the kindness of your present family which sustains you now. When you see them as your own relatives and remember their kindness, you will be able to generate an attitude of cherishing them, taking them to your heart.

Another method of generating an altruistic attitude is to exchange yourself with others. This is possible because all other sentient beings are the same as you in wanting happiness and not wanting suffering. They are also the same as you in having the capacity and the opportunity to get rid of suffering and attain happiness. Like you, all sentient beings have the right to eliminate suffering and attain maximum happiness. Although you are the same from all these perspectives, all other sentient beings are countless. And yet you are not unrelated to them, because in worldly terms you are very much dependent on them. Even when you meditate on the path, you do so by focusing on sentient beings. Finally, ultimate enlightenment, known as the effortless spontaneous achievement of others' purposes, is achieved in dependence on them. Thus, we are related to and dependent on sentient beings when we are in cyclic existence, during the path, and finally at the time of the fruit.

Now, seeing that you have this close connection with all other sentient beings, it is foolish to neglect their welfare to pursue the interests of only one being—yourself. On the other hand, it is wise to neglect the interests of one for the benefit of the rest, who are the majority of sentient beings. All the pleasures and facilities that we enjoy in this life, such as wealth, possessions, fame, and friendship, are all obtained in dependence on other beings. We cannot think of enjoying anything by our own efforts alone, without their help. In this modern age especially, everything we enjoy—food, clothing, and everything else—is produced by various manufacturing companies in which other people work. Almost nothing is grown or produced in your own small garden or courtyard.

We eat canned fruit which is produced by the hands of other human beings. When we travel in an airplane, we depend on the work and facilities provided by the many people who are involved in running that airplane. In our modern society we cannot think of surviving without depending on other human beings. Equally, without other human beings you would have neither reputation nor fame. Even though you may have acquired certain qualities that are the basis of your fame and reputation, if other people do not know about them, there is no question of your becoming famous.

If you think carefully, even your enemy, whom you usually view as an opponent and completely dislike, gives you the chance to generate many qualities like patience, courage, and strength. There is a teaching by Shantideva in his chapter on patience [in *The Way of the Bodhisattva*] that is pertinent here about how to generate patience with respect to your enemy and to regard him as precious. This is especially important for a Buddhist practitioner. If you are able to see how you can gain these kinds of qualities from your enemy, you will also be able to generate kind feelings toward him.

If you are able to generate such a positive mind toward your enemy, who is normally an object of contempt, you will have no trouble in generating a feeling of care and concern toward neutral beings or, of course, toward your friends. In order to generate such a mental attitude, it is not necessary that you recognize all the sentient beings individually. You can, for example, infer that all trees have certain common characteristics from the qualities of one particular tree without having to know each and every individual tree. Similarly, you can conclude that all living beings are the same in wanting happiness and not wanting suffering by examining your own situation. By doing so, you will easily generate compassion, which is an aspiration thinking how nice it would be if all sentient beings could eliminate suffering. If you are able to generate a clear understanding of the sufferings of sentient beings, you will also be able to generate love, which is to think how nice it would be if all sentient beings met with happiness.

Based on these two aspirations—love and compassion—you will generate the special attitude of taking responsibility for getting rid of these sufferings yourself, and this will induce the mind that wishes to attain the highest enlightenment for the sake of all sentient beings. This altruistic aspiration for enlightenment for the sake of all sentient beings is called the mind of enlightenment. The way to measure your generation of the mind of enlightenment and determination to be free was explained earlier.

The Need to Realize Emptiness

From this point on, the text explains the nature of emptiness and the wisdom that realizes it. The first verse explains the need to generate this wisdom realizing the nature of emptiness. There are various kinds of wisdom: wisdom understanding conventional phenomena such as the various sciences, and wisdom understanding the ultimate, real nature of phenomena. If you do not possess wisdom realizing the ultimate mode of existence, no matter how strong your determination to be free or your aspiration for enlightenment may be, you will not be able to shift the conception of true existence, the root cause of cyclic existence. Therefore, you should make an effort to realize dependent arising.

> *Without the wisdom realizing the mode of existence,*
> *Even though you familiarize yourself with the determination*
>   *to be free and the mind of enlightenment,*
> *The root of cyclic existence cannot be cut.*
> *Therefore, make an effort to realize dependent arising.*

Common explanations of the meaning of dependent arising, such as the dependent arising of cause and effect, are accepted by all Buddhist traditions. But this verse refers to subtle dependent arising; something's coming into existence in dependence on its parts. In other words, there are conditioned relations in which particular effects or phenomena arise merely in dependence on a particular cause and condition. Another meaning of dependent arising is the existence of things relative to others. For example, when we talk about the part of a whole body, we call it a part in relation to the whole; similarly, the whole is only a whole in relation to its parts. From this point of view, the part and whole are related to and dependent on each other. Likewise, qualities like long and short have a relative sense because we use these terms to describe objects in relation to other objects.

At another level, phenomena are also called dependent arisings, because they arise in dependence on their basis of designation, and they are dependent on the mind that designates them. The first meaning of dependent arising applies only to conditioned phenomena, whereas the last two meanings apply to all phenomena, conditioned impermanent phenomena and unconditioned permanent phenomena.

The dependent arising referred to in this line is the subtlest one, in which it is explained in terms of existing merely by name and designation by thought. In other words, when we say that phenomena exist through the power of terms and designations and in dependence on designations, we are explaining dependent arising as it appears, as mere existence due to the power of name. From the ultimate point of view, that is mere emptiness of inherent existence. This means that since a phenomenon cannot come into being from its own side, it lacks inherent existence and is dependent on other conditions. Here other conditions refer to designation and the designating thought. The phenomenon exists merely by the power of that designation and as such it is empty of self-sufficient existence. Conversely, since it is empty of self-sufficient existence it exists through the power of designation.

So these are explanations of subtle emptiness. When we talk about the meaning of emptiness, we are talking about something being empty of its object of negation. Phenomena are empty of independent existence, inherent existence, and existence from their own side. These three—independent existence, inherent existence, and existence from its own side—are the objects of negation. Emptiness thus means being empty of these objects of negation. This is said because phenomena are dependent on something else; they are dependent on the name and the thought by which they are designated.

When we explain that they are dependent on their parts, name and designation, we are also stating that they do not have inherent existence, because dependence and independence are opposite terms. Phenomena are either dependent or independent; they cannot be both. Since these terms are mutually exclusive, a phenomenon can only be one or the other; it cannot be something in between. For example, human being and horse are opposites but not direct opposites, because there can be a third category, such as a dog, which is neither horse nor human being. But human being and nonhuman being are direct opposites and if we say that there are only two categories of phenomena, those that are either human being or nonhuman being, there cannot be a third category. So through the reasoning of dependent arising, lack of inherent existence can be established.

When we use the term *emptiness*, it has some similarity to our usual idea of absence of something or voidness. But if you think that emptiness is the mere absence of anything, then your understanding is incomplete. We should understand emptiness as absence of inherent existence. Because they lack inherent existence, phenomena do not have an independent existence, yet they are existent. This understanding of emptiness can be gained through understanding the meaning of dependent arising, because dependent arising means that phenomena are dependent on something else. They do not exist independently, nor do they exist from their own side. If phenomena exist in dependence on something else, this clearly shows that they do exist.

Sometimes emptiness is explained as the meaning of the Middle Way, which means the center that has eliminated the two extremes. One extreme is to think that if phenomena do not exist inherently, they do not exist at all—the extreme of nihilism. The other is to think that if phenomena exist, they must exist inherently—the extreme of eternalism. If we have a good understanding of emptiness, on the one hand we will understand that, since phenomena exist in dependence on thought and name and so on, they have nominal existence; that is, they do exist. This avoids the extreme of nihilism. On the other hand, when you think about how phenomena exist in dependence on thought and name, it is clear that they do not have an independent existence. This avoids the extreme of eternalism. If it were something that did not exist at all, then to say that it depended on something else would not make any sense. The next verse clarifies this point.

One who sees the infallible cause and effect
Of all phenomena in cyclic existence and beyond
And destroys all perceptions (of inherent existence)
Has entered the path which pleases the Buddha.

This means that if you are able clearly to assert the infallibility of dependent arising, such that you are able to generate an ascertainment of it, and if, without harming the presentation of dependent arising, you are able to destroy the perception that things exist inherently, then you have entered the path that pleases the Buddha. The first two lines clearly explain that one who sees cause and effect, within and beyond cyclic existence, as infallible, who can posit the existence and actual function of cause and effect, rather than their nonexistence, is able to eliminate the extreme of nihilism. The next two lines explain that through understanding the function of cause and effect, you will understand that although things exist, they do not exist independently or inherently, and you will be able to destroy the conception that things exist inherently.

So, these lines explain that although cause and effect function, they do not function in an inherent way. In fact, inherent existence is the object of negation, and it is what should be destroyed by true perception. This eliminates the extreme of permanence. In general, the whole of Buddhist teaching can be subsumed under four statements: all conditioned phenomena are impermanent, all contaminated things are suffering, all phenomena are empty and do not have self-existence, and nirvana is peace. From these four, it is clear that most schools of Buddhist tenets, with the exception of certain subschools such as the Vatsiputriyas, accept the explanation of selflessness.

The selflessness that is accepted by all the four different schools of Buddhist tenets is the lack of a self-supporting or self-sufficient person. The meaning of the lack of a substantial, self-supporting person is that there is no person who is completely independent of the mental and physical aggregates. If you view the mental and physical aggregates as the subject to be controlled and the person as the controller, and if you view this controller, a person, as something completely independent of those aggregates, you are maintaining a view of the existence of a substantial, self-supporting person.

All four schools of Buddhist tenets accept that there is no such person independent of his physical and mental aggregates. This understanding weakens our strong yearning for the person, the enjoyer of happiness and suffering, to be something solid, but it seems that it is not very effective in weakening the attachment, anger and so on, that is generated by observing other objects of enjoyment. In general, attachment, hatred, and so on, which are generated in relation to ourselves are stronger, so we think of "my" object of enjoyment, "my" relative, and "my" rosary.

If the object of enjoyment does not belong to you, then you may not have a very strong sense of an independent, self-supporting person, but if you possess something, then that feeling is stronger. This is clear if you compare the two attitudes before and after buying something, let us say a watch. First you buy it, then you start thinking, "This is my watch" and "These are my clothes" and so forth. So because of that feeling of "mine," the feeling of possessing that thing, you generate a very strong sense of the person to whom it belongs. Such a person is called a substantially self-sufficient person. If you talk about nonexistence of such a substantial, self-sufficient person to people who have a strong sense of the existence of such a person, it will help reduce their attachment to their possessions.

In addition to this explanation of the selflessness of persons, when we study the highest schools of tenets, that is, the Mind Only and Middle Way schools, we find subtler explanations of the selflessness not only of persons, but also of phenomena. With respect to the Mind Only School's explanation, when we relate to different objects of enjoyment, such as form and sound, they appear to us due to the awakening of imprints on our consciousnesses. So, according to the Mind Only explanation, all the various phenomena appear to us and we experience and enjoy them merely due to the awakening of the imprint left on the mind. In other words, all phenomena are of the nature of the mind and do not have any external existence.

This is one explanation of the meaning of emptiness and is a means to reduce attachment toward objects of enjoyment. But the Middle Way explanation is that no phenomena, whether the person, the enjoyer, or the object of enjoyment, exist inherently from their own side, because they are merely designated by thought. Thought designates the name, and then the phenomenon comes into being. Phenomena do not have an existence from their own side, other than being designated by the terms and thoughts of the mind. According to this explanation, all phenomena have their own character and their own nature, but all these characteristics of specific phenomena exist in dependence on something else; they do not have a specific mode of existence from their own side.

Within the Middle School there are two interpretations of the meaning of emptiness. According to the Middle Way Autonomy [or Autonomist] School, all phenomena exist, but their existence comes about as a product of two conditions. On the one hand, a valid mind should designate the name and the term to that particular phenomenon, and at the same time the phenomenon should also exist from its own side. When these two conditions are met, the phenomenon comes into existence. Other than being designated by the mind, there are no phenomena which come forth from their own side.

The subtlest explanation is found in the Middle Way Consequentialist School, which says that although there are things like form, sound, mountain, house, and so forth that we can point to, they do not exist in the way we ordinarily perceive them. Usually phenomena appear to our consciousness as if they existed from their own side, but the Consequentialists say that phenomena do not exist from their own side at all. They have only a conventional and a nominal existence. Therefore, if phenomena existed in the way they appear to us, when we try to analyze, examine, and find the object of designation, it should become clearer and clearer. But this is not so. When we try to analyze and examine the nature of phenomena we have perceived, we are unable to find them; instead, they disappear. This shows that phenomena do not have any inherent existence and do not exist from their own side.

According to the Autonomy School, the measure by which to prove that things exist is existence from their own side. But the Consequentialists say things do not exist from their own side at all, because they are merely designated by the mind. For them, a phenomenon's existence from its own side is the object of negation, and the lack of such inherent existence or existence from its own side is the meaning of emptiness.

If you are able to perceive the real nature of phenomena by realizing that they do not exist inherently, but in dependence on causes and conditions, such as designation by name and thought, you will have entered the path pleasing to the Buddha. Usually, when an object, form, or sound appears to us, it appears as if it had an independent or solid existence not dependent on causes, conditions, names, thoughts, and so forth. But that is not a real mode of existence. Therefore, if you understand that they exist in dependence on these things, and you thereby eliminate the misunderstanding that phenomena exist independently, you have understood the right path.

On the other hand, you might think about how all phenomena appear and the infallibility of their dependent arising, but be unable to generate the realization that they are empty of inherent existence, or when you think about the emptiness of phenomena or their lack of inherent existence, you might be unable to accept the infallibility of their dependent arising. When you have to alternate these two understandings and are unable to think of them simultaneously, you have not yet realized the thought of the Buddha. As the following verse says:

Appearances are infallible dependent arisings;
Emptiness is free of assertions.
As long as these two understandings are seen as separate,
One has not yet realized the intent of the Buddha.

Although phenomena do not have inherent existence, they have nominal existence. When we see the reflection of our own face in the mirror, the reflection is not the face itself. In other words, the reflection is empty of the real face, because it is only a reflection and not the real face at all. Even though the reflection of the face is not the face, because of the assembly of causes and conditions, the reflection of the face arises. The reflection is completely empty of being the real face, and yet it is very much there. It was produced by causes and conditions, and it will disintegrate due to causes and conditions. Similarly, phenomena have a nominal existence, although they have no existence independent of causes and conditions.

If you examine yourself or any other phenomena carefully in this way, you will find that although all phenomena appear to exist inherently, no phenomena exist from their own side or as they appear to us. However, they do have nominal existence, which produces results, is functional, and its activities are infallible.

> At the time when these two realizations are simultaneous and
> don't have to alternate,
> From the mere sight of infallible dependent arising comes
> ascertainment
> Which completely destroys all modes of grasping.
> At that time, the analysis of the profound view is complete.

If you familiarize your mind with this, a time will come when you do not have to alternate the two understandings: the understanding of the meaning of dependent arising and that of emptiness of inherent existence. Then you will understand the meaning of emptiness of inherent existence by merely understanding the meaning of dependent arising, without relying on any other reason. Merely by seeing that dependent arising is infallible, you will be able to destroy completely the misconception of the true existence of phenomena, without relying on other conditions. When you are able to generate an understanding of dependent arising or emptiness of inherent existence as meaning the same, you have gained a complete understanding of the view of the real nature of phenomena.

Now we will complete the rest of the text of the *Three Principal Aspects of the Path*. When we think about phenomena's lack of inherent existence, we should start our investigation with our own person and try to find out whether this "I" or person has inherent existence or not. Find out who the person is and separate out the whole physical and consciousness aggregate by asking whether my brain is me, or my hand is me, or whether the other parts of the body are me. When analyzed in this way, then the "I" is unfindable. You cannot identify the "I" with any of these factors, neither the whole physical body nor parts of it or consciousness and its various levels.

If you think about the physical body itself and try to find out what it is, whether it is the hand and so forth, it will be unfindable. Similarly, if you analyze a particular table to find out what it is, whether it is its color or its shape or the wood of which it is made, you will not be able to point to any particular quality of the table as the table.

When you are not able to find things through this mode of analysis, it does not mean that they do not exist. That would contradict reason and your own experience. Phenomena's unfindability under scrutiny indicates that they do not have any objective existence from their own side and that they do exist as posited or designated by the mind. There is no other way of establishing them. Since they do not have any objective existence independent of thought, their existence is dependent on the power of the object, the designation. Therefore, phenomena have a conventional or nominal existence.

But when you are not analyzing or experimenting or studying in that particular manner and phenomena appear to you in their usual way, they appear to exist independently from their own side. It does not appear to you that they have only a nominal or conventional existence. But since you have some understanding through analysis and study, when things ordinarily appear to you as existing independently, you will be able to think,

"Although phenomena do not have inherent existence, to my impure mind they appear to exist independently and inherently." In other words, if as a result of your study you compare phenomena's ordinary mode of appearance and the way things appear under investigation, you will understand the wrong way in which phenomena appear when you are not analyzing them, and then you will be able to identify the object of negation, inherent existence.

Therefore, when you are in an actual meditation session, it is important to ascertain through reasoning that things exist merely by designation and do not have an independent existence from their own side. However, as soon as you arise from meditation, things will appear in the ordinary way. Then, due to the understanding you generated during the meditation session, even though phenomena appear as if they exist inherently or independently, you will be able to confirm that although they appear in this way, this is not how they exist. It is from this point of view that the next verse says:

> Also, the extreme of existence is eliminated by the appearances
> And the extreme of nonexistence is eliminated by the emptiness,
> And if the mode of the arising of cause and effect from emptiness
> is known,
> You will not be captivated by the view that grasps at extremes.

This means that if you are able to understand that all phenomena exist conventionally, you will be able to eliminate the extreme of permanence, and by understanding that things do not have inherent existence, you will be able to eliminate the extreme of total nihilism or annihilation. In other words, you will be able to understand the nature of phenomena, that they exist conventionally and nominally but are empty of inherent existence. Due to their not existing inherently, things appear as causes and effects. If you are able to generate an understanding of such mode of existence, you will not be overpowered or captivated by the wrong view of the two extremes, permanence and nihilism.

Concluding Verse

Finally, the concluding verse says:

Thus when you have realized the essentials
Of the three principal aspects of the path accordingly,
Seek solitude and generate the power of effort,
And quickly actualize your ultimate purpose, my son.

The concluding advice is that it is not enough to have mere scriptural understanding. Having understood the meaning of the three principal aspects of the path, it is your responsibility to retire to an isolated place and put them sincerely into practice. Having understood the meaning of practice, you must engage in it with clarity because the aim and purpose of study is the attainment of omniscience, but it can only be gained through practice. So Je Tsongkhapa advises us to practice well.

Therefore, as explained above, first establish some understanding of the view that phenomena lack inherent existence, then repeatedly make your mind familiar with that understanding so that through familiarity your ascertainment will become clearer, deeper, and stabler. Moreover, as our mind at present is strongly influenced by distraction and excitement, it is very difficult for it to stay calmly on one object even for a short time. Under such conditions, even if you have realized the ultimate view, it is difficult to make it manifest.

In order to have a direct perception of emptiness, it is important to develop a calmly abiding mind through meditation. There are two techniques for doing so: one accords with the explanation you find in the sutras, and the other, which is found in the tantras, depends on deity yoga. This latter method is the more profound. In the tantras too, there are two levels, according to the deity yoga found in the lower classes of tantra and in the highest class of tantra.

In the Highest Yoga Tantra there is a special mode of doing deity yoga and achieving a calmly abiding mind by employing the subtle wind and the subtle mind. When you actualize a calmly abiding mind through that process, what is known as a union of calm abiding and special insight into emptiness is achieved.

If we explain this union of special insight and calm abiding merely according to the nature of the meditative stabilization, there is no certainty that it will become a cause of enlightenment. No doubt because of the attainment of special insight it is a Buddhist practice, but it is less certain that the mere union of calm abiding and special insight will become a cause of enlightenment. Whether it becomes a cause of liberation or omniscience depends on the motivation. Therefore, we need a determination to be free from cyclic existence as a foundation, and then, based on care and concern for the benefit of all sentient beings, an altruistic aspiration for enlightenment. If you then practice the yoga of the union of special insight and calmly abiding mind, it will become an active force for attaining enlightenment.

In order for such practice to be fruitful, it is important that you first receive tantric teachings. In order to receive tantric teachings to ripen your mental continuum, you must first receive initiation to make your mind fertile. Therefore, it is important to practice a combination of method and wisdom. When we engage the altruistic aspiration to attain enlightenment for the sake of all sentient beings, it will influence and support the view understanding the real nature of phenomena, and in turn, our realization of emptiness, the real nature of the phenomena, will also influence and support our aspiration for enlightenment. This mode of practice is known as the union of method and wisdom.

When you follow the tantric path, you first generate a mind wishing to attain enlightenment for the sake of all sentient beings, and then, influenced by this altruistic aspiration, generate the wisdom realizing emptiness, the real nature of phenomena, and on the basis of this realization, generate the deity. In other words, it is the wisdom apprehending the emptiness itself that is generated into the form of a deity. If you again focus on the nature of the deity itself, you will find that even the deity does not exist from its own side. Then you visualize the deity as the truth body that you will ultimately attain when you attain enlightenment.

So, the technique for meditating on both method and wisdom is very important and includes meditation on the extensive circle of the deity as well as on its profound emptiness. The unity of both method and wisdom is involved in this tantric practice, because on the one hand you think about the nature of the deity itself, which is visualizing the real nature of phenomena, and then on the other hand you think of the deity itself as the truth body that you will attain when you become enlightened, which is to think about the object of your attainment. So this is also a meditation on the aspiration for enlightenment.

Through this process of deity yoga, you are practicing both the method and the wisdom at the same time. This is what makes the path so quick and successful. When you follow the Highest Yoga Tantra especially, there are techniques to make manifest the subtlest wind and subtlest consciousness. Through special techniques you will be able to stop the coarser, defiled levels of wind and consciousness and make their subtlest levels manifest.

Whether you follow the sutra or tantra path, if you want to practice in this way, you should first lay a solid foundation in the practice of morality or discipline.

There are many levels of discipline to be observed, starting from the discipline of individual emancipation, which is like the foundation of all the higher levels of discipline. It is sometimes referred to as the discipline of the Hearers, and it is on the basis of this that you generate the discipline of the Bodhisattva, on the basis of which in turn you generate the discipline of Mantra.

QUESTIONS AND ANSWERS

Would Your Holiness clarify whether the determination to achieve liberation is not linked at all with the conception of true existence or the conception of phenomena as inherently existent?

Usually, when we talk about generating a strong wish to be free from cyclic existence, a mind wishing to attain liberation, with reference to a person who has really understood through study that there is such a thing as liberation, and that it is something that can actually be achieved, who has a deep understanding based on reason, then we can say that his wish to attain liberation is not defiled by a conception of true existence or a conception of phenomena as inherently existent. This is because a person can usually have a valid cognition of liberation only after realizing emptiness. If you have understood the meaning of emptiness, then even though you may not have uprooted the conception of true existence completely, neither the liberation that has to be established nor the path that establishes it is polluted by the conception of true existence. Therefore, we can say that the wish to attain liberation is not assisted by the conception of true existence or the conception of phenomena as inherently existent.

However, in the case of ordinary beings like us, who do not have a correct or authentic understanding of liberation's mode of existence, but merely a wish to attain it, while no doubt the wish is genuine, due to not understanding the real nature of phenomena, we might see liberation itself as truly or inherently existent. In other words, not having a good understanding of phenomena's lack of inherent existence, the wish to attain liberation is polluted by the conception of true existence.

In a verse of sutra the Buddha says that if, on seeing the illusory image of a beautiful woman, you feel a desire for her, it is foolish to regret it later when you realize that she was only an illusion, because there was no woman there in the first place. Similarly, if you think of liberation as truly existent, although it is not, then it is true to say that your aspiration toward liberation is not authentic.

Can we use a term like the "bliss of liberation"?

Yes, of course, because when we attain liberation, it is only the complete cessation of delusions. Otherwise one is still a person with a physical body. There is a feeling of pleasure and happiness of having attained liberation, although there is no craving for that blissful feeling. For example, if we speak in tantric terms, then a superior individual being who has eliminated the conception of true existence has the wisdom of great bliss within his mental stream, and that bliss is a real bliss. I think it is also appropriate to speak of the bliss of an individual at the stage of no longer training. So, we can say that even the Buddha has a feeling of pleasure, and therefore we can speak of the bliss of liberation.

But if you are asking this question from the point of view of whether liberation itself is bliss, then it is not, because it is an impersonal phenomenon. Actually, liberation or cessation is a quality, a complete cessation of delusion within the particular person who has attained and actualized liberation. With reference to that person and when he or she attains liberation, it is the person himself or herself who experiences bliss. So, if you ask whether the person experiences the bliss of liberation, the answer is yes, but if you ask whether liberation itself is bliss, then the answer is negative.

How is meditation related to getting rid of the suffering of sentient beings?

When a Bodhisattva actually engages in the training prior to enlightenment, he not only meditates on qualities like compassion and altruism, he actually engages in putting the six perfections into practice. Of the six perfections, giving and ethical discipline are directly related to the benefit of sentient beings. Similarly, a Bodhisattva also engages in the four means of gathering disciples, such as giving things that sentient beings need, speaking pleasantly, and so forth. The generation of compassion and love in meditation actually generates the intention and the practices of giving; observing ethical discipline and so on are the actual expression of that intention in action. Therefore, practical application and meditation go together side by side. You will also find mention of the state of equipoise and the subsequent achievement. During meditative equipoise you engage in meditation, and during the postmeditative state you arise from meditation and engage in collecting merit. This means practically engaging in activities that directly benefit sentient beings.

How is one's aspiration toward liberation related to the experience of suffering?

In order to generate a wish to attain liberation, you should first be able to see the faults of cyclic existence. But at the same time, if you do not have an understanding of the possibility of attaining liberation, then merely seeing the faults and sufferings of cyclic existence is not enough. There are many cases where people are faced with suffering but are unaware of the possibility of attaining liberation. Not finding a solution to their problems, in frustration they commit suicide or harm themselves in other ways.

When the Hearers and the Solitary Buddhas have destroyed delusions completely and become Foe Destroyers, do they possess a neutral consciousness or neutral mind?

Yes, they have neutral consciousness. After having attained the status of a Foe Destroyer [Arhat], the Hearers and Solitary Buddhas not only have a neutral consciousness, but also employ other qualities like harsh speech and referring to others as inferior persons and so on. Although these kinds of actions are not provoked by delusions like anger and attachment, they arise as a result of being well acquainted with negative qualities in the past, which now express themselves physically, verbally, and mentally in bad ways.

People who have not realized emptiness see all phenomena as existing inherently, and because of that they generate anger, attachment, and so forth. But how do those people who have realized emptiness generate anger and attachment since the realization of emptiness is a direct antidote to the experience of the conception of true existence?

The demarcation between these two experiences is that those who have realized emptiness do not have a conception of true existence which views things as inherently existent. Although things appear to them as inherently existent, they do not have a conception of true existence. Even to those who have attained higher grounds and become Foe Destroyers, things appear to exist inherently. So there is no certainty that those for whom things appear to exist inherently should have attachment and anger. Therefore, anger and other delusions are generated not only when things appear to exist truly, but when there is also a determination that things have true existence. It is not possible to eliminate delusions and afflictions completely, merely by seeing emptiness or merely by realizing selflessness. You have not only to realize emptiness or selflessness, you also have to become well acquainted with it. When you not only understand emptiness but also see it directly, you attain what we call the path of seeing. And when you attain the path of seeing, you are able temporarily to suppress all superficial manifestations of delusions. Still, you have only suppressed the manifestations of these delusions and have not finally eliminated their seeds. The innate delusions are still present.

Even after you have gained direct realization of emptiness, there are higher paths, such as the path of seeing and path of meditation. Intellectually acquired delusions are those that are eliminated by the path of seeing and are thus eliminated when one sees emptiness directly. They come about as a result of studying mistaken philosophical ideas. In other words, they are products of wrong views. When you see emptiness or ultimate reality directly, then naturally, intellectually acquired delusions, products of wrong view, are automatically eliminated. Therefore, you have to become thoroughly familiar with this realization of the true nature of phenomena. Then gradually as you attain the path of meditation, you will be able to eliminate the very root cause of delusions. Now, how is this conception of true existence, or the conception that things exist inherently, responsible for generating delusions like anger, attachment, and so forth? Normally speaking, it is not necessarily the case that wherever there is a conception of true existence, delusions like attachment and anger are generated, because there are occasions when you have only a conception of true existence. But wherever there is attachment or anger, it follows that it is due to a conception of the true existence of phenomena. When you generate attachment, you not only see the object as something interesting or attractive, but you see it as something totally attractive, totally interesting, and existing inherently from its own side. Because of that kind of misconception of phenomena, you generate strong attachment.

Similarly, when you see something as uninteresting or unattractive, you do not see it just like that; you see it as totally uninteresting and unattractive. This is because you have a conception of the true existence of phenomena. The principal cause of all these different delusions, like attachment and anger, is the conception of "I" and "mine." First you generate attachment toward the "I," and because of this you start to generate all kinds of other delusions. Usually, you actually do not think about what this "I" is, but when it arises automatically, you have a strong sense of an "I" which is not just nominally existent, but a solid "I" existing inherently from its own side.

Recognizing the existence of a conventional "I" is all right, but when you exaggerate it as having an independent existence, it is wrong. That is the wrong view of transitory collection. Because you have that kind of conception of the true existence of the "I," you generate other delusions like the conception of "mine," thinking, "This or that is mine." When you have this conception of things as "mine," you divide everything into two classes: those that you like, which you think of as mine, as interesting, as my friend and so on, based on which you generate a lot of attachment; and those that do not belong to you or that have harmed you or are likely to harm you, you classify into a different category and neglect them. Because of your conception of the "I" and the feeling that you are somehow supreme, someone very important, you become proud. Due to this pride, when you don't know something, you generate deluded doubt, and when you encounter a challenge from people who have qualities or wealth similar to your own, you generate the delusions of jealousy and competitiveness toward them.

What is the meaning of a definite action and an indefinite action?

A definite action is one all of whose requisite parts are complete: for example, having made the preparations for doing a particular action, actually doing it, and finally thinking that you have done the right thing. If you have committed an action through such a process, the result will be definite, so it is called a definite action.

On the other hand, if you have not generated the intention to commit a particular action, then, even if you have done something, the result will not be definite. So, it is called an indefinite action. In general, there are many kinds of actions explained in Asanga's *Compendium of Manifest Knowledge* (*Abhidharma Samuccaya*): actions that are committed and not accumulated, actions that are accumulated and not committed, and actions that are both committed and accumulated. Actions that are accumulated and not committed are definite actions. Actions that are committed and not accumulated are indefinite actions because, for example, of not being motivated.

Now, to explain this point more clearly, let us take the example of killing an animal. Generally speaking, killing leads to bad rebirth. But if you kill a particular animal without intending to kill it, for instance if you unknowingly trample on an insect and kill it, but then realizing what you have done you generate a strong sense of regret, the result will be indefinite. Because you have actually killed the insect, you have committed the action of killing it, but you have not accumulated the action because you did not intend to kill it. In this case the result is not definite, which means that this act of killing will not lead to the normal result, bad rebirth, because of the absence of intention and having subsequently felt regret. However, since the act of killing was committed, it will bear its own fruit. It does not lead to profit.

How is it possible, especially for a person who comes from the West, to generate a sense of renunciation, an unwillingness to enjoy the pleasures of the world in which we are living?

It is not likely that everyone would generate a spirit of renunciation, nor is it necessary, because of people's diverse mental interests and inclinations. Some take rather a fancy to cyclic existence. So what should we do? If we take the point of view of a Buddhist and strive to attain liberation, then we have to train the mind in this way. If you just glance at the Western way of life, you may see many superficial attractions, the ample modern facilities and so on. But if you examine it on a deeper level, Westerners are not immune to the general worldly sufferings of birth, old age, sickness, and death, and are especially stricken with feelings of competitiveness and jealousy. I am sure that these disturb your happiness, so they are termed the sufferings of cyclic existence.

We can also classify suffering into three levels: the suffering of suffering, the suffering of change, and pervasive compositional suffering. This last one, pervasive compositional suffering, refers to the fact that our physical body, projected by contaminated actions and delusions, itself acts as the basis for experiencing all the different levels of suffering. It is important to know the various levels and stages of sufferings and how to do meditation. In general, if you have no anxiety, no troubles, and no worries, that is best. We think of practicing the Buddha's doctrine because we have some suffering, some anxiety, but if you don't have these, then there is no need to practice; just enjoy yourself.

Since we have this conception of a truly existent self, is it possible to benefit other beings?

It is possible. Actually there are two kinds of mistaken attitude with regard to the self: one is to hold it as inherently existent, the other is the self-centered attitude. If you have a very strongly self-centered attitude, perpetually concerned about your own well-being and nothing else, you will automatically neglect the welfare of other beings. The conception of a truly existent self is difficult to get rid of, but while you are doing so you can also train in the altruistic attitude concerned with the welfare of other sentient beings and engage in activities to benefit them. Hearer Foe Destroyers and Solitary-Buddha Foe Destroyers have destroyed the delusions with their seeds and have realized the real nature of phenomena. Thus they have eliminated the conception of true existence, but because of their self-centered attitude, they may not care much for the welfare of other sentient beings. However, it is also possible for a Bodhisattva to belong to the Vaibhashika School of tenets, which does not assert emptiness of true existence. So, although that Bodhisattva may not have eliminated the seed of the conception of true existence, but because he has trained in developing an attitude of concern for others, he will work with total dedication for the benefit of other sentient beings.

Chapter 4

JE TSONGKHAPA'S *ABRIDGED STAGES OF THE PATH TO ENLIGHTENMENT*

There is a good gathering of people here from different walks of life, including some who have come from Tibet. When we lived in free Tibet, we had every opportunity to do Dharma practice, but unfortunately we have faced some difficulties since then. Today, we are gathered here not to listen to some story or other, but to listen to the Buddha-dharma. It is important to transform your body, speech, and mind, to attain enlightenment if you can. So, at least during the sessions of these teachings, make an attempt to turn your mind toward spiritual practice. Try to keep in mind whatever meaning you get from these teachings and make yourself familiar with it. Listening to Dharma is not just an academic pursuit. It is meant for taming and transforming the mind. So it is important that, as a result of listening to the Dharma, we should make some transformation in our lives.

Usually before a teaching we recite the verses for taking refuge in the Buddha, Dharma, and Sangha, and generating the awakening mind, which is the essence of the Buddha's teaching. The first two lines are: "I go for refuge until I am enlightened to the Buddha, Dharma, and Sangha." Taking refuge is to trust and confide in the Buddha, Dharma, and Sangha from the depth of your mind. Entrusting yourself to the Buddha, Dharma, and Sangha is what distinguishes you as a Buddhist. It is important to have a clear understanding of the nature of the Buddha, Dharma, and Sangha. This is achieved through study, thinking, and meditation. Ordinary people, without such understanding, who simply follow the prevailing tradition, saying, "I take refuge in the Lama; I take refuge in the Buddha, Dharma, and Sangha," without understanding the nature of the Buddha, Dharma, and Sangha, cannot take refuge in a profound way. They have not gained real conviction through reason or study. Therefore, there can be different levels of taking refuge depending upon your interest, your study, and your intelligence.

The real way to take refuge in the Buddha, Dharma, and Sangha is to emulate their example. You make a determination to become the Buddha and the Dharma yourself, to generate the Dharma within your own mental continuum. When we talk about taking refuge, there are various ways of going about it. Usually, we take refuge in someone who has the capacity to give us shelter or protection. If there are people who have the capacity to remove our sufferings or help us, in a way we take refuge in them. On the other hand, if you are capable of fulfilling all your responsibilities yourself, you live somewhat independently and do not have to take refuge in others.

Therefore, there are two levels of taking refuge in the Buddha, Dharma, and Sangha. The first is to consider yourself on a lower level without ever thinking of becoming a Buddha. The second level is to take refuge in the Buddha, Dharma, and Sangha with the aspiration that you yourself will become a Buddha and generate the Dharma within your mind. That kind of taking refuge is more profound and more courageous. It all depends on the mental level of the individual.

Then you generate the awakening mind. The last two lines of the traditional verse say: "Through the virtuous qualities accumulated by giving, observing ethical discipline, and so forth, may I attain Buddhahood for the benefit of all sentient beings." This clearly explains that the purpose of engaging in the practice of the Buddha-dharma is not for your personal welfare alone, but to attain enlightenment for the benefit of all sentient beings. That is an extremely wonderful and noble attitude, something we should all aspire to. If you have such an awakening mind, it is the source of all excellent qualities.

When you recite this verse, taking refuge in the Buddha, Dharma, and Sangha, and generating the awakening mind, you should dedicate whatever virtuous qualities you do to the benefit of all sentient beings. The teacher should explain the teaching with that motivation, and the listener should also listen with that motivation. Whatever Dharma practices you do, whether you do prostrations or circumambulations, you should do them with this motivation. That way, all your virtuous qualities will become a cause for attaining enlightenment for the benefit of all sentient beings. If you think about the meaning of this one verse when you recite it, your practice will become profound. Think about it in such a way that you are really able to generate a strong feeling within your mind.

Usually we recite this verse three times. We do so to make sure that we think about the meaning and, through repeatedly thinking about the meaning of this verse, we make some change in the feeling within our minds. Therefore, sometimes it is useful to recite it not only three times, but even ten. Sometimes you can concentrate only on the first two lines, taking refuge in the Buddha, Dharma, and Sangha. Focus your mind on the meaning of those two lines. When you are able to generate a really strong feeling, recite only the lines about generating the awakening mind. Remember that you are doing all these practices in order to attain enlightenment for the benefit of all sentient beings. That may be more effective in making a change within your mind.

Whatever virtuous practices you do, if right in the beginning you think about the meaning of taking refuge in the Buddha, Dharma, and Sangha, and generating the awakening mind, all your practices will become very effective. Otherwise, reciting certain prayers might become no different from playing a tape recorder. Buddhist practice, like all the different religious traditions, is meant for transforming the mind; the way this is done in Buddhist practice is through meditation or mental training. Practices related to the mind are subtler and more difficult than practices related to other senses. So, even if you move your lips elegantly when you recite your prayers, if you do not have the correct mental attitude you are not doing real Buddhist practice.

Especially when we have the opportunity to do Buddhist practice, it is important to understand the main thrust of the Buddha's teaching. The Buddha-dharma is to be done through the mind. If we are simply content with practices like circumambulation and so forth, forgetting the mental practice, then it is doubtful whether our practice is really Buddhist. Sometimes, when we have ample time on our hands, it can be very comfortable to do circumambulations or prostrations. But if you go with a talkative friend, exchanging gossip and so forth, it is not a religious practice. It is possible to do circumambulation while thinking of deceiving such and such a person, or making money, but you are just wasting your time because you are thinking about doing various negativities. People who observe you might feel, and you yourself might feel, that you are doing religious practice, but actually you are not, because your mind is turned in another direction.

Now, what does doing Dharma practice through the mind mean? For example, if you are angry and are seeing the faults of anger and the benefits of a calm mind, you reduce your anger. Then if, by focusing on what or whoever made you angry, you generate a more loving attitude by thinking about the benefits of love and kindness, you will be able to transform your earlier attitude. If you think that this person is similar to you in wanting happiness and not wanting suffering, you will be able to generate a real feeling of compassion toward him or her. That is real Dharma practice. That is how your mind can be transformed. Your earlier harmful intention is now transformed into a loving attitude. It is extremely difficult, but it is wonderful. That is real Dharma practice. This is also why we say that Buddhist practice is done by the mind.

If we voluntarily profess to be Buddhists and profess to be followers of the Buddha, it is our responsibility to follow the

Buddha's instructions. It is our duty and responsibility to reduce and eliminate anger, attachment, and hatred. We are followers of the Buddha; in our homes we have images of the Buddha. We also go on pilgrimage and generate great respect for images of Buddha Shakyamuni. But if we accept Buddha Shakyamuni as our teacher and if we like his teaching, then it is important to follow it. At least we can do those things which please the Buddha and not those things which displease him. If we do not engage in such a practice, then we are simply deceiving ourselves and deceiving Buddha Shakyamuni when we say that we take refuge in the Buddha, Dharma, and Sangha.

Now, when I climb on the throne to give you the teaching, it would be unworthy of me to be proud that I am the Dalai Lama and so forth. I am a *bhikshu*, a follower of Buddha Shakyamuni, who cherishes the instruction and teaching of Buddha Shakyamuni and sincerely tries to practice what Buddha Shakyamuni teaches. I practice his teaching not simply to please him, not simply to flatter him; I am not following his practice because all my happiness is in the hands of the Buddha. I am following the teaching of the Buddha because it is beneficial for me in the long run. We all want happiness and do not want suffering. And this wish will not last just for the next few days or few years, but for many lives to come. Whether we have happiness or not is in our own hands. In order to find happiness in the long run and not to encounter suffering, we have to work hard. The root of suffering is ignorance, anger, and attachment. Seeing these negativities as the enemy, and cherishing the qualities of the awakening mind, the wisdom understanding emptiness, and so forth, is all for our own benefit. Therefore, as a follower of Buddha Shakyamuni, I am practicing what he taught. Although he taught the four noble truths and the two truths [conventional and ultimate truth] 2,500 years ago, each time I think about them they become more true; my conviction about them increases.

I always think of myself as an ordinary *bhikshu*, an ordinary follower of the Buddha. Other people are the same as me. Therefore, it may be useful to discuss what I know with you and with that kind of motivation, a motivation to benefit, I give these teachings. Even if we are able to benefit just one person, it fulfills the teaching of the Buddha. The Buddha himself first generated the awakening mind, then he accumulated extensive merit, and finally he attained enlightenment. He did all this for the benefit of sentient beings. He followed his practice for countless aeons without getting discouraged and finally attained enlightenment. This was possible because he had the most wonderful cause: the awakening mind. Therefore, if through our own teaching, or through our own good behavior, we are able to make even one person lead a positive way of life or cause happiness to arise within the mind of that person, it is a great service to the Buddha-dharma, but it also fulfills our own benefit.

Whatever Dharma practices we do should be done with the right motivation. Generally speaking, to habituate ourselves with positive qualities is extremely difficult, while acquaintance with negative activities comes automatically. Therefore, the ancient Kadampa masters used to say that accumulating negative activities is like a stone rolling down a steep slope, but engaging into positive practice is like driving water upstream or leading an exhausted horse. Whether we are awake or asleep, disturbing emotions automatically arise. This is then manifest in our daily behavior. We engage in negative activities even knowing they are wrong.

Since we have found this precious human birth, and we have come together to listen to the teaching, it is important that we should generate a positive motivation. Only then will listening to the teaching become a spiritual practice. When we talk about accumulating positive deeds and eliminating negative deeds, we do so not because the Buddha has told us to, but because the Buddha's teaching is based on the natural law of cause and effect. When he taught the four noble truths, he also explained the way cause and effect works. Happiness arises in dependence on causes and conditions, and suffering too arises in dependence on causes and conditions; this is a law of nature. The happiness we experience in this very life, whether it is material prosperity, better education, or whatever, comes about as a result of accumulating the necessary causes and conditions.

These different causes and conditions arise in direct relation to human behavior, which is related to our human way of thinking. And these different concepts or ways of thinking within the human being do not arise without cause or condition. Human beings have a physical body, and to some extent different conceptual thoughts arise because of the condition of the physical body. For example, if you are physically well and healthy, you feel mentally relaxed and happy. For consciousness to arise, there has to be an external object as the focus of that mind, and when it also reacts with the physical circumstances, that mind arises. Whether you call it the brain, or whatever physical reality you attribute to the mind, it is not only the physical substance that gives rise to the mind.

The mind is something which has clarity and the capacity to know. The formation of the physical human body starts with the union of the father's and mother's sperm and egg. As it develops, consciousness also takes part. But the actual substance of the mind is not the physical body, but a previous mind. The feelings of happiness and suffering that we encounter should be traced not only to the physical body, but also to the subtlest mind. Therefore, in tantric teachings we find explanation of the subtlest mind, called primordial clear light mind. When we talk about the continuity of life, it is explained in terms of the continuity of the clear light mind.

We have different experiences because of our behavior, and our different behaviors arise because of different mental attitudes. Basically we are all the same in wanting happiness and not wanting suffering. If you were to ask even people who seem to be cruel and bent on fighting or waging war whether they really want to fight, the answer will be negative. They also are similar to us in wanting happiness and not wanting suffering. We engage in foul activities because we are overpowered by ignorance. Ignorance is so strong that despite our wanting something else, we are compelled to engage in destructive activities. We see destructive activities throughout the world, which shows the great potency of the human mind to control everything.

Our feelings of happiness and suffering are very much dependent on our behavior, which is very much related to our way of thinking. Those mental attitudes which are negative and unworthy should be reduced and eliminated. We should identify constructive kinds of mind and promote and develop them; this method of transforming the mind is what we call Dharma or spiritual practice. That is why the Buddha's teaching says that we should not do evil acts. We should do positive acts because we want happiness and don't want suffering. And happiness comes from doing positive acts, while suffering comes from doing negative acts.

Since the mind is like a spring, the source of our stream of experience, it is important to control this source of experience—in other words, transform the mind. Politicians try to control people's minds with programs like class struggle and so forth, but as these are mainly based not on transforming the mind but on how to gain victory for your own party and defeat the other party, therefore they are always unsuccessful. The method for transforming the mind is to see that whatever we do, if the result will be negative, we should not do it. If we can see that by doing something it will lead to happiness and peace, then we can happily do it.

When the Buddha taught the four noble truths and introduced true suffering, he did so not to depress us or make us feel sad. If there were no means to remove suffering, then there would be no need to talk about it. But the Buddha did not speak only about true suffering; he also spoke about the causes of suffering and the possibility of removing that suffering, the path leading to the cessation of that suffering. Negativities and disturbing emotions are temporary but have a certain force. If we familiarize our minds with the antidotes to these negative minds, we can definitely defeat them. True cessation or nirvana refers to our mind being completely free from disturbing emotions and sufferings. If it is possible to attain such a state, it is worthwhile for us to find the proper method to do so and to work to achieve it.

First it is important to know the benefits of engaging in such practice and the disadvantages of not doing so.

Someone who has no knowledge at all about the Buddha's teachings might be full of disturbing emotions, but he might feel that these are just the daily habits of the mind and take them for granted. If we speak to him about removing these negativities, he might just ignore it or accept anger, attachment, and so forth as part of life. There are definitely disadvantages to such a course, because when our minds are clouded by disturbing emotions, even if we have wealth, friends, and everything we desire, we may not be able to experience happiness. On the other hand, if we reduce and remove disturbing emotions and generate the positive qualities explained in the teaching, we will get real mental determination and courage.

When we are afflicted by disturbing emotions like anger and attachment, we suffer fear, low self-esteem, depression, and so forth. Therefore, it is important to reduce the negative aspects of the mind and increase its positive aspects. Then we will really start to experience happiness. Of course, external material facilities are a cause and condition for happiness, but they are not the ultimate source. The ultimate source of happiness is within our mind.

Buddhism is a teaching which is very much related to human behavior, and it is divided into philosophy, or view, and conduct. The conduct is not to harm other sentient beings. That is the behavior of a Buddhist. The philosophy is that your own happiness is related to other people. Therefore, cherish other people, do not harm them; as a result you will have happiness. If, on the other hand, you ignore and neglect the welfare of other people, you will not have happiness, because your happiness and suffering do not occur in isolation. If there is happiness and peace in society, in your neighborhood, in the whole world, then we will all have happiness. This is dependent arising, the theory of relativity.

Buddhism does not teach about a creator, nor does it say that things arise without causes and conditions. If you deceive other people for your happiness, it is a foolish way of trying to achieve happiness. Usually, when there is an opportunity, we bully other people. When we are able to deceive someone, we do it without hesitation. And if we are unable to do anything else, we start criticizing or narrating someone's negative qualities to create enmity between other people. Then, when we encounter a problem and seek those people's help, they simply laugh at us.

If, from the outset, you behave as if you are related to your friends, neighbors, and people living around you, when you are faced with some problem, your neighbors will all help without being asked. We are social animals. We definitely have to depend upon each other. This theory of relativity and dependent arising is the Buddhist philosophy. All conditioned phenomena arise in dependence on causes and conditions. Therefore, our happiness and suffering also arise due to causes and conditions. In short, the Buddha advised: if possible, benefit other people; if you are unable to benefit other people, at least refrain from harming them.

Now let us look at this text by Je Tsongkhapa, the *Abridged Stages of the Path to Enlightenment*. It is called the *Song of Experience* because it is based on his own experience and realization. When we talk about the "Stages of the Path" to enlightenment, it refers to the content or subject of the teaching. Enlightenment is the goal to be achieved. Enlightenment here refers to that great enlightenment which is Buddhahood. The first part of the Tibetan word for enlightenment means to purify all negativities. But it does not mean the momentary cessation of these disturbing emotions. That will always take place. It is a law of nature. Whatever is impermanent ceases momentarily. Here we are talking about the cessation or removal of these disturbing emotions through the use of certain powerful antidotes. The second part of the Tibetan word means to generate positive qualities. Purification mainly refers to the three poisons—anger, attachment, and ignorance—especially the imprints left behind by ignorance, which are the obstructions to Buddhahood. When we remove the imprint of ignorance, the innate power of the mind to see the actual nature of phenomena manifests.

The potency of the mind to see the actual nature of phenomena is its inherent quality. It is obscured by the obstructions to enlightenment. Buddhahood is the goal, and it is achieved through the mind. We are talking about achieving enlightenment within our mind. We are not referring to enlightenment as some other peaceful place. If it were somewhere else, we might, instead of purifying our mind, adopt some other measures, such as traveling by airplane or train. Enlightenment is achieved with our mind, by purifying all our negative disturbing emotions individually one by one and actualizing all positive qualities one by one. This is usually called the path.

There are different stages to the process of removing the disturbing emotions. To begin with, we simply weaken or reduce the delusions. Gradually, through the force of countermeasures, we strengthen positive qualities. In this way we completely eradicate and remove the negative delusions. Eventually we attain a state where even if the causes and conditions are present, disturbing emotions do not arise. We achieve a state of cessation of these disturbing emotions which is called the true cessation. And the path responsible for achieving that true cessation is called the true path. The direct counterforce that removes the root cause of suffering is the wisdom understanding emptiness. Other qualities, like love and compassion, contribute to removing it, but do not directly eradicate these negative imprints or seeds.

When we meditate continuously on the wisdom understanding emptiness, the clarity of our understanding gradually increases. To start with, we are unable to understand the nature of the object correctly because our minds are obscured by ignorance. To counter that, we familiarize our minds with the wisdom understanding emptiness. When we attain the nondualistic path of a superior being, it is called the true path. The total cessation of disturbing emotions within your mind is called the true cessation. It is also called the true Dharma, which is our real protector.

Therefore, when we talk about the Stages of the Path, this is the path.

Since the ultimate state of Buddhahood is a state of complete purification of the mind, while we are training we enter into the process of purifying the mind of negativities. In order to generate such a true path and true cessation within our minds, even at our ordinary level it is important to remove the grosser levels of disturbing emotions and the negative conduct that is induced by them. We should promote all positive qualities individually and remove all negativities individually. That practice is called the path. The *Stages of the Path* does not explain these different rules of the path at random. It explains the path in a systematic order. Therefore, it is called the *Stages of the Path*.

Even in achieving the first path, which is called the path of accumulation, there are different techniques depending upon your mental intelligence. The process of meditation also differs. The *Stages of the Path* explains systematically what kind of meditation you should do first, second, and so forth. Therefore, it is called "stages" or "order" of the path. In one sense, all the words of the Buddha and the commentaries on them can be categorized as stages of the path because they explain the different levels of the path. But the usage of this term, "Stages of the Path," actually came into existence after Atisha.

The main subject of these teachings is the generation of the awakening mind. It is a Great Vehicle teaching. When you meditate on the stages of the path of the Great Vehicle, they are based on the stages of the path of the foundational vehicles. The Great Vehicle teaching is of two categories, sutra and tantra. Sutra teachings explain the generation of the awakening mind and engaging in the practices of a Bodhisattva, the practice of the six perfections. Based on that, the vehicle of tantra is explained.

So the main focus of the *Stages of the Path* is on the generation of the awakening mind. As preliminary practices, the topics described in the foundational vehicle are also explained. Then, within the Great Vehicle teachings that explain the practice of the six perfections, the most important are practices of calm abiding and special insight. It is on the basis of these that we engage in the practice of tantra as a sort of ultimate practice.

I bow down to the greatest of the Shakyas,
Whose body is formed by ten million perfect virtues,

Whose speech fulfills the hopes of limitless beings,
Whose mind perceives everything as it is.

I bow down to Manjushri and to Maitreya,
The noblest sons of that peerless teacher,
Whose emanations appear in innumerable fields,
Taking on the task of the Conqueror's deeds

I bow at the feet of Nagarjuna and Asanga,
Adorning this world, famed throughout the three realms,
Who, in the sense intended, wrote commentaries
On the "Mother of the Conquerors," so hard to fathom.

I bow to Dipamkara, who held a treasury of instructions,
Summarizing without error all the main points
Of the paths of the profound view and extensive conduct,
Passed down faithfully from these two great trailblazers.

I bow with respect to the spiritual teachers,
The eye through which to see the myriad scriptures,
The best gateway to liberation for the fortunate.
Moved by compassion, they skillfully illuminate.

Of the different levels of sutra teaching, the most profound is the teaching on the wisdom understanding emptiness. Generally, the *Stages of the Path* is categorized as a text on the perfection of wisdom. Therefore, its main source of reference among the words of the Buddha is the *Perfection of Wisdom* sutras. Of course, when emptiness is being explained, the stages of the path are also explained. The *Stages of the Path* is mainly based on the texts of the great Indian pioneers, Asanga and Nagarjuna, who wrote their own commentaries without depending on the works of other scholars. Nagarjuna especially focused on the meaning of emptiness, and Asanga focused on explaining the stages of the path.

Nagarjuna's principal work is the text called *Root Wisdom*. His main disciples were Aryadeva, who composed the wonderful text the *Four Hundred Verses*, and Chandrakirti. Of course, there was Bhavaviveka, too, but when it comes to conclusive and detailed explanation, Chandrakirti's commentary is one of the most excellent texts.

For the explanation of the Stages of the Path we have the tradition coming from Asanga to Vasubhandu, and so forth. Both these traditions were received intact by Atisha. Although he had countless disciples, because of his past prayers, the great master Dromton Gyalwai Jungney, a Tibetan nomad, was Atisha's main disciple. He was an *upasaka* and a great scholar. The six teachings of the Kadampa, which are mainly based on a more extensive mode of explanation, were passed down by him. Then there is the tradition distinguished by the kind of instruction which was later called the threefold tradition of the Kadampa. And from Atisha there came the ear-whispered transmission.

The Stages of the Path started with Atisha. The Kadampa practices earlier than Atisha are called the ancient Kadampa practices, while those that come from Atisha are called the new Kadampa transmissions. For example, the *Seven Treasures* of the great Longchenpa explains the Stages of the Path. Similarly, other Tibetan Buddhist schools also explain the Stages of the Path. Practice of the great breakthrough of the Nyingma tradition is possible only on the basis of the Stages of the Path. The text called the *Oral Transmission of the Lama* explains the entire Stages of the Path. Similarly, Gampopa, who is regarded as one of the greatest disciples of Milarepa, also explains the Stages of the Path in his *Jewel Ornament of Liberation*. The *Three Traditions* and the *Three Visions* in the Sakya tradition also explain the Stages of the Path. All these different Tibetan schools or traditions, even though they use different terminology, all explain the Stages of the Path. Of course, there are different ways of explaining it. Even in the texts of Je Tsongkhapa, the order of the *Great Exposition* and the *Middling Exposition* are quite different from what we have here in this abridged version of the *Stages of the Path*. And there is another version in the *Mind Training Like the Rays of the Sun*.

We first engage in practices of the foundational level, which involve thinking about suffering and the determination to be free of it. That topic for the individual of initial aptitude contains the complete path for that kind of person, based on his or her intelligence and aptitude. Having trained in the practices of the initial level, if he or she next hears about the relationship between cause and effect, then that person has one whole practice. Similarly, at the middle level, after having trained in generating a determination to be free, if he or she simply wants to do the practice of renunciation, the whole process of renouncing cyclic existence is available. According to this method of explaining the Stages of the Path, based on training the individual, whether you are a person of initial, middling, or great capacity, there are special supplements to practice. Therefore, even though the *Stages of the Path* explains the practices to be done by an individual at the initial level, the aim is to lead that individual to the middle level and then on to the greater level. But if a person does not have the capacity to engage into all this systematic practice, then he or she can find a complete practice in the teaching of the initial level alone.

I received this *Song of Experience* or *Abridged Stages of the Path to Enlightenment* first from Taktra Rinpoche. After that I received one commentary from Ling Rinpoche and one commentary from Trijang Rinpoche. So, I received three commentaries from these three different masters.

In explaining the greatness of the teaching, the text says:

These stages of the path to enlightenment have come down
Intact from Nagarjuna and Asanga,
Crown jewels among the wise of the world,
Banners of fame, preeminent among living beings.

These instructions are a powerful king of jewels,
Since they fulfill all wishes of those in the nine states.
They are a glorious ocean of excellent explanation,
For they bring together a thousand rivers of good scriptural
    statements.

These Stages of the Path to Enlightenment, which come down to us through Nagarjuna and Asanga, fulfill the hopes and wishes of countless sentient beings. They fulfill both our temporary wishes and the ultimate wish, which is the attainment of Buddhahood. All the stages of practice from the practice of thinking about the preciousness of human life up to the attainment of Buddhahood are explained in the *Stages of the Path,* or the three levels of practice. Since it fulfills the wishes of sentient beings, it is like a precious jewel. The *Stages of the Path* contains all the essential practices of the great teachings, both the words of the Buddha and the commentaries of the great spiritual masters. Therefore, it is like a great ocean into which many rivers flow.

> *You will know that the teachings are without contradictions;*
> *How to take all the scriptures as personal instructions;*
> *You will easily discover the Conqueror's intentions, and will also*
>   *be protected from the abyss of great error.*

The greatness of the *Stages of the Path* teaching is that since it condenses all the essential teachings of the great spiritual masters right from the Buddha, we can understand the noncontradictory spirit of all these different levels of teachings. All these different teachings are useful instructions through which we can easily find the intention of Buddha Shakyamuni. The different explanations that we find in the teaching of the Buddha and in the different commentaries were given to address the needs of different students or different sentient beings. At first glance, we may find these teachings to be literally contradictory. And if we are unable to fathom the intrinsic meaning of these teachings, we might get the impression that some of these teachings are to be practiced and some are not. We might feel that these masters contradict each other. But when we gradually work through the practice of the Stages of the Path, from how to rely on a spiritual teacher to the attainment of a Buddha, we find that the teachings are presented in three stages to help practitioners of different mental attitudes according to their different capacities. All the different levels of teachings are to be practiced, but we can start from the level which is suitable to our minds.

In addition, we can see all these teachings as great instructions. Whether they belong to the sutras or tantras, we find that these teachings do not contradict each other. We have different texts, like the *Treasury of Knowledge,* which explains the diverse nature of different levels of phenomena, and the *Ornament of Clear Realization,* which explains the different levels of the path. Looking at these different texts, we might get the feeling that some of these teachings are meant for experience and some are meant only for scholarship. This is a clear indication of being unable to see all the scriptures as great instructions or advice. But if we study a text like the *Stages of the Path,* we will be able to collect all these teachings together, thinking that this particular line of teaching is useful in relation to this or that kind of experience. Therefore, you will be able to see all these teachings as great instructions or advice for your experience.

Good understanding of the different stages of the path is the basis for correct realization. Therefore, the third reason why the *Stages of the Path* is great is that through it we can easily find the ultimate thought of the Buddha. By practicing it we gain realization, through which we increase our conviction in the authenticity of the thought of the Buddha. When we develop such a conviction, we will automatically discard our negative way of life and will treat even one letter of the teaching of the Buddha with great respect.

Then what intelligent person would not be enthralled by
These stages of the path of the three kinds of people, the superlative
    instructions, followed by many of good fortune,
Wise individuals of both India and Tibet?

Because the stages of the path have been arranged systematically, it is easy to practice. These are some of the reasons why the *Stages of the Path* teaching is great. Therefore, the great scholars of Tibet and India relied on this supreme instruction. Then Tsongkhapa asks whether it is possible for someone to claim to be intelligent without being attracted to the stages of the path. Someone who has very strong positive karmic imprints within his or her mind may not have to work through all these different stages of the path; for them a slight causal condition might induce certain realizations. But the general procedure is to do the practice in accordance with the *Stages of the Path.*

Next, it explains how to impart this teaching and the benefits of listening to and explaining this teaching.

Since it's certain you powerfully accumulate
All the benefits of explaining or hearing the excellent teachings
By just once teaching or listening to this concise version
Summarizing the essence of all the scriptures—think about it!

Since the *Stages of the Path* is an abbreviation of all the great excellent teachings, if we recite this teaching just once or listen to it once, we will accumulate the extensive merit to be derived from giving or hearing all those teachings. Therefore, we should listen to or impart this teaching with the intention of transforming our minds. We should point our finger at ourselves and think of transforming our own mental attitude to attain Buddhahood. Otherwise, despite all these extensive levels of teachings being given to transform the mind, we could simply become great scholars. These teachings will become mere academic knowledge that will not touch the mind at all. As a result we will not be able to make any transformation within our minds.

Therefore, when we listen to or impart such teachings, it is important that we do so with a correct motivation, free of all faults. Listening to the teaching is important. It is also possible that by simply reading the text we will understand it, but if we listen to an experienced lama's explanation, it will enhance our own experience. It will be extremely effective for transforming the mind. So, while actually listening to the teaching, you should not be like a pot turned upside down, or like a dirty pot, or like a pot with a leaky bottom. You should also generate the six kinds of positive feeling, such as imagining yourself as a sick person, the Dharma as medicine, the teacher as a physician, and so forth.

The lama should explain the teaching with right motivation. The more he cares about conveying the teaching, the greater will be his own realization. Teaching a text to someone else is different from reading it alone by yourself. Sometimes, when you read it alone, you may gallop through the text but fail to get a clear understanding. If you are explaining it to someone, you have to be more careful. You will gain clear insight into certain things you were unable to understand before. I have found many great *geshes* who became realized after becoming a *geshe* because they spent their time explaining texts to their students. Whether you are able to do circumambulations or prostrations or not, what is more important is to sincerely teach the meaning of the texts to students. That is more beneficial. Then, at the end you should dedicate all the virtuous qualities you have accumulated for the benefit of all sentient beings.

The next point is how to rely on the spiritual friend. Relying on the spiritual friend is referred to as the root of the practice of the *Stages of the Path*. If we have that as the basis, the rest of our practice will be successful. The text says:

> *The root which firmly establishes an auspicious connection*
> *To a store of diverse good now and hereafter*
> *Is, with effort, to rely properly in thought and deed*
> *On the excellent spiritual friends who show you the path.*
>
> *Seeing this, never give them up, even at the cost of your life,*
> *And please them with the gift of doing what they instruct.*
> *This is what my revered and holy teacher did,*
> *And I, who seek liberation, will do likewise.*

Whatever excellent qualities we experience in this life or the life hereafter, relying on the spiritual friend makes an auspicious beginning leading to success in our subsequent practices. If we have the necessary causes and conditions right at the beginning, it is natural that our subsequent practices will be successful. And unless we accumulate the correct causes and conditions in the beginning, the desired result will not be achieved. This is a kind of law of nature. If you want to achieve success in something, you must accumulate the causes and conditions. Whether it is scientific development or economic progress, it will be achieved through systematic planning. By systematic planning I mean that whatever you need or require in the future, you should prepare accordingly. Follow the first step, the second step, the third step—prepare all the necessary causes and conditions in their systematic order and implement them. Then you will achieve the result you seek.

Dharma practice is concerned with achieving success in our future lives. What we mainly seek is peace and happiness. Peace and happiness come about through effecting the right causes and conditions. Simply praying for peace and happiness will not bring you what you want.

This is a matter of dependent arising. If you really desire all the excellent qualities of this life and the life hereafter, you should follow the law of dependent arising. Someone becomes a sublime spiritual friend not because he or she is wealthy or renowned. Buddhahood is something we achieve within our minds. It is a mental quality. That ultimate mental quality is achieved through following the stages of the path. This means that we gradually remove the different levels of disturbing emotions and achieve the different levels of qualities. The spiritual friend should have listened to the teachings extensively and should have extensive experience of their practice. But if he or she is someone who, despite having a name, has no knowledge, or is someone who has knowledge but has no experience, he or she will find it difficult to guide other people.

Tsongkhapa says in the *Great Exposition of the Stages of the Path* that if you really want to help other people tame their minds, you must first tame your own mind. If you have not disciplined or tamed your own mind, you cannot really help discipline other people's minds. Disciplining the mind does not come about through very brief practice. It requires stability. So such training or disciplining of the mind does not take place over a few days or even a few months. It should be done over many years. When you gradually transform and discipline your mind through such effort, it will be a real transformation, a real disciplining of the mind. If you do not discipline your mind in a steady, systematic way, you may sometimes be able to behave as if you are very disciplined by practicing giving and so forth, but it will not be long-lasting. I am not saying that this is not useful, but that it is not a real transformation of the mind, a real disciplining of the mind.

In order to discipline your mind thoroughly, it is important to do continuous practice. We see people who seem to be very disciplined and very well behaved for a few months and even for a few years. But later on they behave very negatively, so this is a clear indication that they did not follow a systematic practice. Our enemies, disturbing emotions, are extremely clever and cunning. When I was young, I was told that you have to be extremely careful about *nagas*, otherwise they watch you everywhere and whenever they find an opportunity they will harm you. Of course, that was just a story. What is true is that disturbing emotions are extremely clever. The only work they have to do is to harm us, to destroy us, to bring us suffering. We should be able to discover the nature of our disturbing emotions. We easily discern the nature of our fellow human beings. If someone we know is cunning or deceitful, we immediately note it. So let us try to discover the same tendency, even a worse tendency, in the disturbing emotions. It is foolish that we point out the negative behavior of other people but overlook the misconception of self and self-centeredness that slumber peacefully within us.

What qualifies a spiritual friend? The *Ornament of Sutras* explains ten qualities that someone who teaches the sutras should fulfill. Such a spiritual friend should be completely disciplined, peaceful, and knowledgeable, and so forth. Tsongkhapa says that if you are looking for a spiritual friend, you should first discover the qualities that make a spiritual friend. If you are a spiritual teacher who wants to gather more disciples or students, you should examine whether you have the necessary qualities. If you don't do this, some risk is involved. You might initially take someone as your spiritual friend without analyzing his qualities, and later on, disgusted with that person's behavior, you might turn away from him or her, which involves a risk for you both.

To begin with, instead of accepting someone as a spiritual teacher and receiving teachings from him, it is advisable simply to talk with him or her. Otherwise, you can simply listen to teachings from a certain person without entrusting yourself completely to him or her. After some time, when you have examined his or her good qualities, you can safely take that person as your spiritual friend. To start with, you have to spy on your teacher. Only when you are sure you can really trust this person should you accept him or her as your teacher. There is a saying that you should not adopt someone as your teacher in the way that a dog runs after a piece of meat.

Once you have adopted someone as your teacher, even if you find some fault in him or her, you should neither focus on it nor declare it to others. Take a neutral stance. It is also said that you should see everything the spiritual friend does as good. This has a particular meaning in a particular context. You should not take it at its face value. It is clearly explained that if a spiritual friend says something which is completely against the general instruction of the Buddha, you have every reason to question him or her. If the spiritual teacher's instruction completely contradicts the general teaching of the Buddha, you should disregard it. Of course, if your spiritual teacher has excellent qualities, but his instructions contradict the general instruction of the Buddha in some way, you should question him. If your spiritual teacher is a really authentic master, even though his instructions may appear to be contradictory, he will be able to explain the noncontradictory spirit of his teaching.

You should sincerely rely on the spiritual friend, even at the cost of your life, in terms of your thoughts and in terms of your practice. Once you have accepted someone as your spiritual teacher, if you can, try to see him or her as a manifestation of the Buddha. However, the main thing is to generate respect and appreciation for his or her knowledge and qualities, and so remember his or her kindness. If you act in accordance with his or her thought and instruction, all your behavior will automatically become virtuous. If you are close to your spiritual teacher, your faults will automatically cease and your qualities will automatically increase.

In order to mold your body, speech, and mind in accordance with the wishes of the spiritual teacher, you should first generate faith. Educated parents take care of their children by sending them to school and making sure that they receive an education. On the other hand, illiterate parents, because of their own illiteracy, do not care much about the education of their children. Similarly, it is very important for us to have the right spiritual teacher. We need someone to emulate. Even in ordinary life we depend on a teacher, whatever profession we adopt. For instance, you cannot simply become a great artist using your own intelligence. But if you are guided by someone who really knows about art, you will be successful in your work.

When I was learning how to write the headless Tibetan script, I was very fond of writing the one with a head, the capital letters. By reading the scriptures and using my own initiative, I was able to write in capital letters. But later, when I started learning from someone how to write them, I found that the proper way, the way you hold the pen, the way you move your hand, and so forth, were completely different. Similarly, when it comes to transforming the mind, it is important to depend on someone who knows how to do it. This is why having a spiritual teacher is important.

Now the important question at this juncture is whether it is really possible for someone to be a Buddha, completely enlightened, without fault and possessing all qualities. Take the example of a human being. There is no individual who right from birth is angry and remains so until he or she dies. There are occasions when we become angry, but there are occasions when we become compassionate and full of love. So even if you are a very angry person, you will not remain angry all the time. This clearly shows that the mind, which has two qualities of clarity and awareness, and disturbing emotions are two separate things. Even though there are occasions when we generate anger and attachment, there are also occasions when the fundamental mind is free from these negativities.

From our own experience we know that there are various aspects of the mind based on the fundamental clarity of the mind. There are occasions when we generate anger, compassion, and so forth toward the same object, but there is no occasion when we generate anger and compassion toward that object at the same time. They cannot arise together at the same time, which shows that these are different aspects of the mind. When we generate disturbing emotions like anger and attachment, we have a strong sense of self, a strong feeling of it. The more we have this misconception of self, the greater will be our anger and attachment. This feeling of "I" or self is sometimes so overpowering that we might think we could touch it. This feeling of self definitely strengthens anger and attachment, but it is not the ultimate nature of the mind.

We can understand by inference that the disturbing emotions can be removed. In addition, the misconception of self has an antidote, which is the understanding of selflessness. Therefore, Buddhahood is something existent, and it is something we can attain. If a Buddha exists, he became enlightened for the benefit of other sentient beings. He accumulated positive qualities for the benefit of all other sentient beings. So, we can also assume that, directly or indirectly, Buddhas are always assisting us toward the positive path. Even so, only our spiritual teacher, who instructs us directly, takes us by the hand toward the true path.

Through reasons such as these we can come to the conclusion that the spiritual teacher is a manifestation of the Buddha. When we think in this way, we are focusing more on the qualities of the spiritual teacher and the unreliability of our own perception. By remembering the qualities of the spiritual teacher, we recall that in those terms he or she may be equal to the Buddha, but in terms of kindness, the spiritual teacher is kinder to us than even the Buddha.

Having relied on a spiritual teacher, how do we engage in the practice? How can we extract the meaning of this human birth? The attainment of higher status is our goal, and the explanation of how to attain it is the teaching for the first stage of the practice. It is for individuals of initial capacity. Finding the root cause of suffering is the middle teaching. Having recognized suffering and determined to free yourself from cyclic existence, if, faced with the sufferings of other sentient beings, you are able to generate compassion, love, and altruism for them, you can engage in the practice of the six perfections. This practice is for individuals of the highest capacity. The next verse explains the importance of a human rebirth.

> *This life of liberty surpasses a wish-granting jewel, and you'll find*
> *the like of it only this once.*
> *It's rare and easily lost, brief as lightning in the sky. With this in*
> *mind, understand that all worldly actions*
> *Are like chaff tossed in the air, so you must constantly*
> *Make best use of this life, day and night.*
> *This is what my revered and holy teacher did, and I, who seek*
> *liberation, will do likewise.*

If nirvana and enlightenment exist and can be achieved, then we must achieve them. The way to do so is to transform and discipline the mind. To do that we need determination, which we can arouse through reason. Only human beings are able to use reason. Gods and demigods are something we do not see directly. But among those we can see, the different categories of animals and so forth, human beings have the greatest intelligence. No other creature has such wonderful intelligence as human beings. Therefore, human existence is extremely precious. But if we spend our precious life overwhelmed by disturbing emotions like attachment, anger, and so forth, it would seem that we have only taken birth to harm other people.

When we took birth, we brought great suffering to our mothers. If we depended on our mother's milk, we survived due to her kindness. And even if we did not depend on mother's milk, we must have depended on the milk of some other animal, so we depended on their kindness for our survival. Likewise, our very life was dependent on the kindness of other sentient beings. So right from the time of our birth until we are able to take care of ourselves, our existence is possible only due to the kindness of many other people. We are able to survive by depending on the suffering and kindness of many other people. But once we are able to take care of ourselves, if, instead of repaying the kindness of others, we are merely destructive, swayed only by attachment, anger, and so forth, it is extremely unfortunate. In that case it would have been better to have been born as an animal rather than as a human being. At least animals are less destructive than those kinds of human beings. Leading such a life, it is better to be dead than alive.

We see various destructive people in different parts of the world. Not only do such people experience unhappiness, but they destroy the happiness of others. They may have power, but they do not experience happiness. If people who have power, wealth, and intelligence are unable to use their power and wealth constructively to make other people happy, then it would be better if they did not live. It is important to be able to employ this great resource of human intelligence to help other people. At least it should not be a source of trouble for other people.

In the context of transforming the mind, human life is extremely important. On the basis of human intelligence we can generate the precious awakening mind. The awakening mind is regarded as like a precious jewel. Caring more about the welfare of other people than about yourself is more precious than a jewel. Such a precious jewel can be produced by the human mind.

So, having taken birth in this world, if we use our precious life for destructive activities, nothing could be worse. Those of us who have encountered the Buddha-dharma have the opportunity to use our intelligence. One courageous person can give new direction to other human beings and bring happiness to other sentient beings. On the other hand, if we use our minds negatively, one person alone can destroy thousands of people and animals. Human intelligence has the capacity for constructive and destructive activity. Attaining the higher status of birth as a human being or a god can be achieved by practicing the ten virtues, the six perfections, and so forth, as a human being. Indeed, by engaging in sincere practice of the three trainings of ethics, meditative stabilization, and wisdom, we will be able to attain nirvana. Moreover, we can also attain the ultimate state of Buddhahood. Therefore, this human life is said to be more precious than a precious jewel.

It is natural that if something is precious, it will be difficult to find. Human life is very precious, and its causes are difficult to achieve, yet on this occasion we have found such a precious opportunity. But not only is it difficult to find, it is easily lost, like lightning in the sky. Whatever is born is subject to death, and at the time of death it is only the imprints of the positive virtuous activities that you have done which will help you in the next life. Otherwise, at the time of death we leave everything behind: our relatives and wealth, and even our highly cherished body. Therefore, we should make a determination to engage in Dharma practice. By reflecting on the reality of death and gaining a strong conviction in it, we can come to see all the petty activities of the world as meaningless and inspire ourselves to engage in practice day and night.

In this very world there are more than five billion people. We all want happiness and do not want suffering. This is a fundamental common quality of us all, yet we adopt different measures to meet it, based on our interest and mental capacity. Some people make their sole aim the accumulation of wealth. Others do not involve themselves only with material prosperity, but also try to ensure mental stability.

One category of humanity views spiritual practice as like poison or opium. Seeing it as an instrument of exploitation, they see spiritual practice as a fault and try to eliminate it. Another category of humanity believes that it is not only material prosperity that brings happiness. Consequently, they engage in spiritual practice to achieve mental peace and happiness. A third category adopts a neutral stance. It neither tries to eliminate spiritual practice nor to adopt it. They simply engage in their day-to-day activities. Whether we practice the Dharma or not, the important thing is that we all want happiness. If we compare those who believe in spiritual practice with those who do not, we will find that those who engage in spiritual practice have more mental stability and more mental happiness. So we can conclude that what we are doing is unmistaken.

Of course, as individuals we are not all perfect. We do encounter various negative experiences, but even then we have the ability to endure the sufferings we encounter. What is more, when we engage in spiritual practice, we accumulate positive actions, which are a cause for future happiness. Those who deny spiritual practice not only exhaust the fruit of what they have done earlier, but they do not accumulate causes and conditions for future happiness.

Even in exile we Tibetans have enough food to eat and enough clothes to wear. I think this is a positive result of our spiritual practice. It is because we are contented that we have enough things for our use. I think this is a clear indication that Tibetans have more spiritual merit than those who do not engage in practice. After the Chinese came to Tibet, they implemented their revolution and redistributed wealth to those who were poor. But we found that gradually those people who used to be wealthy were always successful and became prosperous again. Even if you allot wealth to those who did not have it before, because they lack the necessary merit, they tend to be unsuccessful and become poor again.

Success or the lack of it relates to the force of positive action that we have accumulated in the past. Therefore, whatever certain people do, they are always successful, while others work very hard but do not meet with success. There are unseen causes and conditions which are responsible for one person's success and for the failure of others.

Those of us who have a spiritual practice will be able to face problems and at the same time engage in positive thinking to be able to prepare for our long-term future. Therefore, having accepted spiritual practice, it is not only beneficial for many lives to come, but it is actually very helpful in our daily life. If we expect all happiness to come from material prosperity, we are deceiving ourselves. We cannot deny that material prosperity brings comfort, because we do possess a physical body. But the main source of happiness is derived from mental tranquility and transformation of the mind.

It is not enough that we profess to be Buddhists. We should continue paying attention to the meaning taught in the Buddha's teachings. We may have great reverence for the Buddha, Dharma, and Sangha, but we do not make much effort or attempt to study the Dharma texts. We tend to think that Dharma texts should be studied by monks in monasteries. Yet, whether you are an ordained person or a layperson, it is extremely important to know what the Buddha taught.

When we pay homage to the image of the Buddha, it is not simply enough that we bow down to the image of the Buddha. We should know why we are paying homage to that image. In order to know what Buddha Shakyamuni's qualities are, it is important to study his teachings. Just as you would judge a person's behavior or his attitude through listening to what he says, you should find out the validity of Buddha Shakyamuni himself by listening to his teachings. It is not enough simply to come and attend a teaching without trying to understand the meaning. What is more important is that in your daily life you should try to study different texts. The way to start is initially to pick a short scripture and try to understand the main points. When you have understood the outline of the text, you can study it in more detail. Then you can turn to more complicated texts and so enhance your spiritual education. It is extremely important that ordained persons, the monks and nuns, engage in serious Dharma training and study. The purpose of your study should be the attainment of Buddhahood for the benefit of all other sentient beings. If you study with that motivation, whatever you do will become an important cause for accumulating positive virtue for the benefit of all suffering sentient beings.

We have been discussing the methods for training an individual of initial mental capacity. At that level, the suffering of bad states of rebirth is like true suffering and the ten unwholesome deeds are like the true origin of suffering. Liberation from bad states of rebirth and attainment of higher status is like true cessation. The path to attain that higher status is practice of the ten wholesome actions, which is like the true path. In order to practice the ten wholesome deeds sincerely, we need to recognize the objects of refuge, that is, the Buddha, Dharma, and Sangha.

The better we understand the Buddha, Dharma, and Sangha as the object of refuge, the better will be our understanding of the relationship between cause and effect.

When you die, you can't be sure not to take a bad rebirth.
Only the Three Jewels offer certain protection from such fears.
Therefore, make your practice of refuge steadfast
And follow its precepts without any lapse.

This depends on sound knowledge of black and white actions and
*   their effects,*
And adopting and discarding them in the right way.
This is what my revered and holy teacher did,
And I, who seek liberation, will do likewise.

The stages of the path concerning the individual of initial capacity deal mainly with how to rely on a spiritual teacher and how to engage in the means to liberate ourselves from bad states of rebirth. Whether we have a true sense of taking refuge in the Buddha, Dharma, and Sangha depends on whether we have accumulated the necessary causes and conditions. These are having a sense of fear of suffering and seeing the potential of the Buddha, Dharma, and Sangha to help and protect us. In order to protect ourselves from falling into bad states of rebirth, it is important to think about death and impermanence. If we don't, we might think that we can do the practice later. In the meantime we might meet with death, and having had no time to do spiritual practice, we will fall into bad states of rebirth.

When we think about such bad states of rebirth as the hells and so forth, we might sometimes wonder if they really exist. The *Treasury of Knowledge* not only describes the nature of the different beings in the hells, but even provides calculations to indicate where they are located. Although these measurements may not be entirely accurate, they suggest the possibility of different existences according to their various causes and conditions.

With regard to the formation of the universe, the *Treasury of Knowledge* explains a time when the universe abides, a time when it disintegrates, and a time when it is formed. That formation first takes place from out of empty space as the different elements are gradually formed. These explanations are quite in line with the scientific explanation. It also explains the existence of different sentient beings, such as animals, which leads to the issue of eating meat. If we are able to abstain from eating meat, it is extremely good.

When I was young and staying in the Potala Palace, I often noticed flocks of sheep being driven in by herdsmen at the end of the day. They were being brought to slaughter and, feeling uneasy, I would call someone to release them and would pay handsomely for doing so. At that time I had no thought that by doing so I would prolong my life. My only concern was that these poor animals would die an untimely death. I was able to save the lives of many of those animals. We Tibetans are Buddhists but at the same time we are voracious meat-eaters. When we think about that, it might make us uneasy. In the rest of the world the number of fish and the numbers of different kinds of other small animals that are killed to be eaten is just countless.

Similarly, these days when we can wear clothes made of cotton and stuff other than fur, if instead we simply kill animals for their skins, it is extremely unfortunate. When I think of all these destructive activities in relation to animals, I feel that birth control is good, for if there were fewer human beings there would be less destruction. If we go into detail about the amount of animals that are killed, it is unimaginable. How many hens are being killed every day? How many fish are being killed? I once visited a poultry farm. To begin with, hens are used to lay eggs. During that time they are imprisoned in a metal cage for a few years. Then after two or three years, when they are unable to lay any more eggs, the only place for them to go is the kitchen. When I travel in India, I see small metal cages with a few hens in them outside restaurants. We clearly do not have the slightest feeling about how much these poor birds suffer. We, who are unable to bear even the pain of a needle prick, are totally careless of the sufferings of other animals and birds. As human beings, when we encounter the slightest injustice or suffering, we immediately complain. We go to court. But do these animals have a right to complain? When a stray dog is simply wandering in search of food, we throw stones at it to drive it away. These animals and birds have no courts to complain in; they have no friends from whom to seek support. We proclaim that to kill out of revenge is not good, that human execution is not good, but do the animals have such rights? We tend to think of domestic animals like sheep and goats as something to be bullied without showing the slightest concern for their welfare. The only fortunate thing is that because animals are so ignorant, they may not have as much fear as human beings.

> *Since there won't be swift progress in accomplishing the highest*
> *   path,*
> *Unless you gain a life with all prerequisite features,*
> *Train yourself in creating the causes, so that none are lacking.*
> *Most important is to cleanse karmic obstructions and pollution*
> *By the stains of misdeeds and transgressions through the three*
> *   doors,*
> *So constantly with care apply all four counteractions.*
> *This is what my revered and holy teacher did,*
> *And I, who seek liberation, will do likewise.*
>
> *A real aspiration for freedom won't arise*
> *Without effort to think about the drawbacks of true suffering,*
> *Unless you consider its source—the stages of involvement*
> *In cyclic existence—you will not know how to sever its root.*
> *So cultivate repugnance for it and a wish for freedom*
> *And cherish the knowledge of what binds us to this cyclic process.*
> *This is what my revered and holy teacher did,*
> *And I, who seek liberation, will do likewise.*

If we do not behave properly, when we leave this life, there is no guarantee that we will not also take birth as one of these animals or birds. It is important for us to understand that we encounter suffering because we have harmed other sentient beings. The cause of suffering is unwholesome action. In order to find happiness we must eliminate unwholesome deeds and so free ourselves from suffering. Of the three objects of refuge, the actual protector is the Dharma. We regard the Buddha as precious; we regard the Sangha as precious because the Dharma is so important. It is not because the Buddha is a creator. The Buddha comes into existence because of practice of the causes for the attainment of Buddhahood, which is the true path and the true cessation.

On one level the Dharma can refer to the three collections of scriptures, but the ultimate Dharma is the true cessation attained by eliminating disturbing emotions. When we counter the disturbing emotions and eliminate them at the root, we can attain a state which is free of them. This is called true cessation, which is also known as nirvana or liberation. When we achieve that state within ourselves, we will be protected; we will be saved from suffering. Therefore, our aim should be to attain the true path and true cessation.

We can start by avoiding the ten unwholesome actions. The Tibetan word for disturbing emotion has the sense of being something like suffering. Therefore, when someone is suffering, Tibetans say that that person is subject to disturbing emotions, which means he or she is disturbed or afflicted. Attachment, anger, and so forth are disturbing emotions, and they are so called because as soon as they arise in our minds, we feel unhappy, we encounter suffering, and our mental peace is disturbed. I think this is quite true. For example, here we are all listening to the Dharma in a relaxed way, with calmness of mind. But if we suddenly hear some bad news, it will immediately disturb our minds and we will encounter suffering. Similarly, when we have such negative minds within us, we will be unable to sleep soundly. The moment disturbing emotions arise, the calm and tranquillity of our minds is disturbed, which makes us temporarily unhappy.

When we are overwhelmed by disturbing emotions, we lose our independence, because we almost involuntarily engage in negative deeds. Therefore, the disturbing emotions are responsible for our suffering. The disturbing emotions are our real enemy. We do not want suffering. We want happiness. But these disturbing emotions lead us into suffering. However, it is initially difficult to fight directly with these disturbing emotions when we are unprepared. So, the first stage of the practice, when we don't have the capacity to fight the delusions directly, is to at least refrain from engaging in negative activities. To restrain ourselves from negative activities means not allowing ourselves to become overwhelmed by disturbing emotions. We should restrain ourselves, for example, from throwing stones at someone out of anger. Similarly, you might sometimes go to the market, and out of attachment and delusion you might order a chicken to be slaughtered for you to eat. This is the sort of thing we should restrain ourselves from. So the first stage of practice, which is mainly observed by individuals of initial capacity, is to restrain ourselves and prevent ourselves being overwhelmed by disturbing emotions.

As a second step, we need to establish that all disturbing emotions arise from ignorance or the misconception of self. Then we try to generate the antidote and fight directly with ignorance and the disturbing emotions. Then the third stage of practice is that it is not enough to have removed ignorance and the misconception of self, it is important to remove even the imprints they leave behind, because these imprints are an obstruction to enlightenment for the benefit of all sentient beings.

When we are liberated from the root cause of disturbing emotions, which is ignorance, we attain liberation. And when we eliminate the imprints left behind by the ignorance and the disturbing emotions, we attain Buddhahood. Therefore, by generating the antidotes, we can release ourselves from these different levels of fear. In order to find this right path, it is important to find a proper teacher like the Buddha. All our Dharma practices should be rooted in the notion of dependent arising. And it was Buddha Shakyamuni who had the capacity to voluntarily teach the meaning of dependent arising. Therefore, he is a valid teacher, and the Sangha is the friend who constantly reminds about spiritual practice. The Sangha is like a nurse, always at the bedside of the sick person.

Next the text explains the practice for individuals with greater capacity.

The altruistic intention is the mainstay of the Supreme Vehicle,
The foundation and basis of its powerful activities.
Like an elixir that turns the two stores to gold,
It's a treasure of merit comprising every kind of good.
Knowing this, heroic Bodhisattvas make this precious
And supreme attitude their quintessential practice.
This is what my revered and holy teacher did,
And I, who seek liberation, will do likewise.

First, it describes the generation of the awakening mind, which is an unsurpassable practice, the source of happiness for ourselves and all other sentient beings, and the source of all excellent qualities. *Entering into the Middle Way* says, "Listeners [Hearers] and Solitary Buddhas were born from the Buddha, and the Buddhas were born from Bodhisattvas, and Bodhisattvas were born from compassion and the awakening mind."

When we talk about generating the awakening mind, the exact meaning for the Tibetan words is "extending the mind." Ordinarily, when we always think about our own welfare, our mind is not extended but narrow. When we cease to think only about our own welfare, we give importance to the welfare of others. And when we think about the nature of interdependence, we take account of the importance of other sentient beings achieving happiness and how it is related to our own happiness. So when we care more for the welfare of other sentient beings than for ourselves, we call it "extending the mind."

The actual nature of the awakening mind is that, having engaged in the practice of liberating ourselves from suffering and having identified the nature of the disturbing emotions that obstruct the attainment of nirvana or liberation, we address the possibility of removing even the imprints left behind by ignorance. Since ignorance can be removed, because it is temporary and impermanent, the imprints it leaves behind are also temporary and can be eradicated. These imprints left behind by ignorance obstruct the attainment of Buddhahood.

When we attain Buddhahood, we gain omniscience. Prior to this, the potential of the clear light mind to know everything is obstructed by the imprints of ignorance. As soon as we remove that hindrance, which is called the obstruction to omniscience or knowledge, we achieve Buddhahood. At that level we will be able to know everything, especially the needs and mental dispositions of all suffering sentient beings, which enable us to do only those actions which will definitely benefit other people. If we do not know the needs and attitudes of other people, we will be unable to help them. Even if we have a very good motivation, if we do not know what it is that other people really want, we will not be able to help them. Unless we have a mind which is clearly aware of other people's needs, we will not be able to benefit them. Having generated a wish to benefit other sentient beings, the omniscient mind is extremely important.

There are two levels of generating the awakening mind. One level aspires to work for the benefit of other sentient beings and the other aspires to attain Buddhahood. The aspiration to fulfill the purposes of other sentient beings is the actual cause of the awakening mind, and it is assisted by the aspiration to attain Buddhahood. We have to train on both these levels, which results in a mind possessing two aspects. The awakening mind is a wonderful, excellent, and precious mind. In this life alone, not to speak of developing the fully fledged awakening mind, if you have even a trace of benevolence, you will have more friends around you. More people pat and share their food with a dog which is normally peaceful and calm. But no one approaches or feeds a dog that barks and chases everyone.

Similarly, if one member of a family has calmness of mind, then there will be greater peace within that family. On the other hand, if one member of a family is always angry and impatient, the family is headed for trouble. Usually, when a family is very unsuccessful, people talk about there being hindrances from some other quarter, but I don't think this is true. I think it is more likely something is wrong within the family, which is due to the mental attitude of the members of the family.

If you have a sense of respect, calmness, and patience within your mind, then even if you meet someone you don't know on the road, you easily will be able to make friends with him or her. On the other hand, if you always remain suspicious, even if someone sincerely tells the truth, you will continue to doubt it. Someone may sincerely want to help you, but you will have doubts about it, which will lead to trouble. The reality is that there is nothing to do but depend on the help and kindness of other people. If we always treat other people or other beings as our enemies, if we are always suspicious of them, how can we expect to find lasting happiness? We are naturally sociable, unlike wild animals who go about their lives alone except in the mating season. Whether we like it or not, the reality is that we cannot survive without depending on others. Therefore, it is inappropriate to think only of ourselves, ignoring the welfare of other people. It is extremely important to reduce our self-centered attitude and generate a mind that is concerned for the welfare of other people. The ultimate state of that mind is the generation of the awakening mind.

Once we have such a mind and we generate a determination to sustain it for many lives to come, we will have lighted on the real source of happiness. The practice of generating the awakening mind is like the axis of Great Vehicle practice. If we have such an axis, all other practices will be useful and beneficial. The awakening mind is like an elixir that transforms everything into gold. Whatever extensive activities and conduct we pursue, this mind should be the basis. It is like a precious treasure which comprises all fine qualities. When we make a commitment to generate the awakening mind in order to attain Buddhahood, then whatever we do, whether we are awake or asleep, we will accumulate positive virtues. Because of our earlier determination to attain Buddhahood for the benefit of all other sentient beings, even if we get drunk, our virtuous qualities will go on growing or multiplying. Under the influence of that mind, taking a single footstep, or eating one morsel of food, will become a positive act. Even your inhalation and exhalation of breath will be beneficial to other sentient beings.

Therefore, even those activities which would normally be regarded as negative can become positive, beneficial activities if they are motivated by the awakening mind. This is why the great Bodhisattvas mainly cultivated this supreme, precious mind. That was their main practice, whereas ordinarily our main practice is the recitation of mantras. Henceforth we should recognize that the practice of the awakening mind is the most important practice, and that recitation of mantras and meditation on a personal deity with a multitude of hands and so forth is a secondary practice. Unless our meditation on such deities is based on the practice of the awakening mind, it will not be effective. Just as it is said that the only pathway to attain liberation is the generation of wisdom understanding emptiness, for the attainment of Buddhahood, there is no second path; it is only generation of the awakening mind.

If we try to be clever and ignore the welfare of other people, trying to derive the maximum benefit for ourselves, the result will be negative not only ultimately, but also temporarily. Behaving that way, we will have no friends we can trust. This is what we experience in daily life. The real way of gaining advantage or benefit is to use human intelligence. It is important to use it in such a way that we derive the maximum happiness and benefit, temporarily and in the long run. To ensure long-term happiness, we may temporarily have to undergo minor hardship. As human beings we should use our intelligence in the right way so that we can generate happiness within our own minds and within the minds of all other sentient beings. Since we have found this precious human life, if we can we should try to pursue those paths that are ultimately beneficial for ourselves and other sentient beings. At least we should avoid those activities which limit the happiness of other people.

Having generated the resolution or courage to attain Buddhahood for the benefit of all sentient beings, we have to actually engage in the practices of a Bodhisattva. The Bodhisattva's very purpose in actualizing Buddhahood is to benefit all other sentient beings. Therefore, the practice includes the four means of gathering disciples and the practice of the six perfections. All the practices of a Bodhisattva can be included within these six perfections.

The first concerns giving, about which the text says:

> *Giving is the wish-granting jewel fulfilling the hopes of living beings,*
> *The best weapon with which to cut the knot of miserliness,*
> *A Bodhisattva activity that gives rise to indomitable courage,*
> *And spreads one's fame in the ten directions.*
> *Knowing this, the wise follow the good path*
> *Of completely giving body, possessions, and virtue.*
> *This is what my revered and holy teacher did,*
> *And I, who seek liberation, will do likewise.*

When we engage in the actual practice of giving, we should start with gifts that are easy to make and then gradually extend the scope. This is a great practice, and knowing that, we should ultimately be able to give away our bodies, wealth, and virtuous qualities. The main aim of the practice of giving is to benefit other sentient beings, not to enhance our name and fame, or to enable us to accumulate qualities. The practice is to relieve the sufferings of other sentient beings. Therefore, we should know the proper time and the proper way to give and so forth. For example, medicine, which can be beneficial, given at the wrong time or to the wrong person, can be harmful.

Generally there are three kinds of giving, of which giving the Dharma or teaching is one, and giving material help to birds, hungry dogs, beggars, and so forth is another. For the giving of teaching it is not necessary to be a lama or sit on a high throne to teach. When we give someone a piece of good advice, encouraging him or her to overcome some negative habit, that in fact is giving Dharma. Nevertheless, both from the spiritual and general point of view, giving teaching to other people is a wonderful practice. Doing so, we can develop their intelligence and at the same time increase our own intelligence. The role of teacher is a great opportunity to serve students. If the teacher is sincere and teaches with a proper motivation, the education he or she gives will remain in the student's mind for a long time.

Similarly, the physician who gives the correct medicine to the sick is doing a great service. But if he or she works with sincere motivation to benefit the sick, whether the medicine cures the sickness or not, the patient will feel happy because he or she can trust the doctor. Because of the doctor's concern, the patient feels encouraged and secure. That sense of hope actually contributes to a quicker recovery. Therefore, professions like medicine and teaching, provided they are done with a good motivation, are great opportunities for people to practice Dharma through their work.

If we compare our Buddhist monks and nuns with their Christian counterparts, I think we are lagging far behind in terms of social activities. There are sincere Christian practitioners whose primary goal is fulfilling the words of God. But at the same time they engage in sincere social activities, which also indirectly help develop their tradition. Bearing this in mind, I have often told our monks and nuns that they can also play a great role in social service as teachers or physicians and so forth. This would also contribute directly to the development of the Buddha-dharma.

Among the several thousand monks and nuns in exile, there are indeed a few who, staying in isolation, are doing excellent spiritual practice. In that way they are able to develop real spiritual qualities and personal realization. They are examples of good spiritual practitioners, but it is also important that the ordained be more creative and more helpful in society. Even if you stay in a monastery or a nunnery, you can establish hospitals and schools within your institution. These days, in places like Japan, there are many schools which were established by the monasteries.

Giving Dharma, or giving education and helping sick people as a nurse, are very important, real practices of giving. We can also do the practice of giving through visualization, and pray: "May I also be able to practice as the Bodhisattvas who have reached higher spiritual levels have done."

The next perfection concerns ethics. The text says:

Ethical conduct is water that washes the stains of faulty action,
And moonlight dispelling the hot torment of disturbing emotions.

Glorious like Mount Meru among those of the nine states,
Its power subdues all beings, without use of threats.
Knowing this, the excellent [ones] safeguard, like their eyes,
The rules of conduct to which they're wholly committed.
This is what my revered and holy teacher did,
And I, who seek liberation, will do likewise.

The way to restrain ourselves from faulty or unwholesome deeds is not merely to pray that such faults do not fall upon us. We should first understand what negative activities are, because lack of knowledge is one of the ways in which faults arise. If we do not know what such faults are, even if we are afflicted by them, we will not recognize their presence. Sometimes, though we know the nature of the fault and respect the training, because of the power of disturbing emotions, we engage in negative activities. We have to purify disturbing emotions at the grosser level first, and then at the subtler level.

Another way in which the faults arise is due to carelessness. Although we may not be subject to attachment and anger to begin with, carelessness can provoke them. For example, we watch television or movies containing scenes that can provoke attachment and anger. On the one hand, television is quite beneficial because it informs us about things that are happening in the wider world. It expands our horizons, but it also provides an opportunity for increasing negativities. Watching too many fight scenes can lead us to imitate them in our own behavior. These are ways in which our tranquil mind can be disturbed. It is important, therefore, in our day-to-day lives that we be alert and mindful. We should think, "I am a Buddhist, I am a spiritual practitioner, I am a follower of the Buddha." We should remind ourselves of this again and again.

If you have the opportunity to hunt an animal or kill a bird, at that point you should remember that it is improper as a follower of Buddha Shakyamuni to engage in such a deed. A few years ago I met a very good monk who told me that when he came to Lhasa he saw a Chinese selling a kind of snake which had been killed in a horrible way. When they caught one of these snakes, they would impale it through the eye onto a nail in a plank of wood. He was so horrified by the scene that he requested me to pray for such suffering sentient beings.

Since ancient times we Tibetans have depended on eating meat, but we do not have the bad habit of eating small reptiles and tiny insects. Nor did we have battery poultry farms where thousands of hens are slaughtered. Although Tibetans eat meat, we have always set certain limits to it. Now there is every danger that Tibetans will acquire negative habits from the Chinese. So, when you have an opportunity to take the life of an animal, immediately remind yourself that you are a follower of the Buddha. If you are an ordained person, you should think that since you are wearing a religious robe, which is an indication of being an ordained follower of the Buddha, you should not behave in a way that brings disgrace to others.

To some extent it is true that in ancient times different monasteries would use their combined power to take certain things from other people, which mean they depended on wrong livelihood. There was a degeneration of the Buddha-dharma, and if we make a fine analysis of the causes of such downfalls, it is as Asanga said in his *Thirty-seven Practices*, "Even though you are in the form of a spiritual practitioner, you might engage in nonspiritual practices." In those times we had a kind of completely purified vision, not because we were pure, but because of lack of knowledge about the rest of the world. We took everything so much for granted. As a result, certain activities such as exploitation occurred.

We also have to be careful about our food. As novice monks and nuns as well as fully ordained *bhikshus* we should be careful about the food we take in the afternoon. In general we are not supposed to eat then, but we are allowed to if our diet is insufficient. We can also say that we are unwell and take food after lunch. Let us say that this is correct, but even then we have to be careful and practice to the best of our capacity. As regards eating meat, we also have to be careful. In the texts on monastic discipline, eating meat is not completely prohibited, which is why in countries like Sri Lanka and Thailand they also do not hesitate to eat meat. They take whatever is given to them. But a practitioner of the Great Vehicle should be careful not to take too much meat, since we find in many of the Great Vehicle scriptures that taking meat is prohibited. Certain texts say that the meat we are eating is already lifeless, so there is no harm in it. There are also exceptions to be made for people who have liver problems and so forth, who eat meat for health reasons. But generally speaking, we should try to refrain from too great consumption of meat, especially in small places like Dharamshala.

In all our daily activities, whether we are walking, sleeping, whatever we are doing, those of us who are monks and nuns should always remind ourselves that we are ordained persons. If you become overwhelmed by disturbing emotions, you should not just continue in the same manner, you should confess it. We should put a stop to the faults of our mental and physical activities in dependence on conscientiousness and mindfulness. We should use awareness to discriminate whether something is worth doing or not and then do it with mindfulness. Those of you who have come from Tibet and have been under the Chinese for a long time have had a very good opportunity to develop conscientiousness and mindfulness. You always have to remain alert and aware of what the Chinese are saying and doing. Just as the Chinese have been deceiving you, you have also had to keep the truth from them.

Conscientiousness and mindfulness stop mental distraction. When we strengthen the power of mindfulness and conscientiousness, the subtle internal mental distractions cease. If you do not already have some practice of mindfulness and conscientiousness, it will be extremely difficult for you to start, but through gradual practice you can empower and strengthen it. Using morality as the foundation, we practice meditative stabilization and concentration. Through that we gain at least a strong one-pointed mind, and then we can develop a very powerful discriminative awareness. When we have clear conscientiousness and mindfulness, we will have similar successful results when we do deity yoga practice. Otherwise our practice will just be a rough visualization, which will not be effective.

Ethical conduct is extremely important. There is the ethics of stopping unwholesome deeds, the ethics of amassing virtuous qualities, and, one of the most important purposes of ethics, helping other people. Unless we discipline ourselves, we cannot help other people. Helping other people means more than mere academic study of the scriptures. Therefore, in order to observe ethics for the benefit of other sentient beings, we should first observe the ethics of amassing virtuous qualities, and prior to that we must observe the ethics of refraining from negative conduct. We should observe the practice of the four complete abandonments.

The ethics of refraining from negative conduct is like water that cleanses our mental stream, and cleanses our body, speech, and mind. It is like moonlight dispelling the heat of suffering. When we restrain the disturbing emotions again and again, their strength gradually decreases. Someone who turns away from negative activities, restrains the negative mind, and has a sincere practice of ethics is like Mount Meru standing above all other human beings. This is explained in a text which says that a *bhikshu* who properly observes ethics shines out among others. All beings bow before such a one without his exerting power or force. Knowing this, we must protect and guard ethics, whether it is the ethics of individual liberation, the ethics of the Bodhisattva, or the ethics of tantric practice. We should guard ethics as we would guard our own eyes.

Next is the practice of patience, which is especially important for Bodhisattvas.

> *Patience is the finest adornment of the powerful*
> *And the best austerity to scourge disturbing emotions.*
> *It is the Garuda, the snake of anger's enemy,*
> *And a hard shield against the weapons of harsh language.*
> *Knowing this, grow accustomed in every manner to the stout*
>   *armor of supreme patience.*
> *This is what my revered and holy teacher did,*
> *And I, who seek liberation, will do likewise.*

Buddha Shakyamuni's teaching is based or rooted in compassion, and the opposite of compassion is anger and hatred. The antidote that directly opposes hatred is patience. Therefore, the practice of patience is extremely important. Patience is of various kinds: enduring harm, patiently accepting suffering, and certainty in respect to Dharma practice.

One of the strongest obstructions to the practice of patience is when someone harms us. If we are able to overcome the urge to retaliate, it will be like removing a big boulder from the path, and our practice of patience will be successful. The *Guide to the Bodhisattva's Way of Life* explains in detail how to generate patience and how to employ antidotes. Through such practice we are also preparing for a successful practice of concentration. Similarly, when we talk about successful spiritual practice, we are talking about how to fight disturbing emotions. We are waging a war against disturbing emotions. In the course of fighting disturbing emotions, we will definitely encounter hardship and problems. The disturbing emotions that are our opponents are, if not more powerful than us, at least equally powerful.

The wisdom discriminating right from wrong is what actually fights the war against disturbing emotions. Since disturbing emotions are so powerful, while waging war against them we may get physically and mentally tired. There is also a possibility of losing the spirit to fight anymore, so it is extremely important to undertake the practice of patience, voluntarily accepting suffering. We can take an example from the military exercises. Soldiers do so many exercises in peacetime, voluntarily undergoing hardship so that when they have to fight they are prepared. Therefore, the more we practice patience, the better will we be able to undertake spiritual practice, because we will not be defeated by hardship.

The food of anger is a disturbed mind. I think this is a crucial point. Let us consider the policies of the world's different nations. There are many different policies because by accumulating certain causes and conditions, we experience certain results. And within the cause there are two causes: the immediate cause and the distant cause. Our problem is that we usually only consider the immediate cause and do not even think about the distant cause. Consequently, when the immediate cause comes into effect, there is hardly anything that can be done. The war in former Yugoslavia is an example. Problems have arisen there because of disregarding the distant causes of the trouble. If the right measures had been taken at the time of the distant causes, the present problems could have been prevented. Once things reach a late stage, they are difficult to control.

What Shantideva has said in the *Guide to the Bodhisattva's Way of Life* is absolutely true. The food for anger is a disturbed mind. Imagine, for example, that our minds are upset when we get up on a particular day. Because of this we do not feel like talking to our friends and relatives and we easily get agitated and become angry. In such circumstances the slightest condition can provoke us and anger is aroused within us. If, on the other hand, we had a tranquil, undisturbed mind to begin with, then even if we face a difficult situation, we will not become angry. Therefore, it is important to transform the mind, or train the mind, in such a way that it does not become disturbed. In order to practice patience successfully, we need to think about the faults of disturbing emotions and the qualities of patience.

The practice of patience is the supreme adornment of the powerful and mighty. If we have patience, even when someone accuses or insults us, we will keep smiling. If we have no patience and are overcome by anger, even if our face is normally beautiful, we will immediately become ugly. Patience is a beautiful ornament for everyone, whether we are young or old, a layperson or ordained. Having a clear mind and a smiling face is the best adornment, and of all the different kinds of hardship, the hardship to maintain patience is the most worthwhile.

One of the faults that I see among Tibetans is that unless we are in a crisis we have a tendency to remain relaxed. Nowadays, when there is some relaxation of restrictions on religious practice in Tibet and the food and clothing situation is a little better, we immediately have a tendency to relax. We should recognize that Tibet is still ruled by these same Chinese who have brought so much oppression and suffering upon us. It is the same for those of us in exile. In the beginning, when we had great problems of resettling ourselves, we were all very dedicated and hardworking. Nowadays, when our situation is a little improved, we have a tendency to relax without pushing harder to achieve our ultimate goal. Of course, Tibetans have a unique ability to deal with a crisis, but our weakness is that we relax the moment the crisis is over.

In Tibet today, whatever money Tibetans have, they use it. They give it to the Chinese by visiting Chinese restaurants, going to Chinese tailors to have their clothes stitched instead of going to Tibetan tailors. This is because of lack of awareness. I think we should follow the example of yaks and deer. Once they start butting each other, they keep it up until one of them has completely defeated the other. We should do the same and continue our struggle until we gain control. This should be our attitude, whether we live in Tibet or here in exile.

Next is the practice of effort; the text says:

Armored with unremitting and steady effort,
Scriptural knowledge and insight grow like the waxing moon.
All your activities will become meaningful,
And you will complete successfully whatever you undertake.
Knowing this, Bodhisattvas exert themselves to make
Powerful effort which dispels all laziness.
This is what my revered and holy teacher did,
And I, who seek liberation, will do likewise.

Here we are talking about making an effort toward positive qualities. In fact the Tibetan word for "effort" here refers explicitly to taking delight in virtuous qualities. When we have the armor of right effort, all the spiritual qualities will increase like the waxing moon. There is a saying for students that if you memorize one word a day, after 100 days you will have remembered 100 words. This is the way to increase your positive qualities. Such training is extremely important.

Whether we are concerned with developing inner spiritual realizations or studying the meaning of scriptures, we must make effort like the steady flow of a river. Many of us, myself included, make a very strong effort for a short time and then rest. Our attempts are not persistent like a louse, but sporadic like a flea. The great master Gungthangpa rightly said that for a few days we even forget to take food and make tremendous effort. As soon as we start to study, we want to become a great scholar, but after only a few days we are carried away by distractions. Such people have no qualities at all. Therefore, we must make effort like a steady flow of water. Then all our qualities will multiply and develop, and whatever activities we adopt will be meaningful in accordance with spiritual practice. Whatever work we start we will be able to complete with success. Knowing this, the great Bodhisattvas have made extensive effort to overcome laziness.

Next is meditation on concentration, which is like a king who has control over the mind.

> *Concentration is a king with dominion over the mind.*
> *Once placed, it remains immovable, like the king of mountains.*
> *When directed, it engages with every kind of virtuous object,*
> *And induces the great bliss of a malleable body and mind.*
> *Knowing this, powerful yogis continually practice*
> *Meditative stabilization, which defeats all inimical distraction.*
> *This is what my revered and holy teacher did,*
> *And I, who seek liberation, will do likewise.*

At present we are controlled by our minds, and our minds are overpowered by disturbing emotions, so we involuntarily engage in negative activities. We may generate certain minor virtuous qualities, but because we lack concentration, they tend to be weak. If we had concentration, one-pointedness of mind, it would be quite helpful. For example, when we sleep, most of the grosser levels of consciousness dissolve. If we have some pleasant or unpleasant experience during a dream or nightmare, when we awake we can still feel its influence. Although we know that it took place in a dream while we were asleep, when we wake up we can still feel its impact. If the dream is bad, when we wake up we feel quite negative and our mind is disturbed. When we awake after a good dream, we feel happy. This indicates a great difference in terms of impact between what is experienced by the grosser and subtler levels of mind. Therefore, if our mind is more concentrated, we will have better control over our virtuous practice. For this reason, concentration is called the king of the mind.

Concentration means that when we want to place our mind on a particular object, it will stay there like a mountain. This is how it is explained in terms of meditative stabilization. Whether we do analytical meditation or one-pointed concentration, the attainment of meditative stability is extremely important. Through such practice we will be able to induce the experience of bliss which makes our body and mind functional. Knowing that, great yogis constantly rely on meditative stabilization because it destroys the enemy of mental distraction. Of course, the achievement of one-pointed mind is not a practice unique to Buddhism. But because one-pointedness of mind is so important, we find both in the sutras and tantras explanations of how to achieve a one-pointed mind.

According to the general explanation, we should first think about the importance and qualities of meditative stabilization. In that way we generate a wish to acquire those qualities, we generate faith, and make the right effort, which dispels laziness and attains pliancy. Then we should focus steadily on the object without losing sight of it. Not only should we not lose sight of it, but it is important that the mind should have a clear image of the object. The mind should be intense, sharp, and clear. Lack of clarity of the mind with regard to the object is the result of mental laxity. Being unable to remain with the object is the result of mental excitement. Laxity and excitement are the major hindrances to meditative stabilization. As an antidote to mental laxity we should intensify the one-pointedness of our minds, and when our minds get excited we should calm them down.

On this basis, we should achieve a faultless meditative stabilization, starting with the nine stages of meditative stabilization, such as setting the mind, continuously setting the mind, and so forth. In this way we can achieve a calmly abiding mind. We can take any object to achieve calm abiding, but because there are many advantages and great merit in doing so, according to the sutra tradition we can take an image of Buddha Shakyamuni as our object. When we do tantric practice, we can focus on the deity.

Next is the perfection of wisdom, about which the text says:

Wisdom is the eye for seeing profound suchness.
It's the path which totally uproots worldly existence,
And the treasure of knowledge praised in all the scriptures,
Renowned as the best lamp to dispel the darkness of confusion.
Knowing this, the wise who seek liberation
Cultivate this path with every effort.
This is what my revered and holy teacher did,
And I, who seek liberation, will do likewise.

Wisdom is also called discriminative awareness. Nagarjuna has said that our ultimate object is the attainment of nirvana and enlightenment, and that to achieve them we need faith and compassion assisted by wisdom. Unless the practice of compassion is assisted by wisdom, it will not be effective. Similarly, even if we have faith, it, too, should be assisted by compassion or wisdom. Without wisdom, faith becomes like blind faith. It may not be blind faith exactly, but because we do not see the reason for it, it is like blind faith. In that case we can easily be led onto a wrong path, because we have no proper reason to follow. On the other hand, if we have generated faith based on wisdom and reason, then even if someone tries to mislead us, we will not trust him. Similarly, if our practice of compassion is supported by the practice of wisdom, having taken responsibility for helping other sentient beings, we will be able to achieve the desired goal.

There are various kinds of wisdom, such as the wisdom understanding the five sciences and the wisdom understanding ultimate truth. Since we are dealing here with the achievement of liberation from cyclic existence, we are mainly concerned with ultimate wisdom. Therefore, the text explains that wisdom is like the eye to see profound suchness. Even if we have not realized suchness directly, if we have a good understanding of the meaning of suchness, it will tear up the root of cyclic existence. This is the treasure of all qualities which is praised in all scriptures. Although we find various subjects explained different ways in the scriptures, they all finally come down to the most important point, which is the meaning of dependent arising and emptiness.

Therefore, Tsongkhapa has said in his *Praise of Dependent Arising*, his praise to Buddha Shakyamuni, "All the teaching that you have given boils down to the teaching of dependent arising." This is the best lamp dispelling the darkness of ignorance. Through wisdom we gather many different levels of knowledge. At the highest level it is because of the wisdom understanding selflessness that we are able to overcome the misconception of self. So, knowing this, the wise who desire liberation try to generate wisdom in general and particularly the wisdom understanding ultimate truth.

In order to understand the meaning of suchness, Tsongkhapa himself studied many scriptures by great Indian and Tibetan spiritual teachers. Therefore, because the venerable spiritual teacher has with much effort practiced this path, we should do likewise.

When we talk about the wisdom understanding selflessness, we have to identify what we mean by selflessness. We can have many wisdoms: the wisdom understanding Tibetan, the wisdom understanding Chinese, the wisdom understanding English, and so forth. Similarly, there are many wisdoms in terms of their function, such as great wisdom, clear wisdom, quick wisdom, and so forth. Nowadays, scientists also explain that no one knows the complete potential of the human brain, nor are we able to use our brain fully, which I think is an interesting point. Whether you call it the brain or the human mind, we have a great potential to discover subtle points. Scientists point out that there remain many parts of the brain which are unused or which we are unable to use. This implies that there is no limit to the dimension of the human mind.

When we talk about selflessness, we are talking about the absence of self. We need to know what the self that is being negated here is. The self is negated here in terms of mind. Something which is the objection of negation for the mind is something which does not exist. If it were to exist, mental reasoning could not refute it. If it is an object of negation of the path, it should be existent. When we engage in practice of the path, that object of negation is something that exists but is not useful, so we eliminate it by cultivating the path.

The selflessness we are talking about here is the absence of a self which has never existed before. Now you might ask, if it is a self which is nonexistent, why should we talk about the absence of such a self? Even though such a self is nonexistent, because of our misconception we think that such a self exists. Because of this wrong notion we get confused, and because of that we engage in negative activities. Therefore, what we are trying to establish here is that the self conceived of by a wrong consciousness or wrong mind does not exist. When we come to a conclusion through analysis that such a self is nonexistent, all the other levels of conceptual thought induced by such wrong understanding of self will cease to exist.

Most Buddhist tenets explain about selflessness. There are various levels to the meaning of selflessness: selflessness which is accepted in common by all the four schools of tenets; the unique presentation of the meaning of selflessness; and the self that is to be refuted in terms of the Mind Only School; and also the presentation made by the Middle Way School, whose adherents follow sutra, and the Middle Way Consequentialists. By gradually coming to understand all these different levels of presentation, we should acquire a good understanding of what the object of negation is. Consequently, when we negate the object of negation, we generate the wisdom understanding emptiness.

We have been dealing with the section on the path for individuals of great mental capacity. We have discussed how the generation of the awakening mind is the only way to achieve Buddhahood, the general Bodhisattva practices, and the special training in calm abiding and special insight. We have completed explanation of both calm abiding and special insight, and here we are dealing with the verse which explains that we should practice calm abiding and special insight together.

Single-pointed concentration, alone, is not seen
To have the power to cut the root of cyclic existence.
Wisdom, without a calmly abiding mind, cannot stop
The disturbing emotions, no matter how long you analyze.
Hence, mount the wisdom which perfectly knows reality
On the unswerving steed of calm abiding.
With the sharp weapon of Middle Way reasoning, free from
  extremes,
Which demolishes the focus of extreme conceptions,
Through expansive wisdom which properly analyzes,
Give rise to the intelligence which understands reality.
This is what my revered and holy teacher did,
And I, who seek liberation, will do likewise.

One-pointed mental concentration alone is not enough to tear up the root of cyclic existence. Similarly, even if we have a very profound wisdom understanding the meaning of emptiness, unless we are able to penetrate deep into the object of our meditation, we will not be able to use the full power of the mind. Therefore, we should mount this wisdom that understands the ultimate mode of existence of all phenomena on the horse of unfluctuating calm abiding, and employ the reasoning of the Middle Way, free of the two extremes. Then we will be able to destroy the misconception of self.

No question that familiarity with single-pointedness
Brings about meditative stabilization! But seeing that
Even correct analytical discrimination produces
Immutable stabilization firmly fixed on reality,
Effort to achieve the union of calm abiding and special insight
Is something amazingly admirable.
This is what my revered and holy teacher did,
And I, who seek liberation, will do likewise.

We will achieve meditative stabilization not only through one-pointed concentration, but also through the mind's engaging in discriminative analysis, which also induces a stable mind. Therefore, we should make effort in both these practices.

> *Cultivating space-like emptiness during meditative equipoise*
> *And illusion-like emptiness in the subsequent period*
> *Unifies skillful means and wisdom, which is praised*
> *As that which makes the deeds of Bodhisattvas go beyond.*
> *Having understood this, it is the custom of the fortunate*
> *Not to be satisfied with a partial path.*
> *This is what my revered and holy teacher did,*
> *And I, who seek liberation, will do likewise.*

During meditative stabilization we meditate on the meaning of emptiness as having the nature of space. In other words, we have reflected on the meaning of the selflessness of persons and the selflessness of phenomena by using various logical reasonings, such as the reason of dependent arising, the reason eliminating the four extremes, and so forth. Based on these various kinds of logical reasonings, we have eliminated the object of negation and have then meditated on that. Since we have gained a good understanding of the meaning of emptiness during meditative stabilization, when things appear to us as having intrinsic existence, we can reflect that although things appear this way, this is all because of ignorance and my negative mind.

Because of the force of our earlier understanding, we will be able to see everything as an illusion. Although things appear to have intrinsic existence, in actuality they are devoid of it. Therefore, our understanding during the postmeditative state will also empower our meditational practice. And successful meditational practice will influence the postmeditative state. In that way, we will be able to use method and wisdom together. They will contribute to each other rather than contradict each other. These two practices contribute to the achievement of the two bodies of the Buddha, the form body and the truth body. Therefore, it is important to engage in a full, rather than a partial practice of the path.

This is the common requirement for both supreme paths,
For the causal and resultant Great Vehicle.
Once it is properly developed, turn to a skilled captain as protector
And venture on the high seas of the classes of tantra,
Following the complete oral instructions.
You thereby make your life of freedom and fortune meaningful.
This is what my revered and holy teacher did,
And I, who seek liberation, will do likewise.

First we should listen well to the meaning of positive practice. Then we should reflect on the meaning of what we have heard and engage in meditation. Through hearing, thinking, and meditation we should generate the path, and by depending on the instruction and guidance of a skillful Vajra master, a great scholar and realized being, we should enter onto the great ocean of tantra. If we are able to supplement tantric practice with the practice of sutra, we will achieve the full instruction and make our lives meaningful. Even if we are unable to attain the state of Buddhahood in this very life, because we have engaged in a complete practice, we will leave a deep imprint on our minds. Through successive lives we will travel from happiness to happiness and finally attain Buddhahood.

There may be quite a few among us, including myself, who are addicted to Dharma practice and always participate in these kinds of religious teachings. But there may also be many people who are hearing such teachings over an extended duration for the first time. The important thing is to keep what you have learned in your mind and to sustain the practice. Since you have received this commentary to the *Abridged Stages of the Path*, try to read it and reflect on the meaning. As you read the text, try to remember the meaning that has been explained, and try to understand it. Once you are sure about the meaning, you should reflect and meditate on it again and again so that it will remain deep within your mind.

Therefore, you should first find out what to meditate on, and then you should meditate continuously and make your mind familiar with the practice or the teaching. First glance over the entire stages of the path, and then, when you engage in the actual practice to gain experience, start from the beginning and acquire experience in a systematic and orderly way. A time will come when you will have a good understanding of the essence of the whole *Stages of the Path* teaching. If you meditate further on that, the object you have been meditating on will become close to your mind. At that time you can be sure that if you meditate, it will be useful and successful. In that way, you will gain experience of the subject based on your practice of meditation. Gradually you will reach a stage where you do not have to make much effort to make your mind stay on the object.

Experience based on effort means that there is a stage when you reflect on a particular meaning of the text using reason and logic. You will be able to focus your mind on it and know what it means, but you may not be able to understand or meditate on it without using reason and logic. That means you are making effort to understand the text. If you do such practice continuously, you will gradually achieve the level called effortless engagement, where your mind will not need to use reason and logic to understand the meaning. At the present time we are so overwhelmed by disturbing emotions that they never lose their hold on us, they are always with us. If you make your mind familiar with the positive practices too, a time will come when the positive influence is so strong that you cannot escape it.

In all four Tibetan Buddhist traditions we find guru-yoga practices very important and helpful, so they have a crucial role. You can do whatever guru-yoga practice belongs to your particular tradition.

This completes the *Abridged Stages of the Path*. The next lines explain the purpose for which Tsongkhapa composed this text, and dedicate the virtue of having done so.

> *I have explained in words easy to understand*
> *The complete path which pleases the Conquerors,*
> *To familiarize myself with it*

And also to help others who are fortunate.
Through the virtue created, may all living beings
Never be separated from this pure and good path.
This was the prayer made by my revered and holy teacher,
And I, who seek liberation, make the same prayer.
It is through the spiritual mentor's kindness
That one encounters the teaching of the unsurpassable teacher.
I therefore dedicate this virtue so that all living beings
May be cared for by excellent spiritual friends.
May I and others be reborn as the main followers
Of my spiritual teacher Losang Drakpa
In the Joyous Land or the Land of Bliss
Or in whatever pure realm in which he dwells.
First seek extensively to hear many teachings,
Then view the whole textual tradition as personal advice,
Finally practice continually, day and night,
And dedicate it all to the flourishing of the teachings.

Chapter 5

GENERATING THE MIND OF ENLIGHTENMENT

We value ourselves highly, as all sentient beings do. I value myself highly, not because I am grateful to myself, or kind to myself, but because we have a natural and spontaneous regard for our own worth. Because all sentient beings regard themselves as precious, everybody is entitled to dispel their suffering and work for their own future happiness. Everyone has an equal right to avoid suffering and work for happiness, because we live interdependently with each other.

Leave aside the question of attaining Buddhahood, even in the ordinary insignificant events that occur in our lives, our happiness is dependent on others. For example, the facilities we have at a gathering and our coming together to teach and listen to teachings are dependent on those who first bought the land, leveled it, and put up the buildings. The completion of these facilities is the fruit of all those people's work.

In my own case, I have been able to live due to the kindness of others, not through my own qualities alone or because I am self-sufficient. I have depended on others for my food, for my drink, for my clothes and shelter. All these provisions come about due to the kindness of other sentient beings; none of them come about through any superhuman self-sufficient qualities I may possess. If I had any such self-sustaining qualities, I could have lived in an unpopulated, isolated empty valley. But, actually, I could not survive in such a place at all. I have to live where there are other people.

This shows that human beings have to live in dependence on their fellow human beings. And it is misguided to show ill will toward those on whom you must depend. We behave in this way due to our ignorance. It is a stupid mistake to conduct yourself in that way. In our lives we rely on the support of all the kind sentient beings. This is why religious knowledge is a necessary part of our outlook. Similarly, cultivation of spiritual qualities like compassion and love, which are the roots of religion, are possible only with reference to an object. From this point of view we can see how sentient beings are kind to each of us by providing an easy opportunity to generate love and compassion.

If you have not already generated compassion, then you can generate it. If you have generated it, you can increase it. In the end, the way to attain the state of an omniscient conqueror is derived from this practice of love and compassion. But if there were no sentient beings, we would not be able to generate love and compassion. If there were no sentient beings, we would not have the courage and determination to generate this mind.

If we think carefully, from a wider perspective we owe our entire present and future collection of good qualities to the kindness of sentient beings. When you are strongly motivated to work for others, you can lead a meaningful life. When you have a strong inclination to benefit others, you will find that you are always happy.

Just as it is a reality that all your temporary and ultimate happiness is dependent upon kind sentient beings, so internally, too, the more you concern yourself with others' welfare, the happier you will be. It is only natural that when you have such an altruistic attitude, you will find personal happiness.

The stronger your inclination to neglect others' welfare and think only of yourself, the unhappier you will be. When you have the will to help others, you will be happy in the present and it will bring you benefit in the future. On the other hand, if you are self-centered and inclined to neglect others, eventually it will bring misfortune upon you. In short, a self-centered attitude will bring destruction upon yourself and others. The mind which is concerned for others brings happiness to yourself and others. Therefore, concern for others is the root of the entire collection of good qualities. Disregarding others out of self-centeredness is the root of all downfalls, like the one-sided solitary peace of nirvana and the suffering in the cycle of existence. It is like a chronic disease.

So, today, when you are able to listen to a Mahayana teaching, the Buddha's teaching on love, compassion, and the mind of enlightenment, even if you cannot put them all into practice, you can at least appreciate them. At such a time we should generate a good motivation, say prayers, and try to generate the mind of enlightenment. If we were to investigate how the Buddhas and Bodhisattvas that we take refuge in today became enlightened, we would find that they generated love, compassion, and the mind of enlightenment. So, in our case too, in order to protect ourselves from our present and ultimate fears, we should put love, compassion, and the mind of enlightenment into practice.

If we were to summarize the essence of the instruction of the heap of 84,000 teachings that the Buddhas and Bodhisattvas have taught, it would consist of the practice of love, compassion, and the mind of enlightenment.

Here and now, the external and internal facilities are available to us. We have an opportunity to practice the Dharma. We must resolve to generate an altruistic wish to help others. If you already have such a mind, you must enhance it.

In order to generate such a mind, the most important thing is to pay constant attention. In your daily life, train in regard to the various aspects and objects of the mind of enlightenment. Gradually reform your negative mind, and finally generate this courageous mind of enlightenment, concerning yourself more with others than yourself.

One factor for generating such a mind is to do so in the presence of lamas and many virtuous friends. You visualize before you the Buddhas and the children of the Buddha as witnesses. Due to the presence of many external and internal factors, you should be able to cultivate a fresh noble mind, and to awaken or nurture the previous predispositions. If you don't have such previous imprints, then it will be a great benefit to establish fresh dispositions.

We are going to go through the ritual for generating the mind of enlightenment together. There are two traditions: one derived from Shantideva, as found in his text the *Compendium of Trainings*, and the tradition passed down from Asanga and Serlingpa. Both of these traditions are to be found in the *Jewel Ornament of Liberation* by Gampopa. Some Tibetan scholars classify two modes for generating the mind: the tradition of the Mind Only School and the Madhyamika [Middle Way] tradition. Today, we will do it in accordance with the Mind Only School, the tradition coming from Asanga. We will use this text, the *Jewel Ornament*. According to Jowo Serlingpa, whose tradition comes from Maitreya, through Asanga, there are two processes: generating the aspirational mind of enlightenment and receiving the vows of engaging activity. The mind that you generate is called the aspirational mind with commitments.

So, what is aspiration with commitment? There is a difference between just generating the aspirational mind and receiving the aspirational mind with commitment. When you generate the aspirational mind alone, it is enough simply to wish, "May I attain Buddhahood," or "I will practice until I attain Buddhahood for the sake of sentient beings." Of course, this is not a fully qualified aspirational mind of enlightenment, but it is one way of cultivating the aspirational mind of enlightenment. However, when you generate the aspirational mind with commitment, not only wishing to attain enlightenment for the sake of sentient beings, you must also have the courage to think, "I will never, ever give up this mind that I have generated." This is the way to keep the aspirational mind with commitment.

On this occasion, you will be able to generate the aspirational mind with commitment. Still, there are different kinds of people, and some people might hesitate to take the aspirational mind with commitment, thinking, "I will not be able to practice the trainings"—you can generate the aspirational mind alone.

This is done by first making the supplication, accumulating merit, taking refuge, and performing the special deeds. After that comes the actual generation of the mind.

To do this, the text reads, "The teacher gives the disciples instructions about the disadvantages of the cycle of existence, and generating compassion for sentient beings, faith in the Buddha and the Three Jewels, and paying respect to the spiritual master." Regarding this, the explanation that I gave earlier should suffice. Repeat the following prayers after me:

> O Teacher, kindly pay heed to me. Just as in the past the tathagatas, arhats, the completely and perfectly enlightened Buddhas, and the great and spiritually exalted Bodhisattvas have initially generated the mind of unsurpassed, perfect, and complete enlightenment. Similarly, O Teacher, kindly help me [insert your name] to generate the mind of perfect and complete great enlightenment.

Next, we have to accumulate merit. In some traditions the practice of accumulating merit is done only by making prostrations and offerings, without making confession. But on this occasion we will do the whole seven-branch practice. I do not think there will be any fault in doing more practice. Jigten Gonpo also spoke about "my yoga, the seven-branch practice" and "attainments of the seven-branch practice." So I think it would be good to recite here the full-length ritual of the seven-branch practice. We will do it according to the Arya Samantabhadra Prayer.

You should visualize the Buddhas and their children in the space before you. As our main object we have the image of Shakyamuni Buddha in this temple. You should imagine that it is not just an image but the real Buddha. In the space before you, also visualize the Buddhas and Bodhisattvas of the ten directions. Around you are the protectors of the four directions. Think of them as protecting you against external and internal obstacles to your generating the mind of enlightenment. Imagine that you are surrounded by all mother sentient beings, in the form of human beings, who are experiencing the specific sufferings of the beings of all six realms. Generate love and compassion for them. Generate faith in the Conquerors aspiring faith wishing to gain the qualities of the Buddhas, as well as pure trust in them. On the basis of this, you should think, "I must attain the unsurpassed complete enlightenment for the sake of all the innumerable mother sentient beings."

The foundation for attaining such a state of complete and perfect enlightenment is generation of the precious mind of enlightenment.

Then you should think, "Today, before the Conquerors and their offspring I will generate the mind of the supreme complete enlightenment." For that purpose, first do prostration, make offerings, and confess your misdeeds, rejoice in the virtue of yourself and others, request the turning of the wheel of Dharma, request the Buddhas not to enter into nirvana, and finally recite the dedication. As you recite these prayers, reflect on their meaning within your mind. Since we are to accumulate, purify, and develop by means of this ritual of the seven-branch practice, right from making prostration to the Buddhas and the Bodhisattvas, we should pray with such a motivation.

Then recite the Prayers of Go and Conduct. These practices are concerned with creating merit. They are followed by taking refuge, but as it is not specifically referred to in this text, we can take the words from other texts. Please repeat these lines for taking refuge. The *Ornament of Sutras* says:

Thoroughly engaging, accepting, realizing, and prevailing.

This refers to the specialty of thoroughly engaging in a practice with all sentient beings as the object, the specialty of accepting Buddhahood as the goal to be attained, the specialty of realizing enlightenment, and the specialty of prevailing over the refuge of the Hearers and Solitary Realizers. This line from the *Ornament of Sutras* refers to the speciality of the uncommon Mahayana way of taking refuge.

In short, the object we take refuge in is the Buddha, the One Gone to Bliss; the Dharma is the Mahayana doctrine; and the friends are the exalted Mahayana community. The purpose of taking refuge is not just a wish for personal liberation from fear, but a wish to liberate all mother sentient beings from sufferings and their causes. Focusing on such a purpose and making the wish, "I must attain the state of an omniscient Conqueror," is called the uncommon Mahayana way of taking refuge. Generally, when we take refuge, we also include the exalted Solitary Buddhas and Hearers among the objects of refuge, but here we principally focus on the exalted Mahayana Bodhisattvas and the supreme Mayahana Sangha community. Thinking that the Buddhas and their children actually exist before you and that you are surrounded by all sentient beings, repeat these words three times:

O Buddhas and Bodhisattvas of the ten directions please listen to me.

O Teacher, please listen to me. I by the name of [insert your name], from now until I attain the essence of the mind of enlightenment, I take refuge in the supreme human being, the Supramundane Victor, the Buddha; the supreme Dharma, the Dharma of peace, the state of having eliminated desire; and the supreme assembly, the never-returning Sangha community.

Now comes the actual practice, the actual way to generate the mind of enlightenment. As I mentioned before, there are two ways of generating the mind of enlightenment: to think, "May I attain Buddhahood for the sake of sentient beings," which is the aspirational method, and the aspirational way of generating the mind of enlightenment with commitment, thinking, "I will never give up the mind that I have generated." You should do this if you think you can practice and observe the trainings.

What are the trainings associated with the aspirational mind? If I summarize the points explained in this text, you will understand the four virtuous practices, which are the four causes assisting us not to allow the mind to degenerate in this life or the next life, and the four nonvirtuous factors contributing to the degeneration of the mind of enlightenment.

The four factors protecting the mind of enlightenment from degeneration are: (1) repeatedly recalling the benefits of generating the mind to develop enthusiasm in cultivating it; (2) generating the mind three times during the day and three times at night to actually promote the mind generation. It is for this purpose that we repeatedly recite the verse:

> I go for refuge until enlightenment
> To the Buddha, the Dharma, and the Sangha.
> Through the virtue of giving and so forth,
> May I attain Buddhahood to benefit all sentient beings.

Through the recitation of such verses we should generate the mind of enlightenment again and again, and remind ourselves constantly of the mind we had cultivated earlier. (3) Most important of all, we should not abandon sentient beings for whose sake we have generated the mind of enlightenment. When we think about doing something for all sentient beings, we include them all; no one is left out. After having generated a mind that takes everyone into account, it is possible that one day, in the face of sudden unfortunate circumstances, you might think, "I cannot do anything for this person; may something bad happen to them." Then your wish to help all sentient beings will be shattered. Your mind of enlightenment in relation to all sentient beings will decline. If you abandon one sentient being, your aspiration to help all sentient beings is broken because you did not keep your promise to all sentient beings. Thus, it is very important not to abandon even one sentient being for whose sake you have generated the mind of enlightenment.

Sometimes you may get angry or get into a fight, but you cannot maintain a malicious thought deep within you, thinking, "Just wait, I'll get you one day." Such motivation is absolutely improper. If you cling to such a thought, the mind of enlightenment you have generated will decline. You can practice in this way. You should not abandon your compassion deep down, even in relation to your sworn enemy, and you should not relinquish your love for him or her.

Temporarily you can take action against other people's wrongdoings, as is permitted in the trainings of a Bodhisattva. We find in the *Forty-four Faults of a Bodhisattva's Practice*, that if you do not take appropriate measures to contain the wrongdoing, it is an infraction or fault. So, not to give up the sentient beings for whom you have generated the mind, from the depth of the heart, is the third virtuous practice. (4) The next is accumulating the two collections. These are the four causes helping us not to let the mind of enlightenment decline in this life.

In order not to let the mind decline in future lives, we should understand the four unwholesome practices contributing to the degeneration of the mind of enlightenment and the four virtuous practices contributing to its development. I will not explain the four misdeeds, like deceiving lamas and abbots by telling lies, in detail here. In short, if you practice the four virtuous qualities, you will not be affected by the four nonvirtues. To summarize, the four virtuous practices are:

1. Not to tell lies even at the cost of your life. Of course, sometimes there are situations when you may have to tell lies for the sake of the Dharma or sentient beings in connection with some important issue. But you have to give up telling lies that are without purpose or harmful.

2. Not to be deceitful, to be honest and impartial, with a strong sense of responsibility.

3. To praise the mind of enlightenment by remembering its qualities and never to speak badly of it. If you practice according to the saying, "Generally you have to think of the kindness of all embodied ones. In particular, train in maintaining a pure attitude toward all practitioners," this fault will not occur.

4. Helping others hold on to the practice of complete enlightenment. Making others regret the good actions they have done is called black dharma. The antidote to this is to bring others closer to attaining complete enlightenment, whenever you can. This means anyone, not only those who are near and dear to you.

These are called the four white dharmas. When you practice the four white dharmas, you will avoid the stains of the four black dharmas. And if you think that you can observe these instructions, you should think that not only will you generate the mind of enlightenment, but by focusing on this mind, you will never abandon it. If you cannot maintain this mind, first think, "May I attain unsurpassable complete enlightenment for the sake of sentient beings; and I will attain it." That will be enough.

Those who want to generate the mind of enlightenment, please kneel on your right knee, except for those of you whose legs are stiff or who are unwell. As I said before, with strong faith visualize the Buddha in front of you, and with compassion visualize all sentient beings around you. With a strong determination to attain unsurpassable, complete enlightenment for all sentient beings, repeat the words for generating the mind of enlightenment after me.

> *O Buddhas and Bodhisattvas of the ten directions, please listen to me,*
> *O Teacher, please listen to me.*
> *I by the name [insert your name] have in this and other lives*
>   *planted seeds of virtue through my own practice of generosity,*
>   *ethics, keeping the vows, and other virtues;*
> *Likewise, by asking others to practice and rejoicing at their practice.*
>
> *May these root virtues become a cause to cultivate the mind of*
>   *enlightenment,*
> *Just as in the past, the Sugatas, the Arhats, the perfectly, fully*
>   *enlightened Buddhas,*
> *The great Bodhisattvas seated on the highest ground,*
> *Have generated the mind of enlightenment.*

The first recitation is:

I by the name [insert you name], from now until the attainment of the essence of Buddhahood, in order to liberate those sentient beings who are not liberated, deliver those who are not delivered, give breath to the breathless, and [relieve suffering for] those who have not fully gone beyond suffering, will cultivate the aspiration to attain the unsurpassable, perfect, and complete enlightenment.

At the second recitation, as before, you must think that at this place where we are developing the mind of enlightenment, the Buddhas and their children of the ten directions, the six ornaments and the two supremes of India, the 80 great adepts and the seven lineage holders of the Buddha are actually present. Likewise, from the Land of Snow, visualize the presence here of the 25 disciples of Guru Rinpoche, the eight knowledge-holders among the early Nyingma masters; the five patriarchs of the Sakya, the lamas of the Path and Fruit tradition; the three founders of the Kagyu, Marpa, Milarepa and Gampopa; the three Khampa brothers and Kyobpa Jigten Gonpo among the Kagyu lamas; and Jowo Je, Ngok and Drom of the early Kadam; likewise the great lama Tsongkhapa, the father and his sons, and the lamas of the new Kadampa. Think that the lamas and Bodhisattvas of all four traditions of Tibet who have cultivated the mind of enlightenment, practiced the Dharma, and bequeathed us their wonderful works are present. These great beings should be visualized before you, bearing witness to your taking the precepts for generating the mind of enlightenment.

We are surrounded by all mother sentient beings who have been kind over beginningless time. They desire happiness but are deprived of it, they do not want suffering, but they are immersed in it. All of them like yourself desire happiness and do not want suffering; in this way we are all the same. We are also equal in having the right to have happiness and remove suffering. We are also the same in possessing the Buddha essence within our minds. So, you should think that you have found something very rare when you attained this precious human life and met with the doctrine of the Buddha. In particular, both doctrines of sutra and tantra are present, and you have met with masters of the Mahayana. Therefore, think, "I must seize this opportunity and before long attain the state of an omniscient conqueror for the benefit of all countless sentient beings." By generating such a courageous resolve, you should think, "I will cultivate this mind," and repeat as before.

At the third recitation, you should reflect that self-centeredness is like a poisonous root, while consideration for others is like a medicinal root and the source of the collection of virtue.

Right now, we have attained life as a human being and are able to distinguish between good and bad, right and wrong. We have met with spiritual friends and had the chance to study the Buddha's teachings, and we have had the opportunity to study the excellent works of the scholars and adepts of India and Tibet. From these we have learned the difference between right and wrong; therefore, we must be able to distinguish between right and wrong.

How do we distinguish between right and wrong? We all want not to meet with suffering. The root of suffering is self-centeredness, so we must give it up. We all cherish happiness, and the root of happiness is having concern for others. So, we must generate a considerate attitude toward others and increase whatever consideration we have already generated. What is more, we have to keep on doing this right up to the very end.

If you ask, what is that perfect courage possessing firm resolution that shows concern for others' welfare, it is the thought that cherishes others, the altruistic mind of enlightenment. If you also ask how the precious Buddhas and their offspring, whom we presently visualize as our objects of refuge, did great service to sentient beings and the Buddha-dharma, it is not that they have huge, strong bodies. Milarepa, for example, was physically weak. It is not because of their bodies, or because of their troops or their wealth; it is only because of their wisdom. The difference is the pure thought which benefits others.

The Buddha is faultless, possesses all qualities, and is adorned by the 32 major and 80 minor marks, because he had generated compassion. Dharmakirti's *Commentary on the Compendium of Valid Cognition (Pramanavarttika)* says:

The main causal factor leading to enlightenment is the repeated practice of compassion.

Likewise, in the first verse of homage in the *Compendium of Valid Cognition*, Dignaga mentions that the Buddha became a valid person because he possessed the mind wishing to benefit others. Practice of compassion leads to the practice of wisdom realizing emptiness, which finally leads to the attainment of Buddhahood.

Since the thought of benefiting others is the source of the entire collection of virtue, we should take the Buddhas and their children as our examples and learn from their mode of behavior. And how do they behave? They never maintain harmful intent toward anyone. They maintain a wish to benefit others and display the conduct of benefiting others. If you have such will and conduct yourself in such a way, you have become a follower of the Buddha. On this occasion, when you have the wisdom to join the line of followers of the Buddha and the wisdom to distinguish between right and wrong, there is someone to guide you. You must be careful never knowingly to leap from the cliff.

Today you are at a crossroad. You can either go up or down. You can either head toward permanent happiness or permanent destruction. At present the option is still in your hands. We should aspire to follow the examples of the Buddhas and the Bodhisattvas. In short, from the bottom of your heart generate a genuine aspiration to attain the unsurpassable state of complete enlightenment. If you think you can practice the trainings, you have to resolve never to abandon this mind.

Repeat the words for generating the mind of enlightenment for the third time.

With this we have finished generating the mind of enlightenment. Next, we are told to rejoice. We are very fortunate to have generated such a good mind, when the external and internal circumstances have come together. Never let this good mind decline. When you try to put it into practice, you may find that it is difficult to do something for all sentient beings. But mentally we must have courage to work for the benefit of all sentient beings without holding ill will toward any of them. You will accomplish this, if you try to increase your courage. There is no need to give any additional explanation of the teachings I have already given.

We should all keep this well in mind. There is no need for me to tell those who are accustomed to the practice. If some of you are not very attentive to your practice, you should change your color from now on.

When a family becomes more prosperous, they improve their clothes and eat better food. Today, we have had this opportunity to learn a little about the Dharma and have had some introduction to the meaning of the Dharma. To show that you have become richer in the Dharma wealth, your conduct should improve. You should not speak roughly, and those who are usually quarrelsome and aggressive should be gentler. Those of you who are normally miserly should open your hands. There are some people who, the moment they speak to you, you think are lying. So, try to keep your lies to a minimum and behave honestly. This is very important.

In short, even if you cannot benefit others, at least do not harm them. Keep this in mind. The most important advice I can give you is to keep a kind heart, which is the very life of the teaching. On the basis of a good, kind heart, you should study, say your daily prayers, follow your vocation or training, and do the work by which you earn your livelihood. If you can do this, in future from life to life, there is hope that things will get better and better.

Finally, we should pray and dedicate all our virtuous practice for the flourishing of the Buddha-dharma in general, and in particular that the truth may prevail in Tibet. May the teachings of sutra and tantra flourish once again in Tibet as purely as before. And may that contribute directly and indirectly to the temporary and ultimate happiness of all mother sentient beings.

In short, the protector, Avalokiteshvara,
Made vast prayers before Buddhas and Bodhisattvas
To thoroughly take care of the Land of Snow;
May the good result quickly ripen today.
May we cultivate the supreme precious mind of enlightenment
That has not been cultivated,
And may that which has been cultivated not decline
But flourish higher and higher.

Chapter 6

Dependent Arising

Introduction

For practitioners, it is important to have a right, good motivation. Why are we discussing these matters? Certainly not for money, not for fame, not for our livelihood in this life. We have plenty of other things which bring us more money, more fame, and more enjoyable things. So the main reason is that everyone wants happiness and does not want suffering. This is a point on which there is no argument; everyone agrees. The ways to achieve happiness and the ways to overcome problems differ. There is also a variety of happiness and a variety of sufferings. Here we are not only aiming for temporary relief or temporary benefit; we are thinking of a long-term aim or benefit. As Buddhists, we are not looking for it only in this life, but in life after life, and we are not counting in weeks, months, or years but in lives and aeons.

In this field, money is something useful, but there is a limit to worldly power and worldly things; no doubt there are good things, but there is a limit. From the Buddhist viewpoint, if you have some development of the mind itself, it will go on from life to life. The nature of mind is such that if certain mental qualities have been developed on a sound basis, these qualities will always remain, and not only will they remain, they will increase as time goes on. The good qualities of mind, if developed in the proper way, will eventually increase infinitely. That not only brings happiness in the long term, but will give you more inner strength even in day-to-day life. Keep your mind on these things, with a pure motivation, and listen without going to sleep.

From my side, too, the main motivation is some sincere feeling toward others, some genuine concern for others and their welfare.

Now, how do we develop mental qualities? That brings us to meditation, which means to transform. Without making some special effort, transformation will not take place, so we need effort. Meditation is a matter of making the mind acquainted with some new meaning. It means getting used to the object you are meditating on. As you know, meditation is of an analytical variety in which you analyze the object and then set your mind one-pointedly upon that object. Within analytical meditation there are two types: one, in which the object that is being meditated on is taken as the object of the mode of apprehension of the mind; and the other, in which the so-called object is really the subject, or that type of consciousness into which you are trying to cultivate your mind. When you examine the various types of meditation, there are many different ways of dividing them.

With regard to that on which one is meditating, it seems convenient in Buddhism to make a division into view and behavior. Behavior is the main thing. One's own behavior is what induces one's own happiness in the future, and it is also what brings about others' happiness. For one's behavior to be pure and complete, it is necessary to have a proper view. One's behavior must be well founded in reason, so a proper philosophical view is necessary.

What is the main style of behavior in the Buddhist system? To tame and discipline one's own mind: in other words, nonviolence. In general, the Buddhist vehicles are divided into two types, a Great Vehicle and a Lower Vehicle. The Great Vehicle has the altruistic compassion of helping others as its root, and the Lower Vehicle has compassionate nonharming of others as its root, so the root of all Buddhist teachings is compassion. The Buddha who teaches this doctrine is born from compassion, and the main good quality of a Buddha is his or her great compassion. Among the Three Jewels, the Buddha's greatest quality is great compassion.

The main reason it is suitable to take refuge in a Buddha is because of his great compassion.

The Sangha, the spiritual community, has four qualities of pure enactment of the teaching. The first one means not to answer back in kind if someone comes to harm you or strike you. The second is not to respond with an angry attitude if someone comes at you with an angry attitude. The third is again not answering back when someone challenges you, without anger or violence, but insults mainly using harsh words against you. The fourth is not to retaliate if someone accuses you and embarrasses you. These are called the four practices for virtuous training, which are the special qualities of the Sangha. This is the style of behavior for a monk or nun. The root of these can be traced back to compassion, can't it? Thus, the main qualities of the Sangha derive from compassion; the Three Refuges for Buddhists—the Buddha, Dharma, and Spiritual Community—all have their root in compassion.

All religions are the same in having powerful systems of advice with respect to the teaching on compassion. This basic behavior of nonviolence that has compassion as its root is something that we need not only in our daily lives, but also to solve global problems nation to nation throughout the world.

THE TEACHING OF DEPENDENT ARISING

In general, it seems possible to say that although there are many interpretations of dependent arising, dependent arising is the general view of the Buddhist systems. In Sanskrit, the term for dependent arising is *pratitya samutpada*. *Pratitya* has three different meanings—meaning, relying, and depending—all three of which have roughly the same meaning of "dependence." *Samutpada* means "arising." So the meaning is: arising in dependence upon conditions. When arising in dependence upon factors is explained on a subtle level, understanding it involves an understanding of inherent existence. In order to reflect on the fact that something is empty because of being a dependent arising, one has to understand that "something," that subject about which you are reflecting. So it is necessary to identify the subject, the phenomena that produce pleasure and pain, that harm and help, and so forth.

Prior to understanding that a phenomenon is empty because of being a dependent arising, because of being dependently designated, one has to understand the presentation of cause and effect well. If one does not first understand how certain causes help and harm in certain ways, it is extremely difficult to understand anything about a phenomenon being empty of inherent existence because it is a dependent arising. Therefore, the Supramundane Victor, Buddha, set forth a presentation of dependent arising in connection with the cause and effect of actions in the process of life and cyclic existence, through which to gain a great understanding of the process of cause and effect itself. Thus, there is a mode of procedure of dependent arising which is called the 12 links of dependent arising.

A second level of dependent arising is the dependent arising of phenomena in dependence upon their parts. This implies that there is no phenomenon that does not have parts, so all phenomena exist in dependence upon designation to their parts. There is a third, even deeper level of dependent arising, which stems from the fact that when objects are sought within their basis for designation, there is nothing to be found that is the basis for designation, and thus phenomena have just dependently arisen in the sense of being dependently imputed.

The first level of dependent arising is the arising of phenomena in dependence on causes and conditions, so it applies only to caused phenomena, that is, products. The other two levels of dependent arising apply both to permanent and impermanent, produced and unproduced phenomena.

Buddha set forth dependent arising from a very vast perspective, recorded in detail in the *Rice Seedling Sutra* (*Shalistamba Sutra*), where he says:

> Due to the existence of this, that arises; due to the production of this, that is produced. It is thus: due to the

condition of ignorance, there is compositional action, due
to condition of compositional action there is . . . [and so
on through the 12 links]

When Buddha says, "Due to the existence of this, that arises,"
he is indicating that the phenomena of cyclic existence do not
arise through the force of supervision by a permanent deity, who
is thinking to create this or that, but rather that they arise due to
specific conditions. Then when Buddha says, "Due to the production of this, that is produced," he is indicating that things arise
from causes that are themselves impermanent, that do not arise
from the "generality" or "nature" or some sort of permanent material factor (*prakriti*), as is set forth in the Samkhya system. A third
way that he said it was: "Due to a condition that has such and
such a potential, that arises." This indicates that the phenomena
of cyclic existence are not produced from just any impermanent
causes and conditions, but rather from specific ones that have the
potential to give rise to those specific phenomena.

Thus, in terms of the dependent arising of suffering, how suffering is produced, Buddha showed that suffering has ignorance as
its root cause. This is an impermanent and a specific cause. That
ignorance leads to an action, which deposits potency on the mind,
and so on, the fruit of which is eventually old age and death. With
regard to the 12 branches of dependent arising, there are basically
two different explanations, one in terms of thoroughly afflicted
phenomena, and one in terms of pure phenomena.

Just as in the four noble truths, the root teaching of the Buddha, there are two sets of causes and effects: the effect and cause
of the afflicted side and the effect and cause of the pure side. Similarly, here in the 12 links of dependent arising, in each of the
two types of explanation there is an effect procedure and a cause
procedure. In terms of the four noble truths, true sufferings (the
first truth) are the effects in the afflicted class of phenomena, and
the causes are the second truth, true origins. In the pure class of
phenomena, true cessations (the third truth) are the effect, and
the true paths are their causes.

When it is explained that due to the condition of ignorance, action is produced, this is the procedure of the production of suffering; when it is explained that due to the cessation of ignorance, action ceases, this explains the procedure of the cessation of suffering. Now, each of these is explained both in a forward process and in a reverse process. When it is explained that due to action, consciousness arises; due to consciousness, name and form arise; due to the condition of name and form, the six sources arise; due to those and so on down to old age and death, that is the explanation of the causes that are the sources of suffering.

When it is explained in the reverse process, that the suffering of aging and death that we all know about is produced in dependence on birth; birth is produced in dependence on the potentialized level of action called existence, and so forth, the emphasis then is on the true sufferings themselves, which are the effects of the causes we just saw.

When it is explained that if one ceases ignorance, action ceases, and if action is ceased, consciousness ceases, and down through the 12, this is an explanation of the purified class of phenomena, with the emphasis being on the causes, that is, true paths.

When it is explained in reverse—with the cessation of aging and death depending on the cessation of birth; and the cessation of birth depending on the cessation of the almost potentialized level, called existence; and the cessation of that depending on the cessation of grasping—the emphasis here is on the effects, which in terms of the four noble truths are cessations.

THE WHEEL OF CYCLIC EXISTENCE

This drawing of the wheel of cyclic existence [on page 208] has six sections in it: the upper ones depict the gods, demigods and humans, while the other three depict the bad migrations within cyclic existence. They represent the levels of suffering. Due to what conditions do they arise? The inner circle indicates that these levels of suffering are produced by karma, that is, actions. It is in two halves, the left half depicting virtuous and unfluctuating actions, and the right nonvirtuous actions leading down to the lower realms. Here the people on the left are facing upward, and the people on the right are facing downward.

The source of suffering is karma, which arises from the afflictions of desire, hatred, and ignorance, indicated by the innermost circle. The pig indicates ignorance, the snake indicates hatred, and the rooster indicates desire. In a more correct version of the drawing, the rooster and snake would be coming out of the mouth of the pig, and they would have their mouths on the tail of the pig. This indicates that desire and hatred have ignorance as their root, but the fact that they in turn hold on to the tail of the pig indicates that they act to further and assist each other.

Thus, the drawing shows that the three afflictive emotions of desire, hatred, and ignorance give rise to virtuous and nonvirtuous actions, and these give rise to the various levels of suffering in cyclic existence. What, then, is the order of cause and effect for the arousal of such suffering? This is indicated by the outer ring, symbolizing the 12 links of dependent arising. The fierce being on the outside doesn't indicate a creator deity; he symbolizes impermanence. He shouldn't really have all these ornaments. Once, when I ordered a thangka like this, I had him drawn as a skeleton, for he represents impermanence. The moon indicates liberation. The Buddha is pointing at it, indicating that one should generate the paths that lead to liberation.

The history of this drawing is that the king of a distant land made a present of a jewel to the King of Magadha, and the king felt he did not have anything of equivalent worth to give in return, so he asked Buddha what he should give. Buddha told him to give a drawing like this of the 12 links of dependent arising, with the five sections symbolizing suffering. It is said that when the distant king received the picture and studied it, he attained realization from it.

A traditional Tibetan woodblock print of the wheel of existence
with illustrations of dependent arising around the outer edge.

THE 12 LINKS OF DEPENDENT ARISING

The 12 links are symbolized by the 12 pictures on the outside ring. The first, at the top, shows an old person, blind, using a cane—that indicates ignorance. It is an ignorance which is an obscuration as to the actual mode of being of phenomena. Among the Buddhist philosophical schools there are four main schools of tenets, and among them there are many different divisions, so there are many interpretations of what ignorance is. In general, there is indeed a factor which is a mere nonknowing of how things actually exist, a factor of mere obscuration. Here it is described as a wrong consciousness which conceives the opposite of how things actually do exist. In this sutra [system], 19 different types of ignorance are described, which are the various wrong views related with a beginning, or with extremes. Anyway, the afflictive emotions that we are seeking to be rid of are of two types, innate and artificial.

Artificial afflictions are ones that have philosophical ideas, systems of tenets, or teachings behind them—the mind newly imputes or makes them up through conceptuality. These are not possessed by all sentient beings, and cannot be the ones at the root of the ruination of sentient beings. As Nagarjuna says in his *Seventy Stanzas on Emptiness*: "The consciousness which conceives things produced in dependence upon causes and conditions to ultimately, truly exist was said by the teacher Buddha to be ignorance; from it, the 12 branches of dependent arising occur." This is a consciousness that misapprehends or misconceives phenomena as appearing under their own power, not as dependent.

From the point of view of the different types of objects of this consciousness, there is a conception of the inherent existence of phenomena and of persons, called a conception of a self of phenomena and a conception of a self of persons. There are two types of conception of a self of persons: one is to take cognizance of some other person and consider that person to be inherently existent, and the second type is to take cognizance of one's own person, "I," and consider one's own self to be inherently existent. The latter is called the false view of the transitory collection.

Nagarjuna's point was that the conception of one's own self as inherently existent arises in dependence upon the conception of those bases which are the basis of designation of one's own person, the mind, body, and so forth, as inherently existent. Thus, both are conceptions of inherent existence. The conception of phenomena, mind, body, and so forth, as inherently existent, acts as a cause of conceiving the person that is designated in dependence upon them to be inherently existent.

Another type of conception of a self of persons is the conception that the person is self-sufficient, or substantially existent.

If we consider our own desire and hatred, we see that they are generated with a conception of ourselves, "me," as their basis. Due to the conception of ourselves as so solid, we develop a sense of our own faction and the other's faction, and taking sides, upon which desire and hatred occur. This is the way it happens, isn't it?

There is indeed a conventionally posited "'I," a self, a person that is the doer of actions, the accumulator of karma, the one who experiences the results; definitely, there is such a thing. However, when the feeling of "I" is so strong that it makes trouble, then a sense of a self-instituting "I" has formed, which is an exaggeration beyond what actually exists. A consciousness which conceives of this sort of self-instituting "I" has come about. When this "I" appears to the mind, it doesn't appear as merely designated in dependence on the aggregates of mind and body, does it? Doesn't it appear almost as if it had its own separate entity?

If it did exist the way it appears, then when investigated with the Middle Way of reasoning (Madhyamika), it would get clearer and clearer. However, the fact is that when you search for this "I" using the Middle Way reasoning, it can't be found; but it still appears to our minds as if it were something concrete we could point at, something very definite. Thus, the conflict between the fact that it appears as something very concrete, but if analyzed cannot be found, indicates a conflict between how it appears and how it actually subsists. This is similar to the distinction physicists make between what appears and what actually exists.

Even in our own experience we can identify different levels of desire. For instance, if you go into a store, see some article, and have desire for it, there's one type of desire. Then, after you have bought it and you feel, "It's mine," then there are different levels of appearances and apprehensions here. At the first level, before you have generated desire, there is the mere appearance, the mere recognition of the object. At the second level, when you are feeling, "Oh, this is really good," there's another apprehension of the object. Then, after you've bought it and have made it your own, there is a third level of apprehension of the object.

On the first level, when the object merely appears, it does appear to exist from its own side, to exist inherently. However, the mind is not strongly involved with apprehending the object as existing from its own side, or as existing inherently. But at the second level, the ignorance which conceives of and apprehends the object as existing from its own side (this being the level at which you generate desire toward the object), you do have a concept of the inherent existence of the object and adherence to it as existing

Ignorance

from its own side. There is a subtle level of desire which can exist at the same time as this consciousness conceiving the object to exist inherently. But when that desire becomes stronger, the conception of inherent existence merely acts as its cause, and is not in association with, or existing at the same time as, the desire.

It is important to identify in terms of our own experience that, on the first level, there is the appearance of the object as inherently existent. On the second level, there is a consciousness that agrees with that appearance, which gives rise to desire. Then, at the third level, when you've made the object your own, the concept of ownership becomes involved, and it is as if two very powerful streams of desire have come together. One is an adherence to the object as being inherently pleasant, and the other is the strong conception of its being your own. When these two come together, your desire is extremely strong. If you think about it, is this the way it is?

It is the same for hatred. There is a first level which is conventionally true: for instance, just seeing some object and identifying it as bad. But when it increases to thinking, "Oh, this is really bad," then it produces hatred, and that is the second level. On the third level, if it is bringing harm to oneself, then extremely strong hatred can develop; there are these two levels of hatred. Thus, for both desire and hatred, the ignorance which is the conception of an inherent existence acts as an assistant. So, the one that makes all this trouble is this pig. The obscuration of ignorance serves as the root of the other afflictive emotions. This ignorant consciousness is obscured with respect to the way of being of phenomena. To symbolize that, the person in the picture is blind. Ignorance has no valid cognition as its foundation; it is weak.

The second link is called compositional action because actions serve to compose or bring together—they bring about pleasure and pain. This is symbolized by a potter.

Compositional action

Now, a maker of clay pots is someone who takes clay and forms it into some new object. In this example the potter spins the wheel once, and it will keep turning as long as it is needed, without further exertion. Just so, when an action has been done by a sentient being, that action establishes potency or a predisposition in the mind, or as it is said in the Prasangika system, it produces a state of destructedness. In any case, it has the potential to go on without obstruction to produce its effect eventually. In the meantime, no further condition need be encountered for that potency to remain. If it does not meet with a condition that would actualize it, it will remain potential.

Looking at the effects of the various types of actions, such as rebirth in the desire, form, and formless realms, there are virtuous and nonvirtuous actions, and among the virtuous actions there are meritorious and nonfluctuating actions. In terms of the door, or the approach through which the action is done, there are actions of body, speech, and mind. In terms of the actual entity of the actions themselves, there are actions of intention and intended actions. In terms of whether the effect of the action is definitely to be experienced or not, there are definite and indefinite actions.

Among definite actions, there are actions the effect of which is definitely to be experienced in this lifetime, and those definitely to be experienced in some other lifetime.

Then there are actions which will lead, for instance, to a lifetime as a human, that project the general condition of a lifetime in a human body, and there are other types of actions that fill in the picture, that are called completing actions. They cause the body to be beautiful or ugly, and so forth. Take the example of a human who undergoes many illnesses: the projecting karma was a virtuous action, since the person was born as a human. But the completing actions, which give rise to all the sickness, were nonvirtuous actions. There are also cases where the projecting action or karma was nonvirtuous, and the completing actions were virtuous. In some cases both the projecting and completing causes are virtuous, and there are cases in which both were nonvirtuous.

There is also a division into actions that are done and accumulated according to intention; those that aren't done, but are accumulated according to intention; and those which are neither done nor accumulated according to intention.

There are actions in which the thought is wholesome but the carrying out of it is unwholesome; those in which the thought is unwholesome, but the carrying out seems to be wholesome; those in which both the thought and the carrying out are unwholesome; and those in which the thought and the execution are wholesome. Then there are actions or karmas the effects of which are experienced by a number of beings, and other actions the effect of which are experienced only by one individual.

Suppose one asks, how is an action accumulated? If there is a good motivation and some kind words, some gentle physical action comes which accumulates good karma. The immediate result of such action is to create a peaceful atmosphere, whereas anger, rude words, and bad actions like that immediately create an unpleasant atmosphere.

At first, ignorance happened, and it produced the next stage, action. In the next moment the action itself will cease. At that time, the continuation of consciousness is there. The action imprints a potency or predisposition on the consciousness, and that consciousness that continues on, carrying that imprint up to the time of the fruition of that karma, is the third link, called consciousness. So this moment's action creates immediate results, and in the meantime, it will remain as a potential which eventually brings either a happy, pleasant experience, or an unhappy, painful one. That is the way to create action and how action brings results.

The picture symbolizing the third link, consciousness, is a monkey. Within Buddhism there are different explanations of how many consciousnesses there are. There is one system that asserts only one, others that assert six, another that asserts eight, and one that asserts nine. Most Buddhist systems assert six types of consciousness. The monkey in the main picture seems to be jumping from the tree. It has some connection with the assertion of the system that sets forth only one consciousness. The one consciousness, when it appears at the eye, seems to be eye consciousness; when perceiving from the ear it is ear consciousness, and so forth; but it is really only one consciousness. Anyway, a monkey is a very clever and active sort of animal.

Consciousness

Now the problem is that between the action and the fructi-fication of the action there is a good deal of time. However, all Buddhist systems assert that karmas are not wasted. So, between cause and effect there has to be something that connects the two. Many different assertions are presented regarding what connects the cause with the effect. However, there is a person that exists from the time of the performance of that action, through to the time of the effect of that action. In the Prasangika system, that dependently designated person is the basis of the infusion of that predisposition or potency by that action. As long as a system is unable to present a basis of infusion of predispositions, such as the dependently designated person in the Prasangika system, they have to find an independently existent basis of infusion of the po-tencies. The Mind Only system presents an *alayavijnana*, or mind basis of all, as the basis of infusion of the predispositions. In the Prasangika system, the everlasting or continual basis of infusions of these predispositions is the mere self, the mere "I," the mere person. A temporary basis of infusion of the predispositions is the consciousness.

So now there's an action. The action is done. Right after that action there is a state of destructedness or cessation of that ac-tion, and there's consciousness that infused right at that moment with the predisposition of that action. From that moment right up to just before the moment of conception of the new lifetime, that consciousness is called the consciousness of the causal time. The projected effect caused by the karma accumulated in a single round by compositional factors influenced by ignorance is a birth. The consciousness of the very moment of connection to the next lifetime is called the effect consciousness. It lasts from that mo-ment until the time of the next branch, name, and form, which is an extremely short time.

Name and form

The fourth link is name and form. Here, "name" is the four mental aggregates—feeling, discrimination, compositional factors, and consciousness—and "form" is the aggregate of form. Here it is depicted by people riding in a boat; in other pictures it is depicted by beams leaning against each other, as in sutra. This is in connection with the Mind Only system, in which there is a mental consciousness, an *alayavijnana*, or mind basis of all, and there's form—three beams, like a tripod, supporting each other. The boat symbolizes form, and the people in the boat symbolize the mental aggregates.

How long does name and form last, in terms of the 12 links? It lasts as long as the fetus or embryo has not yet begun to develop the five or six organs, through the "jelly-like" state, and "having little knobs," and so forth, which indicate stages of development of the embryo.

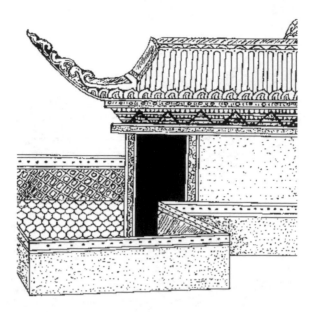

Sources

The fifth link is the six sources, depicted by an empty house, because these are the inner sources of consciousness—the ear, eye, nose, tongue, body sense, and mind—and although the organs are developing at this time, they are not functioning.

After this comes contact, the sixth link of dependent arising. Contact is the point at which objects, sense powers, and consciousness come together. When there is an object, a sense power, and a former moment of consciousness that can act as an immediately preceding condition, a consciousness is generated. Contact is the factor that distinguishes an object as pleasurable, painful, or neutral.

Contact

Consciousness is produced by way of three conditions. The first is called the observed object condition, and it is what causes the consciousness to be generated in the aspect of that object. Then there is the dominant condition, and that is what enables a particular consciousness to apprehend only its respective type of object.

The fact that consciousness is produced as an experiential entity is due to an immediately preceding consciousness, which is the third condition, called the immediately preceding condition. Because there is a meeting with an object and a distinguishing of it, the symbol used in the picture is a kiss. Contact means meeting. Contact is posited as that period during which there is the meeting of object, sense power, and consciousness, and a distinguishing of the object as pleasurable, painful, or neutral, but prior to the production of feeling.

Feeling

The seventh link of dependent arising, feeling, is posited as that factor which experiences pleasure, pain, or neutral feeling. The boundaries of this seventh link are posited in one system as going from the point of the experience of pleasure, pain, or neutral feeling to the point of experiencing the pleasure of copulation. In the picture depicting feeling is someone with an eye pierced by an arrow, because the eye is such that even a very small unpleasant feeling soon feels unbearable. No matter what kind of feeling we experience in our minds, whether pleasurable or painful, it is very effective: we react very strongly with great craving or rejection, we can't stay still, and it drives us on.

The next link is attachment. Both the eighth and ninth links, attachment and grasping, are types of desires. The difference between them is that attachment is a weaker phase of desire, and grasping is a strong phase. There are different divisions of attachment: for instance, desire is an attachment associated with the

Attachment

desire realm. There is desire for existence, which is desire associated with the upper form and formless realms. In one interpretation, desirous attachment is desire for pleasurable feelings; then a
second type of desire is destructive desire, which is a wish to be
separated from unpleasant feelings. Then there is attachment to
mundane or cyclic existence, which is explained as attachment to
the mental and physical aggregates appropriated through a contaminated process of causation. The picture depicting attachment
shows a man drinking beer. That is easy to understand, isn't it? No
matter how much beer you drink, although it makes you fat and
you keep drinking it, there's no satisfaction. Attachment is something that increases desire without any satisfaction. The boundaries are from the time of the fourth link, name and form, until the
ninth link, grasping.

Grasping

Grasping is depicted as a person taking fruit. It is the taking of an object that one desires. There are four different types of grasping. The first is grasping at desires, and the second is grasping at views of self. The third is grasping at bad systems of ethics and conduct, and the fourth is grasping at the remaining types of bad views. These graspings can be described in terms of ordinary householders, or in terms of those who have left the householder's life and are celibate, but have an erroneous view. For instance, if a person who has become temporarily free from desire for the desire realm and has the correct view, seeks to be reborn in a higher realm, in a form or formless realm, some grasping is required. Since there is this type that isn't included, one can see that the four types of grasping don't include all possibilities; the four are set forth to overcome wrong ideas, not to exclude any other alternative.

In dependence upon name and form, sources, contact, and feeling, one generates attachment—attachment to remaining with a pleasurable object or the attachment of seeking to be separate from a painful object. When this type of attachment is strongly produced over and over again, there is grasping of the desired object, and this attachment and grasping serve to activate a karmic potency established by an action in the consciousness. The picture depicting this is a pregnant woman. Just as at this point the karma that would produce the next lifetime is fully potentialized, but not yet manifest, so the pregnant woman has an unborn child inside her womb. Existence is a state of karma, or predisposition established in the consciousness that is fully potentialized.

Existence

This tenth link, existence, lasts from the time of the fully potentialized karma, up to the beginning of the next lifetime. Within it are two divisions of time. One level might be called "directional," as it is directed toward the next lifetime, and the other is "the level of having entered," or being in the process of actually entering. This refers to the potentialized karma in the intermediate state between two lifetimes.

Birth

The eleventh link is the dependent arising of birth. Here the picture shows a woman actually giving birth. The meaning is probably that the woman is in a state of change.

The twelfth link is the dependent arising of aging and death. There are two types of aging. One is the momentary disintegration which takes place immediately after the moment of conception and every moment from then on for the rest of the life. The other type is complete deterioration, which is what we usually think of as aging, becoming old. Then there is death. In between these, there are cries of sorrow, all sorts of suffering: getting what you don't want, not getting what you do want.

Aging and death

Our lives begin with suffering when we are born. The end is death, another type of suffering. In between there is illness, old age, and all kinds of unfortunate things. That is what is called *duhkha* in Sanskrit, suffering, the first noble truth. It is what we don't want, the problem we want to eliminate. It is important to investigate whether there is any way it can be overcome, so it is very important to investigate its cause. It is explained that the origin of the type of suffering that we are undergoing is ignorance.

As long as ignorance, which is the seed of suffering, is there, every minute we may create a certain kind of action or cause of another rebirth. On one consciousness, there is an infinite number of predispositions established by actions motivated by ignorance.

EXPLAINING THE 12 LINKS IN TERMS OF MORE THAN ONE ROUND

We have explained the 12 links of dependent arising in terms of one round, starting from ignorance, with the remaining 11 members coming out of that. But you have to say that at the time this dependent arising operates, there's another dependent arising operating with it. For when you have ignorance, action, and consciousness, between consciousness and name and form you have to have the attachment, grasping, and existence in order to activate the potency in the consciousness for it to produce the lifetime indicated by name and form. The level of fully potentialized karma leads to birth, and at the same time, there will be another set of name and form, sources, and contacts, operating. This is in terms of considering the 12 as one round.

If attachment, grasping, and existence must come between consciousness and name and form, there's another round involved even in their production. Once the first member is ignorance and the last member is aging and death, it might seem as if there were a beginning and end, but when you realize that in order to bring about this one round of the 12-member dependent arising there are other rounds operating at the same time, you realize that there isn't a clean beginning and end. The root of all of it is ignorance, and as long as you have ignorance, there's nothing you can do about getting rid of this process.

With regard to the 12-member dependent arising of a lifetime in a bad transmigration, there is the basic ignorance which is obscuration with respect to the mode of being of phenomena, and there is also ignorance which is obscuration with regard to the relation between actions and their effects. Through that, a nonvirtuous action is produced that deposits a potency in the consciousness, which serves as the projecting cause. The projecting cause is actualized by attachment, grasping, and existence, due to which the effects of suffering in a bad transmigration are produced.

As for the dependent arising of a lifetime of high status within cyclic existence, the basic ignorance is the same, it is obscuration with respect to the mode of subsistence of phenomena, but it is virtuous action that deposits a potency in the consciousness. That projecting cause is nourished by attachment, grasping, and existence, such that it produces the effect of a lifetime in high status. When one reflects on this mode of wandering in cyclic existence by way of these 12 links of dependent arising in relation to others, one's compassion toward them is increased. There are vast methods of meditation on these 12 links in terms of oneself, developing a wish to get out of cyclic existence, and in terms of others, thereby developing increasing compassion.

So that is the mode of dependent arising in terms of the 12 links of the development of a lifetime in cyclic existence.

OTHER ASPECTS OF DEPENDENT ARISING

There is another type of dependent arising which is the dependent arising of imputation or designation in terms of parts. Any physical object has directional parts. Phenomena such as consciousnesses have moments of consciousness. If there were any such thing as a partless particle, one could not discriminate sides, such as left and right, or this side and that side. If you can't discriminate sides in something, no matter how many of these things you put together, you can't have anything bigger than the original one. However, it is the case that gross objects are produced through the coming together of tiny particles. Thus, in terms of investigating physical objects, no matter how small the particle is, it must have directional parts, and it is on the basis of this logic that it is established that there are no physical objects that are partless. With respect to a continuum, if the members did not have earlier and later parts themselves, there would be no possibility of their coming together to form a continuum. Then, with respect to unchanging phenomena such as unproduced space, there are parts or factors such as the eastern or the western quarter, or the part associated with this or that object. Thus, any object, whether it is permanent or impermanent, changing or unchanging, has parts.

When the whole and parts of any particular object appear to our minds, isn't it the case that the whole and parts appear to have their own separate entities? They appear to conceptual thought in this manner, but when you investigate, it is clear that the whole and parts do not have separate entities. When they appear to our minds, the whole seems to have a separate entity from the parts. If it were so, you should be able to find them under analysis, but when you analyze, you can't find any such separate whole and parts. So there is a discrepancy between the way whole and part appear as separate entities and the way they actually exist. However, this doesn't mean that there are no objects or no wholes, because if there were no wholes you couldn't speak of anything as being a part. There are wholes, but their mode of existence is to be posited in dependence upon their parts, and there is no other way for them to exist. Since this is the case, it applies not only to changing or impermanent phenomena, but also to unchanging, permanent phenomena.

There is a yet more profound meaning of dependent arising. When you seek the object designated, you don't come up with anything among or separate from the basis of designation of the object that is different from that object. Take the self or the "I." There is the "I" that is the controller or user of mind and body; "I" is something like the owner, while the mind and body are something like belongings. You can say, "This is my body; today there is something wrong with my body, therefore I'm tired. Today my body is fit, so I'm very fresh." Nobody says that some part of the body is "I." But if in the meantime there is pain in some part of your body, you can say, "'I have pain" or "I'm not well." Similarly, you say "my mind" or "my consciousness." Sometimes you almost fight with your own consciousness, your own memory. Isn't that so? You can say, "I want to improve the sharpness of my mind, I want to train my mind." You appear as the teacher or the trainer of the mind, and the mind appears as the unruly student that is going to be trained. You're going to give it some training in order to make it better.

So both body and mind are belongings; "I" is the owner. But besides mind and body, there is no separate independent entity of "I." There is every indication that there is an "I," but if you investigate, it can't be found. If there is an independent "I," a separate entity—take the Dalai Lama's "I"—it must be here within this boundary; there's no other place you can find it. Now, if you investigate which is the true Dalai Lama, the true Tenzin Gyatso, besides this body and mind there is no substance. Yet, the Dalai Lama is a fact, a man, a monk, a Tibetan, who can speak, who can drink, who can sleep, who can enjoy himself. That is quite enough to prove there is something, yet it can't be found. Among the bases of designation of the "I," there is nothing to be found that is an illustration of the "I" or that is the "I." But does this mean that the "I" doesn't exist? No, it doesn't mean that; the "I" does exist. But since it cannot be found among its bases of designation, one has to say that it exists, not under its own power, but merely through the force of other conditions.

One of the more important conditions in dependence upon which the "I" exists is the conceptuality that posits the "I." Thus, it is said that the "I" and other phenomena exist through the power of conceptuality. Dependent arising here comes to mean: posited in dependence upon a basis of designation; or upon a conceptual consciousness that designates the object; or arising in dependence upon a basis of designation, or upon a conceptual consciousness that designates it. Thus, in the term "dependent arising," *dependent* means depending or relying on some other factor. Once the object depends on something else, it is devoid of being under its own power of being independent. Nevertheless, it arises in dependence upon conditions. Good and bad, cause and effect, oneself and others, whatever the object is, it arises dependently. From the point of view of being dependently arisen, the object is devoid of the extreme of being under its own power. And because in this context of dependence, cause and effect are proper, one can posit them; they are not nonexistent. When one understands this, one is released from the extreme of nonexistence, nihilism. That is the most subtle meaning of dependent arising.

Nowadays, physicists are explaining that objects don't exist just objectively in and of themselves, but that they exist in the context of involvement with a perceiver. I feel that this relation between matter and consciousness is the real place where Eastern philosophy, particularly Buddhist philosophy, and Western science could meet. I think it would be a very happy meeting. Perhaps by the next century, if we carry out more work along these lines, through a joint effort by Buddhist scholars, and also those who have some experience, and pure, unbiased scientists, physicists, working together, investigating, studying, and carrying out deeper research into the relations between matter and consciousness, I think we may find some beautiful things that may be helpful or good, even if they are not considered a practice of Dharma but purely an extension of human knowledge.

Since Buddhist philosophy is somehow connected with science, the Buddhist explanation of consciousness, how it functions, its changes and fluctuations, could make a contribution to the work of scientists studying the human brain and human mind. Sometimes I ask neurologists: What is the function of memory? How does it function? They say they still haven't found the concrete explanation. In that field, too, I think we could work together. Some Western medical people are showing interest in curing certain illnesses through meditation. That also works. This could be another joint project.

In Buddhism the emphasis is on self-creation; there is no creator, so strictly speaking it is not a religion, it is closer to science. From the pure scientist's viewpoint, naturally, Buddhism is a kind of spiritual system. So Buddhism belongs to neither faith nor religion nor to pure science. This provides an opportunity to make a link or bridge between faith and science. I believe that in the future we may have to work to make closer contact between those who are following faith and experience of spiritual value (most people, who simply neglect it, are a different matter), and people who deliberately deny any value to religion. There is constant conflict between these two. If they can be helped to come closer together, it might be worthwhile.

Dependent Arising and Training the Mind

The explanation of the way of taking birth in cyclic existence based on the 12 links of dependent arising is like a presentation of the basis: the contaminated actions, afflictive emotions, and suffering. Now, can the mind be separated from this ignorance or not? This is something you have to look into. No matter what type of consciousness you consider, it is connected with familiarization. No matter how much you develop a mistaken consciousness, since it doesn't have a valid foundation certified by valid cognition, it cannot be increased limitlessly. However, if you become familiar with a nonmistaken consciousness, which has a valid foundation certified by valid cognition, even if you don't train a great deal in it, it will remain with you. To the degree that you continuously familiarize with it, it will increase and eventually can become limitless.

It is said that qualities that depend on the mind have a stable basis. This is because consciousness is said to have no beginning and no end. Mental qualities have a stable basis in that consciousness itself is the basis.

Once a mental quality is in the mind, it is in the mind with a certain force, and you don't have to exert that same force again to bring it up to the initial level. Thus, when you train more, you will increase that quality.

It is in terms of this discussion of no beginning and no end to consciousness that cyclic existence itself is said to have no beginning and no end, which leads to the topic of rebirth. With regard to the one round of dependent arising explained above, for all 12 links to occur, at the slowest it takes three lifetimes, and the fastest they can be completed in is two lifetimes.

The topic of rebirth leads to the topic of reincarnation. Nowadays, there are people who remember their former lifetimes. Recently in India there have been two cases that I have come across, both of small girls. For somebody who accepts former and future lifetimes, there's nothing amazing about this sort of phenomenon. But a person who does not accept former and future lives

231

should come up with some answer: through what sort of condition or causation does this memory take place?

Consciousness also has no end, but reaches its fulfillment in Buddhahood. Now, there's no question of the afflicted levels of mind going on to Buddhahood, or even the coarser levels of consciousness. It is the subtlest level of consciousness that proceeds to and through Buddhahood. This subtlest level has existed since beginningless time and goes on to Buddhahood. When we die, our coarser levels of consciousness dissolve or cease, and the final consciousness that manifests is this most subtle mind of clear light; it is this consciousness that makes the connection to the next lifetime.

The 12 links of dependent arising can also be explained in terms of the obstructions to omniscience, with reference to Bodhisattvas on the three pure Bodhisattva grounds, the eighth, ninth, and tenth grounds.

Since the root of our suffering is ignorance, it is from having an untamed mind that we meet with that root and suffer. Therefore, we have to eliminate the ignorance in our mindstreams that brings us suffering. Through taming the mind we will meet with suffering. Now, since the mind needs to be tamed, there is a mode of taming the mind in terms of the mind itself. Then the trainer and that which is being trained are both the mind. So one has to become skilled in the presentation of mind. In Buddhist teachings, a great deal of time is devoted to this.

Within our consciousness, the most untamed type of mind is called wrong ideas, wrong knowledge, or wrong consciousness. As one hears and becomes accustomed to teachings, one gradually rises to the level of doubt. There are three levels of doubt: the lowest being doubt that tends to what is wrong; the middling being equal doubt, which tends both to what is wrong and to what is right; and the highest being doubt that tends toward what is right. Then, as one trains, more doubt is transformed into correct assumption. From this level, by reflecting on reasons and so forth, one generates inference. Then, by accustoming oneself to the inferential understanding, direct perception which realizes that object is gained.

In order to overcome these wrong consciousnesses or wrong ideas, many absurd consequences are set forth. At the point when you rise to the level of doubt, it is possible to use reasoning to generate an inferential understanding. Through this, one develops the wisdom that discriminates phenomena. In the process, one gradually develops the wisdom arisen from hearing, from thinking, and from meditation.

When one proceeds with this type of practice, one gradually comes to see that there is indeed a possibility of transforming one's consciousness. From this point of view one can become convinced about the practice of nonviolence. This first level is to restrain oneself from engaging in activities that harm others. The second level is to implement the antidotes to the mental factors that motivate bad actions. The third level is to overcome even the predispositions that have been established previously by afflictive emotions. Through reflecting on the view of dependent arising, one sees the faults of cyclic existence, how suffering comes about, and one is drawn into the practice of these levels of nonviolence.

In order to remove the latent predispositions established by the afflictive emotions, it is necessary first to eliminate the afflictive emotions. The removal of the afflictions, as well as of the predispositions established by them, is called the stage of Buddhahood. The mere removal of the afflictive emotions is called the stage of an Arhat or a Foe Destroyer. The practice for overcoming the afflictive emotions and the predispositions established by them is like an offensive engagement. Prior to this, it is important to engage in a defensive line of action, hence the importance of initially restraining ill-deeds of body and speech. The ultimate aim is to attain Buddhahood. But in the implementation of this, one initially has to restrain one's ill-deeds of body and speech. Now, if with a selfish motive one commits a wrong action, such as killing, stealing, lying, adultery, or slander, these bad actions of body and speech not only harm others, but ultimately they will bring suffering upon oneself. Thus, even if one considers merely the violence one is bringing on oneself, it is necessary to restrain wrong actions of body and speech.

For this, it is helpful to reflect on impermanence. No matter how long our life is, there's a limit to it, isn't there? Compared to the formation of the universe, and geological time, the human lifetime is very short. Even then, there isn't any guarantee that we'll live out the usual lifespan of 100 or even 60 years. In these circumstances, to concentrate all your energy, mental as well as physical, on money or on wealth is only helpful for this life, which is uncertain and short. Reflecting on this will help reduce extreme greed, the desire to get something, no matter what the consequences.

Thinking about the current world situation also helps this practice; no matter how good material things become, they can't give the answer to life. Material progress alone is solving some problems, but at the same time it is producing new kinds of problems. Through our own experience we can realize that mere material progress is not sufficient. Thinking along these lines, a conviction will grow, that harming others will bring loss to yourself. This is something to reflect on again and again. Also at this stage, analyze the usefulness of the human brain, the body, and the human condition, for it is really sad to use it in a harmful way. For some people it is helpful to reflect on the three bad levels of transmigration, as hell beings, hungry ghosts, or animals. If it is difficult to believe that there are hell beings, we can just consider the suffering that animals undergo, sufferings we can see with our own eyes. We should think about whether we could stand that sort of suffering if we were born in such circumstances. We can assume that in our minds we already have the predispositions from actions motivated by initial ignorance for rebirth as such animals. We need to think that we have within our continuums the substances which are just ready to develop into that kind of lifetime. And if we were born into that kind of life, what kind of suffering would we have? Up to now we have just been looking at them; now we should imagine: "If I became like that, could I bear it or not?" When you think this way, you discover it's not what you want. Now, what brings about this kind of suffering is violence toward others. This is the first level of reflection on the faults of violence and the need to restrain ill-deeds of body and speech.

Now, there's no guarantee that if you restrain ill-deeds of body and speech in this lifetime you will do so in the next lifetime. Therefore, the best defense is the second level of offensive engagement, training to overcome afflictive emotions. The afflictive emotions that bring us all this trouble are those mentioned in the 12 links of dependent arising. The basis of the afflictions is the ignorance which conceives of objects as inherently existing, which then induces varying degrees of desire, hatred, enmity, jealousy, and so forth. These are the real troublemakers. It is very clear in our present world, at the national or family level, that all difficulties and problems are related to attachment, anger, and jealousy.

When some other person seeks to harm us, we identify that person as an enemy. If this anger, this wish to harm, were the very nature of that person, it would be a different matter. But hatred, anger, and the wish to harm are actually peripheral mental factors affecting the mind. Although we do bad actions, we're not thinking of doing bad actions all the time. It is the same for your enemy. The actual troublemaker is not the person, not the being; it is his or her afflicted mind. The real enemy is within ourselves, not outside. As practitioners, the real battle should take place within ourselves. It will take time, but it is the only way to minimize what I call the bad human qualities. And through this you will get more mental peace, not only in the next life, or after a long time, but day by day. The basic destroyer of our peace of mind is hatred or anger. All bad thoughts are troublemakers, but anger is the most powerful.

OVERCOMING AFFLICTIVE EMOTIONS

To overcome the afflictive emotions it is necessary to get rid of their root, which is the ignorance conceiving of inherent existence. To do this it is necessary to generate a wisdom consciousness that perceives objects in a way exactly opposite to how ignorance perceives its objects. We have to reflect on the fact that objects don't exist inherently, or in and of themselves. It is necessary to develop reasoning to refute the truly existing object that the erroneous consciousness apprehends. In this, the view realizing emptiness is very important. To develop the level of wisdom required to act as an antidote to this ignorance, it is not enough merely to generate an inferential consciousness in dependence upon reasoning. One must bring that inferential understanding to the level of a direct nonconceptual perception of the truth. To do so, it is necessary to have assistance from concentration. Through a deep level of concentration it is possible to develop the meditative stabilization which is a union of a mind of calm abiding and a mind of special insight. So, it is first necessary to achieve a calm abiding or tranquilization of the mind. When one develops one-pointedness and the ability of the mind to remain on its object of observation in a clear and alert manner, it also helps in the daily progress of one's life. One's mind is sharper, more alert, more capable, hence the necessity for setting forth presentations of the way to achieve meditative stabilization (*samadhi*).

Someone who wants to achieve calm abiding of the mind must go to an isolated place and be prepared for it to take a long time. If one works at achieving calm abiding in connection with tantric or mantric practices, it is said to be easier. However, apart from that, just practicing in ordinary life, it is helpful in the early morning just when you wake up to use your clear mind to investigate what sort of a thing the mind is. It will help to keep the mind very alert so it will help the rest of the day. In order to reach the level at which internal subtle distractions have been eliminated and one has a deep level of one-pointedness of mind, it is first necessary to restrain the coarser level, desire and hatred, and the coarse ill-deeds of body and speech. For this, one needs the training in ethics.

In the Buddhist system of ethics there are householders and those who have left the householder's life. Even among householders there are different stages. The reason is that Buddha set forth levels of practice in accordance with the capacity of different people. That is very important. We should follow according to our own mental disposition; then we will get satisfactory results. When you recognize that teachings are set forth for beings of different levels and dispositions, you can develop real respect for the different types of religious systems present throughout the world. Even though differences in philosophy are tremendous, often fundamental, one can see that for various types of beings those philosophies can be appropriate and beneficial. Today we need that kind of mutual respect and mutual understanding. That's very important.

In this connection I very much appreciate and respect the Western monks and nuns here. However, there shouldn't be any rush to take vows. Since Buddha set forth practices in accordance with various different levels, it is important to determine your level and advance gradually within that. And another thing, I feel it is very important that those Westerners who sincerely want to practice Buddha-dharma remain good members of their society. They should remain there, not become isolated. The essence of the Buddhist teaching as it is practiced by Tibetans is also involved with Tibetan culture; it would be a mistake to try to fully Tibetanize and practice a Tibetanized form of Buddhism.

Remain within your society, carry on within your profession, work as a member of your community, and meanwhile implement the Buddha's teaching if you feel it is something useful and effective. We have already established various centers; we should keep them going. But if someone wants to practice Buddha-dharma, it is not necessary to join a center; he can just remain where he is.

We have been discussing ways of combating the afflictions; later we are going to discuss how to develop Bodhichitta, compassion, and how to destroy the obstructions to omniscience, the predispositions established by afflictions. First of all, one trains in ethics, which is the basis; then, through the practice of *samadhi*, the mind is focused and becomes powerful. That focused mind is to be used to meditate on emptiness, by which one gradually overcomes the obstructions, and then gradually the innate obstructions. Finally, one completely overcomes that ignorance which is the conception of inherent existence. That extinguishment is called liberation.

As the protector Nagarjuna said, "Through the extinguishment of contaminated actions and afflictive emotions there is liberation." Contaminated actions are produced from wrong conceptions. Those are produced from conceptual elaborations, and those conceptual elaborations are stopped through emptiness, or cease in emptiness. It is explained in both these ways. In any case, that reality, the emptiness in which all of the afflictive emotions, ignorance, and so forth have been extinguished, is the true cessation that is liberation.

GENERATING THE BODHISATTVA'S ALTRUISTIC ATTITUDE

In terms of this explanation we are at the point of offensive engagement. Through the practice of the three trainings of ethics, meditative stabilization, and wisdom, the afflictive emotions have been destroyed. So now one has arrived at the point where one has to get rid of the predispositions established by the afflictive emotions. To get rid of them is extremely difficult. What is the reason for getting rid of those predispositions? It is because they prevent one from simultaneously knowing all possible objects of knowledge. Therefore, even a person who has achieved the rank of an Arhat, a Foe Destroyer, and has gotten out of cyclic existence, has not fully developed the potential of human consciousness.

The question is how to destroy the predispositions. Here, the actual weapon is the same; it is the wisdom which understands emptiness. However, you also need some powerful backing, great merit; and the way to accumulate great merit constantly is through Bodhichitta, altruism. The person accumulating merit, whose motivation is aimed at liberation and not harming others, is concerned mainly with this single being. In the practice of Bodhichitta, one is concerned with all sentient beings. So because sentient beings are limitless in number, when the consciousness is concerned with them, the meritorious power accumulated is limitless. It is one thing to go for refuge to the Buddha, Dharma, and Spiritual Community out of concern for oneself, but it is another to go for refuge to them out of concern for all sentient beings. These are extremely different in their force because the objects of observation are so different. For the person whose aim is to achieve liberation from cyclic existence for himself, that liberation will be a mere extinguishment of the afflictive emotions. With a more altruistic motivation, one aims for a Buddhahood which is an extinction of both the afflictive emotions and the obstructions to omniscience. Thus, the practices of the second person will be more powerful and will accrue even more powerful merit.

The very nature of the altruistic mind is really precious, marvelous; sometimes we may wonder how the human mind can develop such things. It is fantastic, amazing, to forget oneself, and respect or be concerned with every other being, considering them as dear as oneself. Everybody appreciates such a warm feeling. If someone shows warm feelings to us, how happy we feel. If we can show warm feelings for other people, this is one of the best things in samsara as well as in nirvana. This is the real source of happiness. If you develop even a small experience, it will help you, it will give you peace of mind and inner strength. It will give you the best kind of defense and the best ground for an offensive. It also acts like a teacher, like your best friend, and like your best protector. So it is really something good.

We have already discussed the basic philosophical structure, from which you can draw a conclusion: it is possible to develop such a beautiful mind. The great Indian pandits set out two ways to do this. One is by way of the seven cause-and-effect quintessential instructions, the other is by way of equalizing self and others. In order to generate such a strong altruistic thought, it is necessary to generate the unusual attitude or high resolve of taking upon oneself the burden of helping others. In order to induce this unusual attitude, it is necessary to have a compassion in which one cannot bear to see the suffering of others without doing something about it. Whether those persons are manifestly suffering or have all the causes and conditions to undergo manifest suffering, if one does not have a compassion which is stirring from the depths about that suffering, it will be impossible to induce that great resolve. It is clear from our own experience that it is easier to generate compassion for people who fit in with us, whom we find congenial or pleasant. So prior to generating great compassion, it is necessary to have a technique to place all beings within this class of suitable beings. Thus, the technique is to train in viewing all sentient beings in the way in which you view the being to whom you feel the closest, whether this be your mother or father, a relative, or some other person. In order to recognize beings in this way, it is necessary to view them in an even-minded way. It's helpful here to use your imagination. In front of yourself imagine a person to whom you are very friendly, someone you don't like, and in the middle some neutral person; then examine the type of feeling that you have with respect to these three.

Naturally, when you imagine this, your mind feels close toward your friend; distant from, and sometimes angry with or irritated by, your enemy; and toward the neutral person, nothing. We have to investigate this. From the Buddhist viewpoint, there are endless rebirths. Maybe in the past this friend was our worst enemy. Today the other is acting like an enemy, but maybe in the past was one of the people dearest to us. In the future, too, there is no reason for the enemy always to remain an enemy, or the friend always to remain a friend. There is no such guarantee, even within this life. Today's friend may change within a short time. This is very clear from our family experience and especially among politicians: today a good friend, a good ally, tomorrow the best enemy. Basically the structure of our lives is not stable: sometimes we're successful, sometimes unsuccessful; things are always changing. Therefore, this feeling toward friends and enemies that is so solid or stable is absolutely wrong. There is no reason for such firmness; that is really foolish. Thinking like this will gradually help you to equalize your attitudes to people.

The next step is to think that sooner or later your enemy will be a good friend. So it is better to think of all three persons as being your best friends. We can also investigate the result if we show hatred. It's quite obvious. If we try to develop compassion toward these persons, the result will be good, without doubt. So it is much better to develop an equal, compassionate attitude. Then experiment: turn toward your neighbor on the left, your neighbor on the right, go on down the row. Then extend it to the whole city, the county, then the country, the continent, then the entire humanity of this world; finally, to the infinite sentient beings. That is the way to practice this technique.

Another technique is equalizing and exchanging self and others. Investigate which side is more important, oneself or others. You are one, the other is infinite. Both want happiness and do not want suffering. And both have every right to achieve happiness, to overcome suffering, because both are sentient beings, members of the community of sentient beings. If we ask, "Why do I have the right to be happy?" the ultimate reason is because I want happiness, no other reason. There is a natural feeling of "I," and on that basis we want happiness, which is a correct view. And on that basis we say we have every right to be happy: that is what we call human rights; it is sentient beings' right. The possibility of overcoming suffering is the same; the only difference is, one is a single being, the others are the majority. The conclusion is quite clear: in the context of all sentient beings, just one is nothing important.

Here is something I myself practice and occasionally express to others: imagine on one side the old selfish "I,'" and on the other side a group of poor, needy people. You yourself remain as a neutral or third person. Then judge, which is more important: whether to join this selfish, self-centered, stupid person or these poor, needy, helpless people. If you have a human heart, naturally you will go to their side. Think like this, it will help the altruistic attitude to grow, and then you will realize how bad selfish behavior is. Actually, up to now you have been behaving like that yourself. But if someone says to you, "You are a bad person," then you feel very angry. Why? The main reason is that you do not want to be a bad person. It is in your own hands: if you behave like a good person, then you become a good person. If you are a good person, nobody can put you in the category of bad people. Think about this, for it helps tremendously to develop altruism.

That is one way of practice. Many of you have probably heard me talk about world peace, or family peace, or national peace; the ultimate source of them is altruism, compassion, and love. In all major religions, the essential thing is love and kindness. Now, thinking over these different reasons, as much as you can, will help to develop conviction or determination. With that determination, trying day by day, month by month, year by year, you can improve yourself. With that motivation, every action, whether it is walking, eating, talking, or whatever, accumulates good virtues—limitless virtues.

PRACTICE OF THE SIX PERFECTIONS

Now, from the Buddhist viewpoint, how can one bring help to others? There is the giving of things, such as food, clothing, and shelter. But it has a limit; just as it doesn't bring complete satisfaction to you, it doesn't to others either. Thus, just as it is the case that through your own improvement, through practice, and through the gradual purification of your own mind, you develop more and more happiness, so it is the case for others. For others to understand what they are to adopt and practice in order to achieve this, and what they should stop doing, you have to be fully capable of teaching these topics. Sentient beings are of limitlessly different predispositions, interests, dormant attitudes, and so forth. If you don't develop the exalted activities of body and speech that accord exactly with what other beings need, then full help cannot be given. There is no way to do this unless you overcome the obstructions to omniscience, to knowing everything. It is in the context of seeking help for others that one seeks the state of Buddhahood, in which one has overcome the obstacles to omniscience.

Charity, giving, is a case of training from the depths of one's heart in an attitude of generosity, such that one is not seeking any result or effect of the giving for oneself.

In the Bodhisattva training in ethics, the main practice is to restrain the attitude of seeking one's own benefit, self-centeredness. This will bring about, for instance, an engagement in giving of charity, such that one could not possibly bring harm to others. In order to practice giving properly, one can't do anything that brings harm to others, so in order to bring about giving that is exclusively helpful, one needs this Bodhisattva ethic of restraining self-centeredness.

In order to have pure ethics, it is necessary to cultivate patience. In order to train in the practice of equalizing and exchanging self and others, patience is particularly important. It will be very useful for you to practice using the techniques that Shantideva sets forth in his *Guide to the Bodhisattva's Way of Life*, in both the chapter on patience and the chapter on concentration. The practice of patience establishes the foundation for the equalizing of self and others. This is because the hardest problem we have in generating the Bodhisattva's attitude is developing a sense of affection and closeness for our enemies. When we think of enemies in the context of the practice of patience, not only is an enemy not someone who harms you; instead, an enemy is seen as someone who helps. You come to realize, "There is no way I could cultivate patience about harm to myself unless there was someone out there to harm me." As it is said, there are many beings to whom one can give, but there are very few beings with respect to whom one can practice patience. The value of what is rare is higher, isn't it? Really, the so-called enemy is very kind. Through cultivating patience, the power of one's merit increases, and it can only be done in dependence upon an enemy. Thus, an enemy does not prevent the practice of Dharma; rather, he helps.

In his *Guide to the Bodhisattva's Way of Life*, Shantideva states a hypothetical objection, which is, "Well, the enemy has no motivation to help." The answer is that for something to be helpful it is not necessary for it to have the motivation to help. For instance, true cessations, liberation, the third of the four noble truths, help one greatly, but liberation has no motivation. Even if an enemy doesn't have a wish to help, it is suitable to respect him. The next objection is, "At least cessation, or liberation, does not have the wish to harm me; whereas the enemy—even if he has no wish to help, like liberation—does have the wish to harm." The answer is that because this person has the wish to harm, he becomes an enemy, and you need that enemy in order to cultivate patience. Someone like a doctor, who has no wish to harm, who is trying to help you, cannot provide a situation for the cultivation of patience. So these are the ancient great Bodhisattvas' experiences and their reasons, which are very effective. When you think about it this way, you could only hold on to self-cherishing if you were stubborn, because there is no reason for it, whereas there are plenty of reasons why you should cherish others.

Another important type of patience or forbearance is voluntary acceptance of suffering. Before suffering comes, it is important to engage in techniques to avoid it, but once suffering has begun, it should not be taken as a burden, but as something useful, that can assist you. Another thought is that through undergoing suffering in this lifetime, one can overcome the karma of many ill-deeds accumulated in former lifetimes. It also helps you to see the faults of cyclic existence. The more you see this, the more you will develop a dislike for engaging in ill-deeds. It will help you to see the advantage of liberation. Through your own experience of suffering, you'll be able to infer how others suffer, thus generating compassion. When you think about suffering this way, you may almost come to feel that it is a good opportunity to practice more and to think more.

Then comes effort, which is very important. The effort, like armor, and so forth, is generating a willingness to engage in enthusiastic practice over aeons if need be, in order to bring about development. This helps tremendously in avoiding getting impatient, irritated, or excited over some small, temporary condition. Then comes concentration, then wisdom.

TANTRIC PRACTICE

In the context of altruism, the practices for maturing one's own continuum are the six perfections, and the practices for maturing others are the four ways of gathering students. Among the six perfections, each one is more difficult to achieve and is more important than the previous ones. The last two are concentration and wisdom. In terms of the Sutra Vehicle, there are the 37 harmonies of enlightenment for the sake of achieving liberation, and as in Maitreya's *Ornament of Clear Realization*, there are many variations of paths for the sake of achieving Buddhahood. The root of all these is the meditative stabilization which is a union of the calm abiding of the mind and special insight. As a means for achieving this stabilization quickly and in a powerful way, there is the Mantric or Tantric Vehicle. In the Perfection Vehicle the root of one's practice is the altruistic intention to become enlightened and the view of the emptiness of inherent self-existence. The greatness of Secret Mantra comes by way of meditative stabilization. Thus, it is even said that the scriptures of Secret Mantra are included in the sets of discourses.

How is it, then, that the Secret Mantra Vehicle has a distinctive and more profound way of enhancing the meditative stabilization, which is a union of meditative stabilization and special insight?

With the altruistic intention to become enlightened, one is aiming at a Buddhahood that has a truth body that is the fulfillment of one's own welfare, and a form body which is the fulfillment of others' welfare. Of the two, one is more specifically aiming at the form bodies in order to be of assistance to others. A Buddha's form bodies have the major marks and beauties of a Buddha's body, and one seeks to develop this type of body in the sutra system by practicing the six perfections under the influence of great compassion and the altruistic intention to become enlightened. The distinctive feature of the mantra [system] is that, in addition one engages in a technique that is similar in aspect to the type of form body one is trying to achieve. What one is practicing is concordant in aspect with the fruit one is trying to achieve. In this context, one of the distinctive features of the Secret Mantra Vehicle is an indivisibility of entity of method and wisdom. In the Perfection Vehicle, the sutra-system wisdom is conjoined with or influenced by method, and method is influenced by or conjoined with wisdom. However, the two are not presented as existing in the entity of one consciousness.

How is it that in the mantra [system] there comes to be an indivisibility of method and wisdom? In mantra there is the practice of deity yoga, in which one observes or imagines a divine body, this being in the class of compassionate vast appearances, and through this the collection of merit is accumulated. The very same consciousness ascertains the emptiness of inherent self-existence of that deity's body and thereby one accomplishes the collection of wisdom. This is how in one consciousness there is the indivisible factor of method and wisdom. Although method and wisdom are still separate conceptually, they are present in the entity of one consciousness.

The type of divine body that I am referring to is not the usual divine body of some being, but rather a case of the yogi newly cultivating in meditation an appearance of himself or herself in a divine body. This is what appears to one's own mental consciousness. Thus, when a yogi imagines himself or herself as a deity, and reflects on or realizes the emptiness of inherent existence of that divine body, I think there must be some small difference in the force of the consciousness due to the special object that is the substratum of the emptiness.

In the Perfection Vehicle of the sutra system there are no special techniques through which one purposely engages in trying to cause the substratum or subject, the emptiness of which you are meditating on, to keep appearing; whereas in the mantra system one specifically trains in maintaining the appearance of the divine body in the midst of ascertaining its absence of self-existence.

There is a very important point here, imagining the divine body and ascertaining its emptiness of self-existence within one consciousness. The consciousness is described as the apprehended aspect: that which has the aspect of the apprehended is appearing as a deity in the midst of realizing its emptiness.

There is an even more profound mode of the undifferentiability of entity of method and wisdom. These are practices involving exertion, and there is a special mode of undifferentiability of method and wisdom that comes about by way of the concentrated emphasis that a yogi puts on important places. Due to the substance on which the yogi concentrates, there is a difference in the mode of undifferentiability of method and wisdom. In Highest Yoga Tantra, the substance is the very subtle wind and the very subtle mind. This basis itself is an undifferentiable entity. To practice this level it is necessary forcefully to stop the coarser levels of wind and consciousness. Many different techniques are explained for putting concentrated emphasis on different places in the body and so forth. This is the practice of the channels, the winds, and the essential drops of fluid.

In general, when cultivating special insight, analytical meditation is what is emphasized. In Highest Yoga Tantra, because of these special techniques, stabilizing meditation is what is emphasized when cultivating special insight. At coarser levels of consciousness, in order to ascertain something, it is necessary to analyze and investigate. When one includes the subtler levels of consciousness purposely (not when they happen naturally due to the power of karma), these subtler levels of consciousness (which are states in which the lower states of consciousness have ceased) are very powerful and capable with respect to ascertaining meanings and objects. If at that time you engaged in analysis, this would cause the subtler level to cease and you would return to a coarser level. So one does not analyze at that time, and stabilizing meditation is emphasized.

With regard to the mode of meditation in Highest Yoga Tantra, there are two systems. One emphasizes the extremely subtle wind and the other the extremely subtle mind in order to achieve the Buddha body. In most of the tantras of the New Translation schools, such as *Guhyasamaja*, *Chakrasamvara*, and so forth, the emphasis is on both the extremely subtle wind and the extremely subtle mind in order to bring about the achievement of a Buddha body, whereas in the Kalachakra system the emphasis is put only on the extremely subtle mind. It seems that in Mahamudra, the Great Seal practice, and in Dzogchen, the Great Completeness, the emphasis is mainly on the mind. In general, in Highest Yoga Tantra there is the practice of putting emphasis on the channels, winds, and drops. Within that, one group emphasizes the yoga of the winds, and another concentrates on developing the four joys. There is another group that doesn't emphasize channels, winds, and drops, but puts its emphasis just on sustaining a nonconceptual state, and this latter includes Mahamudra and Dzogchen.

Prior to engaging in the practice of mantra, it is necessary to receive an initiation. Initiation is a matter of one person passing the transmission of a blessing to another person. Although one can gain blessings even from reading books and so forth, there is a difference when one living person transmits a blessing to another, so in Secret Mantra, the lama comes to be valued very highly. One has to take care with respect to a lama; the lama has to take care and the student has to take care. It is said, "When practitioners do not bear the true or proper form of the practice, that is an indication of the degeneration of the Dharma."

Within initiations there are many different variations. It is said that there is no God or Creator, but now with initiation there are a lot of gods. What are these gods? It was said earlier that from the beginning of one's Bodhisattva practice one is wishing and aiming for a state where one can bring vast, effective help to sentient beings. Due to this wishing, this attitude, this aspiration, when one is a Buddha, one spontaneously and without exertion brings about help to other beings. Like the reflection of the moon, which requires someplace for the moon to shine on for it to appear, in a similar way, the spontaneous appearance of form bodies of a Buddha needs beings to whom they appear. Now, whether that reflection appears clearly or unclearly, as big or small, depends upon the vessel on which the moon is shining. Likewise, the form bodies of a Buddha appear spontaneously and without exertion to trainees, in keeping with their interests, dispositions, beliefs, needs, and so forth.

For trainees of the three lower tantras, the form bodies of the Buddhas appear in aspects making use of the five pleasurable attributes of the desire realm—forms, sounds, and so forth—but not in the context of using the bliss arising from the joining of the male and female organs. For those trainees who cannot make use of the path of the pleasurable attributes of the desire realm, the form body appears as a supreme emanation body in the aspect of a fully ordained monk. For a person who has the disposition, capability, and so forth, to practice Highest Yoga Tantra, and whose abilities are activated and manifest, the form bodies appear in the aspect of male and female deities in union.

For those who are capable of using the factor of hatred in the path, the deities appear in a wrathful aspect; for those who are mainly capable of using desire, they appear in a peaceful aspect. It is in this context that three levels of practices or activities are described: practices devoid of desire, vast activities, and the practice or activities of the Great Seal. Just as Shakyamuni Buddha was one person and appeared as one person, there are deities in the tantra sets which appear as one single deity. A deity such as Guhyasamaja, in a mandala of 32 deities, is a case of one deity appearing in 32 different aspects. There are not 32 persons. There is only one, and the rest of the deities are aspects of that one person.

If you use what I've been explaining as a key, you can increase your understanding. After one has received initiation, it is important to keep the pledges and vows.

When the view is explained, it is important to understand that just as when discussing feeling, we can talk about that which feels and that which is felt; so with the view, we can speak about that which is viewed and that which views.

In Highest Yoga Tantra the term *view* is used predominantly in the context of that which views, the subject that views. Although there is no difference with respect to the emptiness that is viewed, there is a difference in the consciousness, the subject that views that emptiness. It is in this context that Sakya Pandita says that sutra and mantra have the same view. There are also many similar statements in Gelug. The reference is to the object that is viewed, emptiness.

There is no difference between the emptiness of sutra and the emptiness of mantra. However, in Sakya, again, it is said that there are four different views of the four initiations in Highest Yoga Tantra. Similarly in Gelug, there is reference to the view of the undifferentiable bliss and wisdom. In such cases the reference is not to the object that is viewed but to the subject that views: the consciousness that is viewing emptiness. There is a difference here, even if there is no difference in terms of the object that is viewed. In Kagyu and Nyingma it is also said that the view of mantra is superior to that of sutra. All of them are referring to a distinctive, more subtle type of consciousness that is viewing.

Now, in Sakya, there is a presentation of the undifferentiability of cyclic existence and nirvana. It is said that one is to settle the question of the undifferentiability of cyclic existence and nirvana in terms of the causal continuum of the basis of all. There are differences of explanation among the Indian pandits and also small differences of explanation within Sakya, but this causal continuum which is the basis of all refers to the reality of the mind. In the *Guhyasamaja Tantra* there are explanations of students of varying capacity. The supreme is the jewel-like person. He or she could be described as the causal continuum which is the basis of all. In Sakya's own system the causal continuum which is the basis of all is identified by Mangto Lhundrup Gyatso, a great scholar, as being the fundamental innate mind of clear light.

In another Sakya system it is identified as all the impure aggregates, constituents, and so on, of a person. It is said that in the causal continuum which is the basis of all, all phenomena of cyclic existence are complete in their characteristics. All the phenomena of the path are complete as high qualities. All the phenomena of Buddhahood are complete in the manner of effects.

With regard to the equality of cyclic existence and nirvana, in the sutra system, as Nagarjuna said, "Cyclic existence and nirvana do not inherently exist: a consciousness that is realizing the emptiness of inherent existence of a sprout and a consciousness that is realizing the emptiness of inherent existence of a divine body are similar." Likewise, when one has understood the meaning of the non-inherent existence of cyclic existence and all true sufferings and sources of suffering have been extinguished, the reality into which they have been extinguished is nirvana. This is the sutra system. Now, the reference in the Sakya presentation to the equality of cyclic existence and nirvana is to view the impure mental and physical aggregates and so forth as primordially existing as pure mental and physical aggregates, constituents, and so forth. According to the thought of the great scholar Lhundrup Gyatso, one views all of the phenomena of cyclic existence and nirvana as the sport or reflection of the fundamental innate mind of clear light. Thus, what we were getting down to here is the fundamental innate mind of clear light.

In the Kagyu system there is the practice of the four yogas. The first is one-pointedness of mind; the second, that which is devoid of conceptual and dualistic elaborations. These two are said to be common with the sutra system. In the first, one is mainly achieving a calm abiding of the mind. With the state of being devoid of elaborations, one is mainly achieving special insight, realizing emptiness. The third, the yoga of one taste, can be considered as an advanced or enhanced type of special insight in which all phenomena of cyclic existence and nirvana have the single taste of the fundamental innate mind of clear light. This brings one again to the mind of clear light and Highest Yoga Tantra. When one advances in this practice, one arrives at the fourth yoga, the yoga of nonmeditation. As Nagarjuna says in his *Five Stages*, which presents the path of *Guhyasamaja*, "When one arrives at the stage of union, there is no new path to be learned." The thought here is the same as the yoga of nonmeditation.

We have to make a difference between mind and basic mind (*sems* and *sems-nyid*), between mind and mindness. Mindness, or basic mind, is the innate truth body, the fundamental innate mind of clear light. Whether appearances are pure or impure, all of them are like waves of the truth body, they appear from the sphere of the truth body. This last point relates to the Mahamudra of the Kagyu.

Then, with regard to the Gelug, if you ask whether the views that were just presented accord with the Madhyamika view in general—they do not. But you could say they accord with the special Madhyamika view of Highest Yoga Tantra, which is concerned with the innate union of bliss and emptiness. On that level, they are the same. In Gelug teachings, in their sutra teachings and even tantra teachings, there is great emphasis on the view as being the object of the view, that which is viewed, the emptiness that is viewed. However, in Gelug there is also a description of this difference in view in terms of the subject. For it is said that all pure and impure phenomena of cyclic existence and nirvana, as well as being the sport of emptiness (the object), are also to be viewed as the sport of the subject, the viewing consciousness, the innate mind of undifferentiable bliss and emptiness. As Nagarjuna says in his *Five Stages*, "The yogi himself or herself abides in the meditative stabilization which is like illusion, and similarly views all phenomena the same way, as being the sport of this basic innate mind of undifferentiable bliss and emptiness."

With respect to Dzogchen, the view of the Great Completeness, the mode of explanation is very different, but it is getting at exactly the same thing. As my source for this, I mainly rely on Dodrupchen Jigme Tenpai Nyima, a really great scholar, as well as a great practitioner, a really remarkable yogi. In the Great Completeness [Dzogchen], the reference is to the fundamental mind of clear light, but the vocabulary used is that of ordinary consciousness. It is necessary to make a difference between *sems* and *rigpa*, or between mind and basic knowledge. In the Nyingma system, Highest Yoga Tantra is divided into three categories: Mahayoga, Anuyoga, and Atiyoga. Atiyoga itself is divided into three classes; the class of mind, the class of the great vastness, and the class of quintessential instructions. As the great Dodrupchen says, "All practitioners of Highest Yoga Tantra in the New and Old Translation schools are practicing just the fundamental innate mind of clear light."

The difference is that in the other systems, in the initial stages of practice, there are many paths that use conceptuality to advance to this other stage. Whereas in the Great Completeness, the practitioner relies on the quintessential instructions, right from the outset, without seeking help from conceptuality; right from the beginning, the emphasis is on the basic knowledge. One puts the emphasis on the basic mind right from the beginning. Thus, it is called the doctrine that is free from exertion.

Because there is tremendous emphasis in the Great Completeness system on the fundamental innate mind of clear light, an uncommon presentation of the two truths, these are called the special two truths. These are called the special two truths. This could be roughly expressed thus: that which is fundamental and innate is the ultimate truth, and anything relative to that is adventitious, a conventional truth. From this point of view, the fundamental innate mind of clear light is empty of all conventional truths, of adventitious phenomena, thus it is an other-emptiness, an emptiness of the other. However, this fundamental innate mind of clear light is said to have a nature of essential purity; thus, it does not pass beyond the nature of the emptiness of inherent existence that is set forth in the middle wheel of Buddhist teaching.

Because this other-emptiness is set forth in the context of compatibility with the emptiness of inherent existence of the middle wheel of the teaching as in Madhyamika, some scholars have called this a good other-emptiness; whereas they have called a teaching of Buddha-nature, or maybe the fundamental mind of clear light, in which one looks down on the middle wheel of teachings and advocates that the fundamental mind of clear light does inherently exist, a bad other-emptiness. Many scholars from all the schools of Tibetan Buddhism—Nyingma, Kagyu, Sakya, Gelug—have specifically refuted the presentation of some sort of final truth that is itself inherently existent. They have refuted a presentation that looks on the emptiness of inherent existence that is taught in the Madhyamika system as a sort of lower teaching, calling it a self-emptiness that is to be looked down upon. That sort of teaching is unsuitable.

The oral transmission from the great adept Dzongsar Khyen-tze Chokyi Lodro says that the presentations of the levels of the path in the Nyingma system are seen from the perspective of a Buddha, whereas in the Sakya system the presentation of the path is mainly in terms of the spiritual experience of a yogi on the path. The presentations in the Gelug system are mainly from the perspective of ordinary sentient beings. This is important to consider, for it can help you overcome a lot of misunderstandings. In his writings Je Tsongkhapa raises many qualms and investigates and eliminates them with respect to the mode of perception of a Buddha. He went into a lot of analysis about how a Buddha sees the various types of phenomena, classed as pure and impure.

While on the path, to create an imprint of putting emphasis on both the wind and the mind with respect to the mode of achieving Buddhahood, one develops a pure illusory body together with the mind of clear light. Now, I mentioned earlier a system that emphasizes just the mind. In the Kalachakra system, in dependence upon achieving a union of a body which is empty form and immutable bliss, Buddhahood is achieved. Then there is another, third mode, a rainbow body, which is the exclusive mode of procedure of the Mother Tantras. In the Nyingma system of the Great Completeness, in dependence upon bringing to completion the four appearances, all of the coarse factors of one's body are consumed, much as in the system of achieving Buddhahood by way of the great transference of a rainbow body.

ABOUT THE AUTHOR

His Holiness the 14th Dalai Lama, Tenzin Gyatso is the spiritual leader of Tibet. He was born on July 6, 1935, in north-eastern Tibet and was recognized two years later as the reincarnation of Thubten Gyatso, the 13th Dalai Lama. He travels extensively – having visited more than 62 countries – giving speeches to promote understanding, kindness, compassion, respect for the environment and, above all, world peace. In 1989, he was awarded the Nobel Peace Prize for his non-violent struggle for the liberation of Tibet.

www.dalailama.com

We hope you enjoyed this Hay House book. If you'd like
to receive our online catalog featuring additional information
on Hay House books and products, or if you'd like to find out
more about the Hay Foundation, please contact:

Hay House UK, Ltd., 292B Kensal Rd., London W10 5BE
Phone: 0-20-8962-1230 • *Fax:* 0-20-8962-1239
www.hayhouse.co.uk • **www.hayfoundation.org**

Published and distributed in the United States by:
Hay House, Inc., P.O. Box 5100, Carlsbad, CA 92018-5100
Phone: (760) 431-7695 or (800) 654-5126 (760) • *Fax:* 431-6948 or (800) 650-5115
www.hayhouse.com®

Published and distributed in Australia by: Hay House Australia Pty. Ltd.,
18/36 Ralph St., Alexandria NSW 2015 • *Phone:* 612-9669-4299
Fax: 612-9669-4144 • www.hayhouse.com.au

Published and distributed in the Republic of South Africa by:
Hay House SA (Pty), Ltd., P.O. Box 990, Witkoppen 2068
Phone/Fax: 27-11-467-8904 • www.hayhouse.co.za

Published in India by: Hay House Publishers India, Muskaan Complex,
Plot No. 3, B-2, Vasant Kunj, New Delhi 110 070 • *Phone:* 91-11-4176-1620
Fax: 91-11-4176-1630 • www.hayhouse.co.in

Distributed in Canada by: Raincoast, 9050 Shaughnessy St.,
Vancouver, B.C. V6P 6E5 • *Phone:* (604) 323-7100 • *Fax:* (604) 323-2600
www.raincoast.com

Take Your Soul on a Vacation

Visit **www.HealYourLife.com**® to regroup, recharge,
and reconnect with your own magnificence. Featuring
blogs, mind-body-spirit news, and life-changing
wisdom from Louise Hay and friends.

Visit **www.HealYourLife.com** today!

JOIN THE HAY HOUSE FAMILY

As the leading self-help, mind, body and spirit publisher in the UK, we'd like to welcome you to our family so that you can enjoy all the benefits our website has to offer.

 **EXTRACTS** from a selection of your favourite author titles

 **COMPETITIONS, PRIZES & SPECIAL OFFERS** Win extracts, money off, downloads and so much more

 **LISTEN** to a range of radio interviews and our latest audio publications

 **CELEBRATE YOUR BIRTHDAY** An inspiring gift will be sent your way

 **LATEST NEWS** Keep up with the latest news from and about our authors

 **ATTEND OUR AUTHOR EVENTS** Be the first to hear about our author events

 **iPHONE APPS** Download your favourite app for your iPhone

 **HAY HOUSE INFORMATION** Ask us anything, all enquiries answered

join us online at **www.hayhouse.co.uk**

 292B Kensal Road, London W10 5BE
T: 020 8962 1230 E: info@hayhouse.co.uk